Landscape Poetics

To Julian

Landscape Poetics

Scottish Textual Practice, 1928–Present

Monika Szuba

EDINBURGH
University Press

Edinburgh University Press is one of the leading university presses in the UK. We publish academic books and journals in our selected subject areas across the humanities and social sciences, combining cutting-edge scholarship with high editorial and production values to produce academic works of lasting importance. For more information visit our website: edinburghuniversitypress.com

© Monika Szuba 2023, 2025

Edinburgh University Press Ltd
13 Infirmary Street
Edinburgh EH1 1LT

First published in hardback by Edinburgh University Press 2023

Typeset in 11/13 Adobe Sabon by
IDSUK (DataConnection) Ltd

A CIP record for this book is available from the British Library

ISBN 978 1 4744 8420 6 (hardback)
ISBN 978 1 4744 8421 3 (paperback)
ISBN 978 1 4744 8422 0 (webready PDF)
ISBN 978 1 4744 8423 7 (epub)

The right of Monika Szuba to be identified as the author of this work has been asserted in accordance with the Copyright, Designs and Patents Act 1988, and the Copyright and Related Rights Regulations 2003 (SI No. 2498).

Contents

Acknowledgements   vi

Introduction: Towards a Phenomenological Reading of the Scottish Landscape   1

1. 'This intricate interplay': The Interconnectedness of Place, Atmosphere and Living Matter in Nan Shepherd   19

2. 'Where are your dictionaries of the wind, the grasses?': Logos of the Landscape in Norman MacCaig's Poetry   63

3. 'A wing's beat and it's gone': Between Transience and Permanence in Kathleen Jamie's Writing   100

4. 'A patch pegged out for closer examination': Thomas A Clark's Poetic Practice   139

5. 'Acts of communal memory': Landscape, Memory and Place Names in Alec Finlay's Work   187

References   213
Index   232

Acknowledgements

This book was written largely during the Covid-19 pandemic, which made work particularly difficult as lockdowns and travel restrictions limited physical access to the natural world (and research). I am grateful to Edinburgh University Press for their flexibility. Special thanks to Michelle Houston for her enthusiasm and encouragement in the early stages of this book, as well as the understanding she demonstrated regarding the deadline. Thank you to Emily Sharp, Elizabeth Fraser, Carla Hepburn, Fiona Conn, Caitlin Murphy, Robert Tuesley Anderson and everyone at Edinburgh University Press for their work.

Among friends, colleagues and students who have inspired and sustained my interest in poetry, landscape, Scottish literature and culture, I would especially like to thank Robin MacKenzie, Alan Spence, Alan and Rae Riach, Camille Manfredi, Lindsay and Donald Blair, Glenda Norquay, Carla Sassi, Paula and Zygmunt Gorszczyńscy, Paulina and Łukasz Kunz, Magdalena and Marcin Muzioł, and Katarzyna Vitkovska. I owe special thanks to Alan Spence for allowing me to use 'Borrowed Landscape' for the epigraph of this book.

I take this opportunity to thank my colleagues at the Institute of English and American Studies, particularly Jean Ward and Tomasz Wiśniewski.

I gratefully acknowledge Thomas A Clark's kind permission to cite his poems. I wish to express my gratitude to Tom and Laurie Clark for their generosity.

At the Scottish Poetry Library I would like to specially thank Toni Velikova, Rod Hunt and Jill Mackintosh. Thanks are also due to the staff at the National Library of Scotland.

I am grateful to Helen Glassford for the permission to use her painting on the cover.

I wish to thank the anonymous readers whose suggestions helped shape the book.

As always, my deepest gratitude to my parents, Wanda and Jan Szuba, for their support.

The cumulative effects of reading, listening and conversations over the years remain immeasurable. Known and unknown debts are hereby gratefully acknowledged.

Portions of Chapter 5 appeared in an earlier form as 'A "monolithic map / of we know not what": Alec Finlay's Chorographic Poetics', in *Literary Invention and the Cartographic Imagination: Early Modern to Late Modern*, edited by Monika Szuba and Julian Wolfreys (Brill, 2022). I am grateful for permission to republish the material here.

Research for this book was partly funded by Narodowe Centrum Nauki from a grant Miniatura 4 'Poetyka krajobrazu: praktyka eksperymentalna we współczesnej literaturze szkockiej' (2020/04/X/HS2/00929) and Program Wsparcia Humanistyki Gdańskiej at the University of Gdańsk Between.Pomiędzy Research Group 'Teatr – Literatura – Zarządzanie' (533-I015-H014-22).

BORROWED LANDSCAPE

open the gate,
borrow the landscape —
it's all yours
Alan Spence

Introduction: Towards a Phenomenological Reading of the Scottish Landscape

In introducing this book, let me address my title. For the purposes of this study, poetics is understood here as poetic theory and practice, the study of various techniques in poetry and the essay. Landscape poetics denotes methods and strategies of engaging with the landscape in poetic and essayistic work, whereby landscape is not perceived as a static, imperial, visual product of the gaze, but a vibrant, engaged, embodied experience: landscape that is seen, thought, felt, imagined, remembered, sensed, enacted, interacting with other beings and entities as materiality and perception combine. Apprehended in this manner, landscape is not just an aesthetic category, but a topographic and ultimately ideological experience. The authors gathered in this book engage in reinventing the perception of landscape: no longer a gazing subject surveying the land, a subject involved in the act of objectification, but an embodied self that enters the landscape, perceiving it more fully.

Landscape

Landscape is a wide-ranging concept used in a broad discussion of spatiality and subjectivity, coined, as Barbara Bender argues, 'in an emergent capitalist world of western Europe by aesthetes, antiquarians and landed gentry' (1993, 1–2) as a way of *seeing* that is predominantly elitist. The act of 'scoping' the land from a particular – usually raised – viewpoint involving distance created 'an ego-centred landscape', or 'a landscape of views and vistas'. Such a perspectival way of seeing was considered 'correct', contrasted with a peasant's 'close-up view' of open fields (Bender 1993, 2). In the last few decades a number of critics have exposed the imperialist aesthetic which has dominated Western landscape art, whereby vision functions as implicitly possessive. Landscape has been considered by some to operate as a site of imperialist control (see Mitchell 1994). A construct in the cultural sphere created in literature and art, which transmit content, landscape is formed by aesthetic, social and environmental elements. The aesthetics of landscape representation becomes an ideological ground. It is viewed as a site of debate over various visions of past, present and future. In recent decades the concept has been re-examined mainly by cultural geographers, ethnographers and anthropologists, resulting in a more comprehensive understanding that involves dynamic cultural, ecological and material processes. As perceptions of the land alter, it is possible to explore landscape as something experienced subjectively, and as something that alters through time and space, depending on gender, class, age, one's socio-economic status, historical conditions and geographical emplacement. Jeff Malpas reminds us that '[e]mbedded in the physical landscape is a landscape of personal and cultural history, of social ordering and symbolism . . . the narratives of the land as enculturated and humanised cannot be prised away from its physical structure' (1999, 187). The fundamentally spectatorial nature of landscape is posited by Raymond Williams, who writes that '[t]he . . . idea of landscape implies separation and observation' (1973, 120).

This approach is shared by Denis Cosgrove, who argues that '[v]isually, space is rendered the property of the individual detached observer' (1985, 48). The categories of detachment and distance are discussed by John Wylie who believes that visual landscape is 'a tool for keeping the world at a distance', whether it is 'an aloof, distanced figure', detached from the life of the land 'gazing upon landscape', 'the explorer scoping out the distances to be mapped', or 'the landowner contemplating their property from a detached vantage-point'. In these situations the distance involved suggests 'an ethically-problematic detachment and indifference – a distance which enables command and control, which facilitates an uncaring and remote perspective' (Wylie 2017, 2). Citing Jean-Luc Nancy's rejection of any possible communion of subject and place in reference to landscape, Wylie argues that landscape introduces estrangement and distance, which in turn makes it 'uncanny, unhomely' (2017, 2). Instead of depicting a 'land' and a 'location' it ought to be presented as a 'dis-location' (Wylie 2017, 2).

The aesthetic response to the Scottish landscape has been witnessed for thousands of years, as the remains of cairns, brochs and henges attest, demonstrating that humanity is intrinsically connected with the landscape rather than separated from it. The popularity of landscape as an object to be gazed upon began in the eighteenth century. Large numbers of travellers undertook journeys to scenic places, usually visiting the same sites as fashion required, as travellers 'hunted' for those landscapes which would fulfil their fantasies of picturesque disrepair. A tour of the Highlands was de rigueur for English Romantic poets. Keats travelled to Scotland to 'gorge wonders', as he described the journey in a letter to a friend, the place described by him as 'beautiful, enchanting, gothic, picturesque, fine, delightful, grand, sublime—a few blisters, etc.' (1818, 268). Wordsworth toured Scottish landscapes, extolling their grandeur and ideal of the sublime, his being an 'egotistical sublime' in which the mountains exist primarily to reflect the poet's emotional state, functioning as a poetic canvas to understand himself. Following the vogue for the Highland Tour, Scottish landscapes became appropriated and commodified: popular views and their characteristic elements such as mist, the rugged peaks, the castles and ruins became objectified and reproduced ad infinitum in a multitude of forms.

An aesthetic category, the picturesque encouraged viewing nature as a painter might in the process of painting a picture. The interest in landscape perceived through the eyes of the great painters dominated people's responses to it in the eighteenth century; as a result, painting, poetry and landscape gardening reflect that particular taste for landscape. Gardens were designed to comply with the picturesque ideal, as people sought to recreate the image of nature represented in eighteenth-century landscape painting, which fossilised views. Classical landscape painting employed a set of established codes in order to create a particular tone which corresponded with the represented motif. The aesthetic of the picturesque created a particular way of viewing landscapes as if they were landscape paintings. This was achieved using Claude glasses which recreated the style of seventeenth-century landscape artist Claude Lorrain (Andrews 1999, 115–18), which made viewing a landscape a doubly mediated experience: through the painter's eyes and subsequently through an accessory which simplified the colour range of the scenery in search of the painterly quality.

Some critics consider the picturesque 'an almost obscene practice' (MacLaren 1988, 111) due to its ties with colonialism. Subsuming the land to the category of the picturesque, tourism became one of the factors that pushed aside the needs of communities, as the commodification of the Scottish landscape combined the commodification of land and the natural world. This trend transformed the landscape into a source of pleasure, presenting it as a playground, or hunting ground in which tourists acted as hunters. Certain Romantic perceptions of place prevail to this day, particularly visible in the tourist industry advertising bothies and wilderness cottages placed in the Scottish landscapes, which are described as 'remote', 'empty', 'vast', 'unique', the place 'quiet', 'lonely', 'the edge of the world' and, more recently, also 'off-grid', promising 'a break away from' the world and an escape from modern life in a pastoral vision. Nature has become a consumer fantasy (McGrath 2019, 28), the wilderness ideal appropriated by capitalist logic. Robin Kelsey writes about 'romantic landscape fantasy' – the 'fantasy of not belonging to the totality of life of a terrestrial expanse' – in which 'landscape is a technique for setting the world at a distance from us . . . so that we can *deny* our involvement, our belonging. Or, rather, so that we can on the one hand claim that we do not belong to the world, while on the other acting as if *it* belongs to *us*, as our *property*' (2007, 204). Framed in this manner, landscape as a mode of representation created 'denial of corporeality, of materiality, of alterity' in Western culture (Kelsey 2007, 204).

Certain critics have noted a shift from the merely visual to a full sensory experience of landscape (Mitchell 1994, 2; Thomson, Howard, Waterton and Atha 2019, xxi; Waterton 2013, 85–6). In this approach, the spectatorial, visual-representational character of landscape is replaced by non-representational modalities which involve incarnate subjectivity, intimate perception and the immediacy of interrelations, whereby involvement is created by sensory acuteness and perceptual unity. The accusations that non-representational theories favour solipsism, presentism and lack of historicity have been countered by discussions of the significance of temporality and memory. The strand of aesthetics which promotes the categories of distance and disinterestedness, positing the division and separation of the subject from the object of appreciation, is contrasted with landscape, understood as 'the re-presentation of a relatedness to place, a re-presentation of a mode of "emplacement"' (Malpas 2011, 7) whereby embodied beings are implicated in engagement and phenomenological experience. The phenomenological-aesthetic approach stands in opposition to the subject/object and mind/body dichotomy implicit in Kant, in which landscape is appreciated as an object from the perspective of a disembodied observer. In this model, disinterested contemplation, passivity and distancing figure predominantly (Pratt, Howarth and Brady 2000, 150). The notion of disinterestedness, which for Kant constitutes an essential element of the aesthetic response, is refuted by Arnold Berleant, who advances the notion of total engagement. The shift has been enabled by environmental aesthetics, which emerged in the second half of the twentieth century and which enquires about different ways in which the appreciation of nature differs from the appreciation of art in a rapprochement between environmental humanities and landscape studies. Berleant's theory of an 'aesthetics of engagement' is aimed at a comprehensive perception of nature: the appreciation of nature for itself, not as an artwork (1992; 1997).

The origins of environmental aesthetics can be traced back to eighteenth-century concepts of nature as an ideal source of aesthetic experience. Nature as an object of aesthetics became a concern with notable thinkers such as Lord Shaftesbury, Addison and Kant. There followed a period in the aftermath of Hegel's highly influential propositions on the philosophy of art, which relegated the aesthetics of nature to oblivion. It was brought into light in 1966 by Ronald Hepburn who, in his 'Contemporary Aesthetics and the Neglect of Natural Beauty' (later republished in *Wonder and Other Essays* [1984, 9–35]), introduced a phenomenological perspective in the aesthetic appreciation of the natural world. In recent years a phenomenological approach based on an unmediated response to the world has led to a rise in non-representational theories concerned with the human body and its coexistence with things (Thomson, Howard, Waterton and Atha 2019; Wylie 2002; Wylie 2005), whereby the visual fuses with the sonorous, tactile and olfactory aspects of the environment. Critics employ Maurice Merleau-Ponty's work on embodiment in order to challenge binary categories such as subject and object and espouse the intertwining of self and landscape (see, e.g., Wylie 2002). The body is not separate from the world, but rather characterised by an 'unparalleled ability to co-evolve with things, taking them in and adding them to different parts of the biological body to produce something which ... resemble[s] a constantly evolving distribution of different hybrids with different reaches' (Thrift 2007, 10). In the embodied being-in-the-world, experience means active engagement with emotions forming in and arriving from the environment, as Merleau-Ponty posits (2004, 97). A true understanding of landscape means that 'it must be felt', Christopher Tilley argues, 'but to convey some of this feeling to others it has to be talked about, recounted, or written and depicted' (1994, 31). Feeling and emotion – as opposed to the merely cognitive response promoted in the Kantian model – are meaningful in human aesthetic response to nature. Merleau-Ponty underlines the intimate nature of the landscape, 'the homeland of our thoughts' (2002, 28) rather than an object to be contemplated in a disembodied, disinterested manner.

Yet one aspect of the phenomenological perspective echoes Kant's approach, namely the emphasis on the immediacy of perception and feeling in the aesthetic response. As participatory aesthetics opposes ocularcentrism with its ensuing dualisms, landscape is not perceived as a flat, immovable image. In an engaged, phenomenological experience of the landscape all its elements are wholly interdependent: objects are never static but remain in a constant state of becoming. Thus conceived, landscape cannot be fixed in an image nor can it be transformed into a representation. Edward S. Casey wonders whether fragments of the world do not speak for themselves, 'Why re-present what is already presented so effectively and thoroughly in ordinary direct experience? . . . as if such representation were more important or more satisfying than experiential immersion' (2002, xiii). The rejection of the observational landscape as a model of nature appreciation entails the immediacy of phenomenological experience in which a chiasmic relation between human beings and the natural world abolishes the false separation of the perceiving subject and the world. As landscapes are created, negotiated and contested in the course of time, the horizons of the subject's life-world are shaped by geographical, cultural and historical elements.

In a narrow perception of landscape understood solely as an aesthetic category, ethics tends to be elided; yet the inclusion of ethical aspects in the philosophy of landscape is necessary for a comprehensive understanding of the subject. As emplaced beings we remain in an ever-renewing relation with others and the world. By proposing that 'every landscape is a place-scape', Jeff Malpas expands the notion of the view beyond a narrowly understood ocular and pictorial mode and into 'the expression and representation of a relation to place' (2011, 7). Relational spatial politics frames space as a challenge of multiplicity, encounter and relation: a 'throwntogetherness' that demands ongoing negotiation, a concept coined by Doreen Massey in her influential work on the connection between a place and a community in which she affirms that social relations are inscribed in the landscape (2005, 149–52). This view becomes expanded in the environmental humanities, whereby landscapes are understood as 'overlaid arrangements of human and non-human living spaces' (Gan et al. 2017, 1) and, as such, approached in this study.

Environment and Ecology

Presently, landscape is perceived as something that needs to be protected and managed. In 2006 Great Britain signed the European Landscape Convention, recognising landscape as an important part of natural heritage. Changes foisted on landscapes by human activity have shaped how the elements of the natural world relate to one another, and has shifted to synchronise with the urgencies of this environmental moment. Anthropogenic pressures, which include changes in land use affecting biodiversity, depleting and displacing animal biomass and leading to defaunation, threaten the future of the landscape as a result of refashioning the environment of numerous species of plants and animals. In the mechanistic view the natural world is denied intrinsic value, perceived as a resource rather than entity, whereby the land is treated as a food factory with no regard for the needs of other beings that grow and live there. Financial incentives destroyed the lives of many Scottish communities as sheep took precedence over people. Such a system based on extraction and accumulation of profit, involving exploitative relations of power, has generated and continues to generate ecological breakdown. The idea of nature commodified lies at the root of environmental and social injustice. The fraught notions of innovation on Scottish land, which have led to forced dispossession and privatisation of commons, has revealed the dark side of the relentless drive for progress, as the concept of improvement has meant displacement and disrupted lives. In a practice of creating artificial scarcity which marks modernity, the legacy of the enclosures continues to haunt the debate on land rights and land reform in Scotland. In its specific context problems include subsuming the land for stalking and grouse shooting, and eliminating species of animals such as predatory birds, which in turn leads to manipulating ecosystems and attacking environmental protection, as in certain parts of the Scottish landscape, which has become overdetermined by extractive practices. Commercial forestry which is aimed at maximising wood production has transformed forests into a stock harvested through clearcut logging in which all the trees in a particular area are removed. Ancient pinewood sites were also damaged in the course of overgrazing from sheep and deer. Many Scottish landscapes are haunted by visions of ancient woodland brimming with biodiversity, the filling of brambles, climbing plants, a temperate rainforest filled with enormous richness of life contrasting with a place denuded of trees, serving as a hunting preserve for grouse shooting and deer stalking. The loss of much of the wildlife shaped the Scottish landscapes in the course of many centuries. Despite conservation efforts, the numbers of capercaillie, the largest grouse in the world whose call composes the sounds of the ancient Caledonian pine forest – becoming extinct in the late eighteenth century and reintroduced in the 1830s – declined again in the late twentieth century. The call of the corncrake was once a familiar sound of the countryside, the bird elusively omnipresent in hay meadows and pastures, but the sound was extinguished by the 1960s due to the mechanisation of agriculture. Although the corncrake has been returned to the Scottish Highlands and Islands thanks to conservation efforts, it remains under threat.

Capercaillie and corncrake are just two examples of the many species of animals and plants the numbers of which have declined or which have disappeared from landscapes. Environmental concerns such as habitat and biodiversity loss shape the landscape together with social concerns which include the ongoing recovery from the Clearances. Confronted with these problems, poets and artists often convey a sense of grief and anxiety that characterise our environmental moment and hope of socially just, ecologically regenerative production, while addressing a future for the landscape in which exploitation of the land is replaced by a world of lived sensibility. This hope is already present in the visionary ecological work of Patrick Geddes whose profound biological understanding of ecosystems of the primacy of life – *all* life – over economic value may be encompassed by the oft-repeated phrase 'by leaves we live'.

Of the five authors gathered in this study, three were born before the rise of the new environmentalism of the 1960s (Shepherd in 1893, MacCaig in 1910 and Clark in 1944), yet all, to a lesser or greater degree, reflect the renewed awareness in the human–non-human relations in their work. Although Nan Shepherd's work predates the environmental movement, her remarks about the destruction of the landscape seem prescient today. Norman MacCaig's appreciation of the smallest living beings – frogs, toads, caterpillars – demonstrates an ecological consciousness, as does the long poem 'A Man in Assynt', written in 1967, in which he considers the ownership of the land and hope for its regeneration. Particularly visible in the works published from the 2000s onwards, the heightened awareness of the environmental crisis can be traced in the work of Jamie, Clark and Finlay. With the publication of *The Tree House* in 2004, Jamie's writing entered a new phase, one in which she demonstrates deep engagement with the natural world. The environmental context, particularly the issues concerning the climate crisis, marked the beginnings of Jamie's post as the Makar, or National Poet for Scotland, in 2021. The first poem curated by the poet and premiered during the UN Climate Change Conference in Glasgow (COP26) was 'the people's nature poem' entitled 'The Life Breath Song', a collaborative work originating from being attentive to the natural environment. Finlay's work most explicitly expresses the fate of the commons and the need for land justice in the context of the history of land grabbing, dispossession and consolidation. In the face of lost landscapes and their ongoing disappearance due to historic, social and climatic changes, a sense of melancholia encompasses the past and extends into the future as climate and biodiversity crises are witnessed and recorded with increasing acuity since the first decades of the present millennium. Emotional responses such as nostalgia, mourning, melancholia or 'beautiful sadness' are recognised by Jacky Bowring as part of the landscape experience associated with ethics and empathy (2016, 8), implicated in the picturesque and the sublime. By expanding the boundaries of our care, the authors brought together here demonstrate an ethical stance which involves heightened attention, all acknowledging life existing outside of human language. The statement that 'language is a form in which landscape can come alive' (Tarlo 2011, 10) can be refined: landscape *is* already always alive with language. To cite Maurice Merleau-Ponty:

> the whole landscape is overrun with words . . . And in a sense, . . . language is everything, since it is the voice of no one, since it is the very voice of the things, the waves, and the forests. And what we have to understand is that there is no dialectical reversal from one of these views to the other; we do not have to reassemble them into a synthesis: they are two aspects of the reversibility which is the ultimate truth. (1968, 155)

In a reversible movement, language permeates landscape and landscape suffuses language. Poetic practice registers place before it formulates meaning or offers itself to interpretation as landscape poetics becomes woven into being from voice, body and text.

About This Book

The assumption that the landscape is a view comprehended exclusively by the eye is explored and challenged by the five Scottish writers that this study brings together. Aware of the ethics of perception embedded in the various representational modalities, the poets productively resist, contend and challenge the imperialist urge to take dominion of the land. In my discussion of the authors' work, I continue to employ a phenomenological perspective which I developed in *Contemporary Scottish Poetry and the Natural World: Burnside, Jamie, Robertson and White* (2019), which focused on the intertwining of human self and the natural world. In following this thread of enquiry, I build upon the investigations of the engagement of active participation, whereby self in the analysed texts is an active participant and perceptual agent. The concept of landscape employed in this study embraces its ambiguous status, challenging the understanding of landscape as a static image which is viewed and mimetically reproduced. Marked by topophilia (Tuan 1974, 93), the authors' textual translation of the embodied relation with the landscape apprehends landscape not as a static image or source of the picturesque, but as being in a constant process of change. They demonstrate attempts to find authentic ways in which the relationship between humans and the natural world can be evoked and manifested – if not represented, as they become aware of the limitations of mimesis. Thus informed by environmental imagination, their work demonstrates a range of possible ways of reinventing landscape.

As already indicated, in the context of Scottish literature the notion of the landscape is politically as well as ethically and aesthetically fraught. Thus poetic practice may become a form of resistance to historical, social and, increasingly also, environmental injustice in contestation with the established order. In the process of mediation the poets enter into a relationship not of mastery but an open engagement with the land as landscape, and this in turn becomes a form of discourse uncovering semantic relations between language, structure, history, geography. Based on communication coursing between various, internally related agents, this discourse cannot be delimited: continuously changing, it lacks fixed boundaries. Mediated, mobile landscapes of modern and contemporary poetry, essay and practice, involve modes of attentiveness reckoning with flux, geological time, historical and social change. Through a number of embodied practices such as walking, the poets and artists enter the landscape ready for the unexpected encounter, welcoming the gift in the spirit of openness. 'We must perceive in order to move but we must also move in order to perceive,' as James Gibson argues (1979, 223). The right to roam, which distinguishes Scotland from England, ensures a freedom to wander and ramble, opening the self to diverse landscapes. Walking around creates 'the unity that pertains to place'

(Malpas 2012, 60), further established by undertaking various lifeworld activities as 'embodied agents' in relation to others (ibid., 203), entwining the self with the landscape. Through movement, landscape unfolds and opens before us. In recent years, walking has sparked renewed theoretical interest as a method of enquiry (see, e.g., Borthwick, Marland and Stenning 2020; Ingold and Vergunst 2008). In the work discussed in this book landscapes are predominantly experienced through walking, whether in the Cairngorms, the Highlands and Islands, or by means of proxy walking, the latter offering an experience of the landscape that goes against discourses of ableism present in some strands of writing which engages with nature.

The dynamics of human–environment relation reveals symbolic and material aspects of landscape. Composed of living and non-living beings, alongside which we have existed for at least five thousand years, or since our Neolithic ancestors first cleared the forests to farm the land, landscape extends onto other participants in it, as their poetic practice widens the circle, offering a reminder that landscape contains a vast number of beings and things. 'The topographies of landscapes are constantly evolving,' as Doreen Massey writes (2006, 34). The authors discussed in this volume are concerned with the dynamic exchange between the embodied consciousness and the world in an act of perception which encompasses animate and animating landscape presences endowed with life and giving life to the living power, constituting in turn a sentient environment which listens and speaks. To describe contemporary Scottish poetry as 'the over-populated eco-kailyard' (Lyon 2010, 55) therefore relegates the work of many authors to a sentimental literary patch, dismissing its diversity and scope, and implicitly undermines the role the kailyard played in constructions of Scottishness (see Bold 1983; Cook 1999). As this book aims to demonstrate, Scottish writing is exploratory, engaged, diverse, testing and contesting the notions of space, place and environment as well as the relation of the individual to culture, language, memory and history. In their multifaceted and heterogeneous work centred around the embodied subject and the materiality of place, the authors form a shared and yet diverse response to how humans inhabit the land. The idea of community, important to Scottish literature, is expanded in the work of the authors discussed and encompasses all living beings through the revelation of an entanglement of human communities and natural ecosystems. The pastoral desire to consider nature in nostalgic terms as home, refuge or perfect whole is productively addressed and challenged by the authors brought together in this study. Their writing is antipastoral in its preoccupation with temporality, as dreams of centred wholeness yield to provisionality and eccentricity, exploring the question of time's entanglement with place.

The present study engages with twentieth- and twenty-first-century artistic practices and critical poetics, offering critical exploration of the relationship between writing and landscape, literary form and cultural identity. It attempts to provide a diversified, but not exclusive, framework for critical engagement, with a view to offering to the reader insights into authors, focusing on poetry, essay and material practice. It is concerned with place, environment and locus encompassing various regions of Scotland, but focusing mainly on non-urban spaces. It continues a discussion on modalities of the natural world in Scottish literature and art undertaken by Louisa Gairn in *Ecology and Modern Scottish Literature* (2008) and Camille Manfredi in *Nature and Space in Contemporary Scottish Writing and Art* (2019) but proposes a view on a number of distinct ways in which the selected authors and artists engage with the landscape in an intimate connection between self and world, subject and place. The discussed texts evoke a distinctive world where landscape, language and subject are inextricably connected, taking into account complex pasts of the land and people. The aim of the volume is not to provide historical, social or biographical context, but to focus on close readings of the selected works in order to highlight the relations between various agents in the landscape as evoked in the work considered. By communicating individual experience in a significant way, the authors trace the changing meanings of the Scottish landscapes. Tending towards localised knowledge, they demonstrate attention to minute details of the landscape with a heightened perception and through imagination. By discarding the primacy of vision, the engagement of the sensual is realised through immediate presence. While landscape as an expression of nationality is particularly strong in Scotland, in non-representational approaches the politics of landscape is given less prominence than in representational landscape studies (Harvey 2015, 918–20), and in accordance with this approach the present study focuses on a mutual entanglement of the human self and natureculture, which reveals a range of possible ways of entering in a relationship with the natural world. The importance that all five authors attach to dynamism and flux as predicates of the natural world calls attention to the mutual entanglement of human and non-human beings and things.

Confronted with various temporalities, Scottish authors evoke sublimity originating in the realisation of deep time – a time when landscapes were sculpted into being – and a possible aftermath of anthropogenically induced transformations of the land reaching into deep future. A grasp of geologic materialities combines with apprehension that we share the land with prehistoric ancestors. Their writing and art demonstrates the ways in which memory embedded in the landscape bears relation to identity as a layering of emotions gathered over the years, forming individual identification with place through time (Ryden 1993, 39–40). A combination of memory, a sense of place and identity, landscape nostalgia is a 'longing for a certain being-in-a-place' (Malpas 2012, 168). The significance of memory in the landscape extends onto the collective memory of social and historical events manifested by the physical environment. Many landscapes of Scotland function as places of memory – 'mnemotopes', or 'topographical texts of cultural memory' (Assman 2011, 44). Historical processes which shaped the Scottish land are haunted now by the remnants of former habitations, ruptured landscape marked by displacement, the space of collective memory being a dereliction of the landscape and disintegration of the Gaelic culture.

Apart from environmental haunting, spectral presences in the landscape indicate other kinds of landscape hauntedness such as ancient inhabitation of the land, its material evidence unearthed in archaeological digs, the vagaries of island populations including the event of the evacuation of St Kilda, the Highland Clearances, all powerful reminders that landscapes are inhabited by people. It is a lived landscape which reveals cultural and social dimensions of place marked by layers of temporality. The discussed work indirectly reflects the aftermath of that major social and historical moment on the Scottish land. Witnessing the aftermath of the Clearances, the authors gathered here confront the melancholy brought by the dereliction whereby ruins do not create a sense of the picturesque but offer a reflection on the enduring effects of a depopulated land as well as a sense of our fragile connection with the natural world. In various forms the work of the authors here constitutes a response to the destruction of the Commons. Loss of the Gaelic language largely means losing touch with the landscape and so, in view of this dereliction, they aim at healing the fractured connections through diverse literary and artistic approaches. Witnessing the resilience of Highland people continuing in relation to community, traditional music and language, they are hopeful for the ecological and social regeneration of Scotland. Even if none of the authors discussed in the present study are Gaelic speakers, part of their work is an expression of Gaelic hauntings. The haunting presence of Gaelic is explored by three of the poets in question, MacCaig, Clark and Finlay. In view of MacCaig's deeply-felt ancestral ties with Gaelic culture and the sorrow of not knowing the language, his return to Assynt every summer for forty years was a way to recuperate the ruptured connection. Not a Gaelic speaker, Finlay admits that he has 'regretted and been aware of this lack' (1997, xv). Both Clark and Finlay trace the spectral presence of Gaeldom in place names. Finlay engages with Gaelic poetry in such works as *Còmhlan Bheanntan / A Company of Mountains* (2013) which evoke the landscape of mountain range in Skye and takes inspiration from Sorley MacLean's poem 'Ceann Loch Aoineart'. Scottish correspondences and affinities in Finlay's practice combine with Zen. Such openness to other cultures is characteristic of the work of the authors brought together in this study, which demonstrates the extent of literary and philosophical associations that connect it to Scottish culture and extend beyond it and include antique as well as classical continuities.

Searching for forms of expression that resist human-centred vision, this is writing that challenges a language that does not define but rather seeks to find an open form, 'a living testament to the non-transparency of verbal language' (Abberley et al. 2022, 5). Moving away from writing *about* towards being *with* the landscape and towards the elision of the preposition: writing the landscape. Through seeking the truth, poetry establishes connections between the system of signs and the anthropocentric world of human creation. Eastern influences have enabled the authors gathered in this book to step away from the European viewpoint on the landscape, dominated by distance, objectification and perspectival and ego-centred approaches. The writers in question demonstrate an affinity through their work with Zen practice and aesthetics. The influence of Eastern philosophical systems, particularly that of Zen Buddhism, is present in modern and contemporary Scottish literature thanks to such figures as Nan Shepherd and Neil M. Gunn. One might also acknowledge Norman MacCaig's self-mocking declaration that he is a 'Zen Calvinist' and Kathleen Jamie's travels in Tibet, which exerted a profound effect on her writing. Thomas A Clark's minimalist aesthetic involves a deep engagement with Japanese philosophy and poetry, incorporating Zen Buddhist themes. Finally, Alec Finlay's engagement with Japan manifests itself in a number of works, including an edited anthology of Scottish haiku and short poetic forms, *Atoms of Delight* (2001, the title of which is a reference to Gunn's *The Atom of Delight* [1956] in which he demonstrates an interest in Zen Buddhism) as well as *The Road North* co-created with Ken Cockburn, in which the two poets recreate in the Scottish landscape a work by a seventeenth-century Buddhist monk and poet Bashō, *Oku no Hosomichi* (*The Narrow Road to the Deep North*). In the interconnectedness of the intellect and body manifested particularly by the work of Shepherd, MacCaig and Clark, the authors exemplify the manner in which consciousness extends towards and intertwines with the landscape in a precognitive knowing, and thus offer a phenomenological reading of the world. As Merleau-Ponty explains, phenomenology is a philosophy 'for which the world is already there' and an attempt to achieve 'a direct and primitive contact with the world' (2002, vii), not as an objectification of the world into reducible knowledge but 'an account of space-time and the world as we live them' (2002, vii). Non-dual understanding, theorised by Merleau-Ponty in such concepts as wild knowing, or a way of pure apprehension before categorisation, may be compared to the pre-Christian Celtic mode of apprehension, in which there is a connection between self and environment, as explained by Meg Bateman and John Purser in their insightful, comprehensive study *Window to the West: Culture and Environment in the Scottish Gàidhealtachd* (2020).

Perception which engages the whole body as phenomena and things appear to the subject, emerging in consciousness and interlacing with it, distinguishes the texts in question from conventional responses. The aesthetic categories of the pastoral, the picturesque and the sublime associated with the landscape are tested, contested and challenged by the authors discussed in this study. Aspects of the picturesque in the landscape appear in a subversive form, as the conventional, static viewing of landscape does not respond to the dynamic perception represented by the authors in question. Self-reflectively considered by the poets, the sublime does not represent a dominating experience, while its echoes are nonetheless present in their work. The othering of 'wilderness', which remains part of the Romantic legacy, is actively challenged by authors such as Jamie, who recognises wilderness as a human construct (if occasionally she is unable to resist the appeal of sublimity in her work), and redeemed by Finlay in such projects as *Wild City* (2018). Rather than focusing on constructed notions of landscape as scenery – a source of the ineffable sublime experienced passively – they actively engage with place in a subjective, individual, multisensory experience, bearing witness to the patterns and rhythms of the landscape. The engagement of the embodied self, walking through natural objects in order to explore what Anne Whiston Spirn names 'landscape grammar' (1998, 168). Thus experienced, landscape assumes a multi-dimensional form, differing from the flat, static apprehension dominated by vision.

The selected authors revel in plenitude, yet at the same time they find themselves confronted with the loss of creaturely abundance, noticing the disappearance of habitat and species diversity. The texts represent different degrees and modes of care as the authors recognise a duty to ecology and seek to safeguard the natural world, whereby the preservation of nature constitutes a form of environmental citizenry. Poems concentrating on intimate, small-scale imagery reveal part of the continuum of being in the natural world with a sense of a shared vulnerability of a community of species. MacCaig and Clark's miniature scale contrasts with the vastness of time and space witnessed in a number of Jamie's essays. Landscape intimacy, particularly in the work of such authors as Shepherd, MacCaig and Clark, who return to the same places, exposes a deep familiarity with their features which informs the texts.

Landscape in the work discussed in the present book is not limited to rugged mountain peaks or picturesque valleys but encompasses coastal and archipelagic areas with a large ratio of sea and sky. The texts discussed encompass the landscapes of diverse regions of Scotland: the Highlands and Islands in MacCaig's and Clark's poetry, St Kilda, Rona and the Orkney Islands in Jamie's and Finlay's writing, the Pentland Hills in Jamie's work; and, finally, the Cairngorms in Nan Shepherd's and Alec Finlay's essays, poetry and practice. While this study focuses on poetry, essay and practice mostly concerned with open landscapes, it notes the significance of the natural world in urban settings in the work of Clark and Finlay. Their literary and artistic responses to the built environment maintain close connections with the natural world. The work involves green spaces in cities and include Clark's installations at Charlotte Square in Edinburgh and in New Stobhill Hospital in Glasgow, and Finlay's various works such as *Taigh: a wilding garden* in Edinburgh Botanic Gardens, *Manifesto for Urban Crofts* and Scotland's Covid Memorial in Pollok Country Park, all of which highlight the importance of parks, gardens and other green spaces in an urbanised world, as well as stress the relationship between personal and social landscapes, local cultural and geographic factors which surround garden creation and use, emphasising a contemplative role of verdancy in a modern world. Furthermore, Finlay's work contributes to a contemporary debate about the urban dimensions of land justice and their implications for locally autonomous food systems, which demonstrate alternative ways forward towards democratised land use, based on cooperative ownership models.

Anne Moeglin-Delcroix's argument that artists' books bear 'a close relation to utopia' as they create an 'alternative space' located 'outside established institutions' (2001, n.p.) is embodied by the publications of two of the authors discussed here. Apart from being poets and artists, Clark and Finlay are publishers, having (co-)established small presses in order to publish mainly (but not exclusively) their own work. While Clark's practice oscillates between finding and making, Finlay's work is marked by ecological, social and historical awareness, his term 'place-aware' with which he describes his practice involving complex processes. Jamie's work involves digging the earth; Jamie reaches into the ground, finding artefacts of the people, ancestors, who lived on the land thousands of years before us, imagining the lives that they led, reflecting on the manner in which humans have been transforming the landscape.

This book is not intended as a survey. Rather, it seeks to bring out some of the most important figures in modern Scottish nature writing in order to understand what is distinctive and important about the poetry, prose and practice of the presented authors. I take a selective approach so as to examine how five Scottish authors in the twentieth- and twenty-first century have engaged with the landscape in what has come to be considered a 'post-natural' world. In a post-natural world, as is presented, for instance, by Jamie, there is no nature separate from humans. I am part of nature together with my microbiome, with the gannet and the apple tree. The boundaries between synthetic and natural are fluid: derived from other living organisms, plastic is part of living organisms, those that have existed on earth for millions of years.

Scottish landscape poetry and practice challenge 'the divide between experimental or innovative and traditional or mainstream' which, as Harriet Tarlo has noted, 'has haunted British poetry, in all its many guises, since the nineteen-thirties' (2011, 7). While the practice of some of the authors discussed in this volume can be characterised as environmental, land or visual art, the main focus of this book is textual practice. That part of this study dedicated to minimalism (particularly Clark and Finlay) discusses the manner in which emplacement encourages the participatory response of the perceiver, an embodied experience of such artworks indebted to Merleau-Ponty's philosophy, in particular *Phenomenology of Perception* (1962), which played a fundamental role in establishing a theory of Minimalist installation art in the 1960s, and which is 'organised around a phenomenological model of the viewing subject' (Bishop 2005, 10). Of course, while the principal focus of this book is the poets to whom chapters are dedicated, it is equally important to stress the role of collaborators, Laurie Clark especially, without whom the work of Thomas A Clark would not appear as it does. Laurie Clark contributes importantly to the visual and graphic aspects of Thomas A Clark's poetry in its published form, as he happily acknowledges.

By concentrating on five modern and contemporary Scottish authors, the book offers the proposition of an opening rather than a definitive statement on the subject. While their work displays particular affinities, which I hope will be demonstrated in my discussion, their singularity dictates the open form of this study. Given the scope of the subject, my project is relatively modest. Writing the landscape in the twentieth- and twenty-first century does not constitute a departure from earlier Scottish literature but demonstrates forms of continuity in the appreciation of landscape in Scottish literature, a spirit that permeates the land and surrounding seas. It travels across time and language. It suffices to think about the intertwining of plant, animal and mineral with the self in the eighteenth-century Gaelic poem *Praise of Ben Dorain* by Duncan Ban MacIntyre. There are many other writers and artists in Scotland who might well have figured in a book on landscapes in Scottish modern and contemporary literature. I wish to stress the relevance for contemporary debates on the reassessment of the concept of landscape. Importantly, the work analysed in this study constitutes a shift in perception towards the world which mostly moves away from focusing on human beings and foregrounds correspondences within the natural world, while exploring the topos of the interconnectedness of all beings. I seek to delineate the manner in which the authors reclaim the landscape and the ways in which aesthetic experiences of the natural world are entangled with the ethical dimension of planetary habitation. In drawing attention to these literary and artistic practices, my hope is to stir interest in contemporary approaches to place that inform human/non-human entanglement.

Chapter 1

'This intricate interplay': The Interconnectedness of Place, Atmosphere and Living Matter in Nan Shepherd

Recently, there has been a surge in interest in Nan Shepherd's work. In 2011 Canongate Books published a new edition of *The Living Mountain*, introduced by Robert Macfarlane; four years later Galileo Publishers produced an edition of *In the Cairngorms*, with another foreword by Macfarlane. Shortly after, the first biography, *Into the Mountain: A Life of Nan Shepherd* (2017), was published by Charlotte Peacock. The year 2020 saw Samantha Walton's study *The Living World: Nan Shepherd and Environmental Thought*, which discusses *The Living Mountain* in the context of such themes as ecology, environmentalism and deep time, as well as Kerri Andrews's book entitled *Wanderers: A History of Women Walking* with a chapter devoted to Shepherd. Critical interest in Shepherd's writing (see, for instance, *Modern British Nature Writing, 1789–2020* [2022]) accompanies artistic responses in Rose Strang's series of paintings commissioned by the Folio Society, resulting in an illustrated edition of *The Living Mountain* (2021) as well as *Into the Mountain* (2019), 'a place sensitive performance' choreographed by Simone Kenyon.[1] In contrast with more prolific authors, such as Norman MacCaig, Nan Shepherd's output is modest in volume: between 1928 and 1934 she published three novels, *The Quarry Wood* (1928), *The Weatherhouse* (1930) and *A Pass in the Grampians* (1933), and a collection of poems, *In the Cairngorms* (1934). Then, more than forty years later, there appeared *The Living Mountain* (1977), which may be described as a 'celebratory prose-poem' (Macfarlane 2011, xiv), written during the Second World War. In 2014 a volume of poems,

In the Cairgorms, was published, followed four years later by a collection of Shepherd's writing, *Wild Geese*. This chapter focuses primarily on *The Living Mountain*, addressing fiction and poetry in order to demonstrate the ways in which *The Living Mountain* constitutes a development of Shepherd's views on the landscape.

Shepherd's novels, written in a 'quietly pioneering' (Peacock 2020, n.p.) narrative technique with the occasional use of Doric, the dialect of Aberdeenshire, demonstrate the manner in which modernity affected rural communities. The largely rural nature of Scottish culture of that period accompanies the openness of the Scottish Renaissance's modernist aesthetics, represented by Neil M. Gunn and Lewis Grassic Gibbon, as well as by Hugh MacDiarmid and Willa and Edwin Muir, to mention but a few names. Set in North-East Scotland, in the Cairngorms specifically, Shepherd's writing originates from an authentic intimacy with the landscape, emphasising a familiarity with all of its aspects, experienced and closely observed in all weathers and seasons[2] – the world which spreads between darkness and light, lived at the pace of the changing seasons, in the rhythms of 'island weather' made unstable by large continental mass (2011, 2). Focusing on the material features of the world and phenomenal experience, Shepherd's writing highlights sensual aspects of a subject's being-in-the-world. Shepherd enters *into* the landscape, foregrounding the significance of the body to the world, to others and, reflectively, to the self. Shepherd's writing focuses on the situated, physical nature of being, her prescient work pre-empting developments in phenomenological thought.

According to Robert Macfarlane, Shepherd demonstrates 'an obsession (ocular, oracular) with the eyeball' (2011, xiii), yet in this chapter I argue that Shepherd's concern lies not only in visuality but extends to other sensual and corporeal aspects of a subject's experience of the world, her phenomenological approach echoing Maurice Merleau-Ponty's conceptual reorientation towards embodiment and the flesh of the world. The chapter explores the manner in which mind, body and the landscape intertwine and how the vegetal, animal, mineral and meteorological elements of the world interconnect in Shepherd's work. The discussion focuses on the dynamic, entangled relation between self and world whereby the former is permeated by the latter. Before going further, it is crucial to address a certain important issue that arose while I was researching and writing this volume, as it goes directly to my references to Macfarlane and to his, and my own, acknowledgement of the significance of reading Nan Shepherd through a phenomenological, particularly

Merleau-Pontian lens. To do justice to this, I hope the reader will allow me a slight digression at this juncture.

Published in July 2022, Samantha Walton's impressive monograph on the work of Shepherd in the context of current and recent ecological debates, *The Living World: Nan Shepherd and Environmental Thought*, is, without doubt, an important work on Shepherd's writing. Though not a phenomenologist, Walton nonetheless engages with themes common to phenomenology, especially as phenomenology, ecocriticism, and theories and discussions of the Anthropocene overlap, such as Being, Dwelling, the Self, Oneness, Deep Time, Opening, Abyss and Geopoetics. Walton privileges the interconnections through what she calls the 'complex, interconnected ecology of nature', in a manner that is 'innovative and prescient' (2020, 14). Walton affirms that she is writing 'as much for fans of Nan Shepherd as those who are interested in environmental thought' and each chapter is accordingly shaped by 'a new theme or approach to ecocriticism' (2020, 15). Thus, as Walton continues, and in my view correctly and in a manner which touches closely on some of my own concerns, her book is a political intervention in contemporary ecocriticism, reading Shepherd through this lens in order, on the one hand, to reread retrospectively Shepherd according to the politics as well as the poetics of ecocriticism, thereby unveiling what is putatively 'prescient' while serving the 'Shepherd revival' (2020, 14). Walton's ecocriticism, again, somewhat like my own, shows the way to rethink what are usually considered 'traditional themes explored in the humanities' (2020, 15).

In this, and this is one significant area where we diverge, Walton's book 'uses an ecocritical lens to read Shepherd and draws from historical sources to situate Shepherd's writing in its cultural context' (2020, 16). In this avowal, Walton announces her work as belonging to that British form of historical and ideological critique known as cultural materialism. This is, of course, an undeniably significant intervention, even if in some cases it does sacrifice close reading for the sake of context and ideology. I have no particular issue with Walton's approach, except to acknowledge that her methodology is different from my own, and this brings me to one discussion in particular in Walton's study. In her final chapter, 'Being', Walton engages with 'alternative selves', 'phenomenology', 'selfhood' and 'oneness' (2020, 220ff.), and also '[t]he problem of the "I"' what it means to be a '"self"', singularity and so-called '"authentic" identity' (2020, 221), in a discussion that takes us through Cartesian, Romantic and post-Romantic thought. Walton rehearses, a little too briefly (though, as she says, she is writing for fans of Shepherd and not just academics), notions of Darwinism, a 'Hobbesian universe', the work of William James, and psychoanalysis (2020, 222).

Walton then proceeds to phenomenology, acknowledging the work of Merleau-Ponty and Husserl (2020, 223–5). In the section titled 'Shepherd's Phenomenology', Walton cites Macfarlane's approving nod towards the similarity between Shepherd's work and that of Merleau-Ponty: 'To Macfarlane, "her philosophical conclusions concerning colour-perception, touch and embodied knowledge now read as arrestingly similar to those of Merleau-Ponty" (2011, xxix). Macfarlane even notices a similarity between their expression and diction' (2011, xxx, cit. Walton 2020, 226). At this juncture, Walton makes a rather abrupt turn, asking: 'is it possible that Shepherd could have read Merleau-Ponty's work?' (2020, 226). The question is somewhat stark. There is nothing in the citations of Macfarlane to suggest anything of the kind, the interrogative on Walton's part being something therefore of a non-sequitur. Macfarlane is careful to position his analysis by saying that Shepherd's 'philosophical conclusions' *now read* as arrestingly similar, his reading coming as one after the fact historically of Shepherd's writing. Yet Walton feels the need to create a distance by turning to a biographical commentary that includes the statement that Merleau-Ponty never taught in Aberdeen and that Shepherd, who had studied little French, had no works that Walton was able to find in Shepherd's library. What follows is a commentary on Shepherd's affinity and relationship with other modernists, and the relationship between modernism's techniques and phenomenology. As Walton observes, 'Her writing is intensely phenomenological, grounded in the direct experience' (2020, 207). Further, 'Common to both Shepherd and Merleau-Ponty, then, is the conviction that we are co-present with the world; we are not distinct objects on a static backdrop but part of an "intersubjective world composed of a plurality of anonymous subjects, i.e. subjects which are at the same time a self and an other" (Lau 135)' (2020, 207). However, while, for Walton, phenomenology has its place, it should also be kept in its place, it being 'a critique of European philosophy' (2020, 209); however, 'alternatives to individualist theories of selfhood are fundamental features of diverse global perspectives and traditions. Many of these critiques have important ecological dimensions and can aid in the final excavation of Shepherd's account of "being"' (2020, 209). Thus, while phenomenology is for me the principal mode of critical analysis and a methodology that allows us, to recall Macfarlane, now to read Shepherd in a vital, engaging and relevant manner, for Walton it is merely one mode among others, and we diverge in that she seeks to wrest Shepherd's notion of Being away from a solely phenomenological interpretation. The point to make is that Shepherd's work is so richly overdetermined by different concerns, interests, foci and explorations that it contains multitudes, as it were.

In this, Samantha Walton and I can agree at least: everything begins with the attention to things and phenomena, Shepherd foregrounding the interdependence between humans and the world through an embodied inherence in a slow, deep exploration. The first part of *The Living Mountain* is devoted to elemental being: 'inanimate things', as Shepherd writes, 'rock and water, frost and sun', which are 'the forces that create' the animate things (2011, 48). The mountain is alive with plants, roots and seeds, 'anchoring' (2011, 50) themselves; despite seeming fragility, they have 'roots of a timeless endurance' (2011, 49) or 'knots of life' (2011, 49). Plants and animals are part of 'the mountain's wholeness' (2011, 48), entangled, inextricably related. The hardiness of heather is one example of 'the tenacity of life' (2011, 49). Emphasising the interrelated condition of all things, Shepherd states that 'the very substance of the mountain is in its life' (2011, 51). This sense of relatedness, already present in her poems – a case in point being the sonnet 'Real presence' (2014, 53), which contains the statement 'substance and its essence now are one' (l. 11) – provides the title for the essay collection: 'All are aspects of one entity, the living mountain' (2011, 48). Such phrases demonstrate that in Shepherd's writing the world is not reduced to self: the perceiving I does not have an imperial authority over the world, as it is *of* the world, not separate *from* but inherent *in* it. Nor is it implicitly the supreme ego implied in nineteenth-century landscape painting. The landscape becomes active as the I becomes part of the surrounding world where perception is a not passive state but a performative act. The self makes the world that makes the self. As the senses are combined together, each 'heightened to its most exquisite awareness' (Shepherd 2011, 105), the body is not passive before sensorial stimulation.

In the perceptual paradigm observed by Shepherd, the self is sensually involved *in* and forming an intimate relation *with* the landscape. As all the senses combine together in the experience of the world, there is no distinction between the subject and the object as the perceiver and the perceived condition one another. Marked by the phenomenological apprehension of the world, whereby the sensual body experiences 'a life of the senses so pure, so untouched by any mode of apprehension but their own, that the body may be said to think' (2011, 105), Shepherd's work emphasises the form of an embodied being-in-the-world that is total and momentarily unadulterated. Demonstrating that the human is interdependent and interconnected – 'this network of relationships' (Merleau-Ponty 2002, xxiii) – Shepherd writes of 'this intricate interplay of soil, altitude, weather, and the living tissues of plant and insect' (2011, 59). These bounded identities stress the entangled, '*thirled*' ('bound' or 'tied') nature of being-in-the-world. The world's multitude is revealed throughout by cataloguing phenomena and things as the enumeration of the components of the landscape, serving to highlight its abundance. 'What wealth!', Shepherd exclaims (2011, 106), naming various phenomena: 'its weathers, its airs and lights, its singing burns, its haunted dells, its pinnacles and tarns, its birds and flowers, its snows, its long blue distances' (2011, 90) or 'the sun, scree, soil and water, moss, grass, flower and tree, insect, bird and beast, wind rain and snow – the total mountain' (2011, 105). In the last citation, items are listed in subcategories, combined with a conjunction: mineral, vegetal, animal and atmospherics. The world is 'total' when all these elements combine. Watching the light over the plateau gives the perceiving I the illusion of movement as the eye 'catches' delights (2011, 101), or brief glimpses of passing phenomena and the interplay between them, which suggests ecological enmeshment.

This sense of boundedness forms a major preoccupation of Shepherd's writing, reflected in the recurring references to the entanglement of mind and matter. Inseparable from the body, the mind forms part of a body-subject that thinks and perceives. Shepherd sees the Cairngorms as a group rather than individual peaks. When described in numbers, the physical features of the Cairngorm Mountains may only constitute 'a pallid simulacrum of their reality, which, like every reality that matters ultimately to human beings, is a reality of the mind' (2011, 1). As consciousness enters in an interaction with place, so it expands the measurable world. In all its shapes, the mountain 'tranquillises the mind' (2011, 101), the source of its effect remaining both unknown and unknowable, impossible to explain. The disembodied reason and science which relies upon it prove insufficient. The mind in Shepherd's essay is not a disembodied entity, representing pure reason, but is deeply entangled with place:

> It is, as with all creation, matter impregnated with mind: but the resultant issue is a living spirit, a glow in the consciousness, that perishes when the glow is dead. It is something snatched from non-being, that shadow which creeps in on us continuously and can be held off by continuous creative act. So, simply to look on anything such as a mountain, with the love that penetrates[3] to its essence, is to

widen the domain of being in the vastness of non-being. Man has no other reason for his existence. (2011, 102)

The fabric of experience is braided with the complementary functioning of all senses whereby each informs the others. A 'total experience' (2011, 105) occurs when senses are acute and combined, contrasting with 'living in one sense at a time' (2011, 105), which marks the lost innocence brought by modernity. Through phenomenological being, the transcendental subject is interrelated with the other; the world is total with 'its contours, its colours, its waters and rock, flowers and birds' (2011, 108), all expressing the interconnectedness of being. The perceiving body-subject collapses the distinction between a thing perceived and consciousness. The act of perceiving and the thing perceived are not distinguishable. Self and world exist in a dynamic interchange, the embodied consciousness inherently interleaved with the world. As Merleau-Ponty argues, 'the life of the body, or the flesh, and the life of the psyche are involved in a relationship of reciprocal expression' (2002, 185). The lines of the chiasm intersect momentarily, only to diverge at the point of intersection, the body 'keyed to its highest potential and controlled to a profound harmony deepening into something that resembles trance', a brief chance to 'discover most nearly what it is to be' (2011, 106). Pointing to the impossibility of the disembodied reflection, Shepherd underlines incarnate consciousness as the perceiving body-subject is intimately entwined with and is of the world. Such is Merleau-Ponty's view, Shepherd's affinity with whom was first pointed out by Robert Macfarlane (2011, xxix–xxxii). As Merleau-Ponty argues, 'the presence of the world is . . . the presence of its flesh to my flesh, that I "am of the world" and that I am not it' (1968, 127). Shepherd's representation of self suggests its incompleteness and processual nature: self is never completely or finally constituted, the embodied consciousness forever changeable in a constant intertwining with the world and the dynamic relations are never fully grasped by consciousness as they are lived through. Where action and perception are interconnected, the lived experience proves the hypothesis that there can be no detachment of the subject from the object.

Process extended in time, knowledge is never complete; in effect, the noun is replaced by a verb participle to emphasise its processual nature as '[k]nowing another is endless' (2011, 108). To know the land or, more specifically, the mountain, is '[t]o know Being', which is 'the final grace accorded from the mountain' (2011, 108). Gained through years of a slow and patient gathering of experience, which trickles down with each and every walk into the mountain, it amounts to an intimate knowledge, for '[t]he thing to be known grows with the knowing' (2011, 108). Yet an authentic being in the landscape does not seek 'only sensuous gratification', as Shepherd points out, enumerating various kinds of sensations, craved by some who climb mountains for that sole purpose, such as 'the sensation of height, the sensation of movement, the sensation of speed, the sensation of distance, the sensation of effort, the sensation of ease' (2011, 107). By structuring the sentence around repetition, Shepherd underlines the endless, insatiable, ego-dominated desire to collect experiences. She recognises the immaturity of the approach, driven by ego and focused on oneself, striving to achieve something only for oneself, and in effect ignoring the outside and using it for one's self-centred gain. Behind human-centred matters there is 'the mountain itself, its substance, its strength, its structure, its weathers', as Shepherd notes, thereby moving focus onto the land (2011, xlii–xliii). Someone who goes into the landscape in pursuit of nourishing the ego cannot be said to experience it truly.

Situated in time and place, the perceiving I is not an absolute entity. 'I know myself only insofar as I am inherent in time and in the world, that is, I know myself only in my ambiguity' (2002, 345), writes Merleau-Ponty. The ambiguity of the self is bound with the ambiguity of time [the subject is time and time is the subject (2002, 431–2)]: with the elusive present moment, the embodied consciousness transcends the individual horizons of significance. Rejecting the ego-driven approach which dominates in many mountaineering accounts (and much nature writing, for that matter) focused mainly on reaching the peak and collecting 'achievements', Shepherd is 'a peerer into corners' (2011, xlii), celebrating nooks and crannies, her approach differing from numerous accounts of mountain climbing in that it lacks the obsession with going *up* as she climbs 'back, to the sources' (2011, 3). She celebrates purposeless walking, going out 'merely to be with the mountain' (2011, 15) as 'the mountain gives itself most completely when I have no destination' (2011, 15). In Chapter 2 of *The Living Mountain*, Shepherd reverses the prevailing interest in the verticality (and therefore phallocentric perspective) of the mountains, focusing her writing around the hollows, peering down and around herself rather than up. Challenging the obsession with reaching a peak, Shepherd counters the recesses with the summits, their slow exploration. As one of her characters notices, it is not the heights but depth that matters, as it is the fourth dimension which resides 'down in – hollowness and mud and foul water and bad smells and holes and more mud. Not common mud. It's dissolution – a dimension that won't remain stable' (2017, 114). The concept of a 'spectacular'

(2011, 2) landscape is challenged by Shepherd: the sublime is not experienced through the verticality of the view, but looking at the plateau and watching the small-scale such as 'moss and lichen and sedge, and in June the clumps of Silence – moss campion' (2011, 2). Not seeking dramatic views or spectacular scenery, she continues to return to the same familiar places. For Shepherd, reaching the top is not the goal of climbing, as she devotes more attention to being-in-the-world, to walking *into* it, and not conquering it.

The work of an experienced climber and patient observer, *The Living Mountain* demonstrates an evolution of Shepherd's perception. When she was young, as she recalls, her interest in the mountain equalled an interest in herself as she was 'not interested in the mountain for itself, but for its effect upon me' (2011, 107). Only later did she discover the mountain 'in itself' (2011, 108). The final paragraph of *The Living Mountain* emphasises the interchangeable relation of the embodied consciousness and the land: 'as I penetrate more deeply into the mountain's life, I penetrate also into my own' (2011, 108). Shepherd writes about 'a journey into Being' (2011, 108), comparing it to a Buddhist pilgrimage to the mountain (see the chapter on Finlay, below). The word 'pilgrimage' also recurs in *The Quarry Wood*, where Martha's January walks are described as 'pilgrimages'; taking the form of 'exquisite initiations' (2018, 204); this is when her love of the earth erupts with intensity. (The word 'pilgrimage' will return below during the discussion of light.) Similarly, in *The Living Mountain*, Shepherd writes about a 'journey in pure love' (2011, 106), which becomes synonymous with 'a journey into experience' (2011, 107). The world becomes a revered place of worship, which accords enlightenment, the imaged emphasised through the adjective 'pure', which returns in Shepherd's writing, suggesting a sense of completeness, an unadulterated extract of a thing or phenomenon.

Ecological Enmeshing

Never stopping at a surface view, Shepherd dives within the landscape for an entanglement with matter, penetrating the world and gaining in-depth knowledge. The intertwining of the embodied consciousness with the world pervades her images. In her writing, especially in her 'journey into the mountain' (2011, 88), prepositions assume significance; among those most frequently used, 'into' is particularly favoured. Macfarlane argues that it is a preposition, which 'gains – by means of repeated use – the power of a verb' (2011, xx). Ecological enmeshing is present in the recurrent prepositions 'in', 'into' and 'inside', which create and emphasise the mediation of entangled matter. Shepherd writes about going *into* the mountain and '*into* the hill' (2011, 10), walking '*in* cloud' (2011, 22). Interiority is highlighted when such phrases as a 'sensation *inside*' (2011, 16) of a rock or walking, again, *inside* clouds (2011, 17) appear. In this, going into the mountain equals going into oneself, for to dwell in the world authentically means to be *in* oneself. The exhilaration the embodied self – or 'sheer exuberance of spirit' (2011, 70) – experiences in the landscape is the opposite movement to ecstasy, which Shepherd calls 'that leap out of the self' (2011, 108).[4] As she writes, 'I am not out of myself, but in myself' (2011, 108), whereby to be in oneself means to be 'beyond desire' (2011, 108). In contrast to going into oneself as a result of going into the mountain, Shepherd employs the expression to 'go through the business of living' (2011, 52) to suggest a hasty, unreflective existence. Going 'into' the world, employed by Shepherd frequently, contrasts with going 'through' in the expression cited above as the preposition suggests a careless, quick passage, a 'business', rather than a contemplative existence the image of which is created by the prepositions 'in' and 'into', creating a sense of unrushed, explorative immersion.

Shepherd employs phrases such as '[s]lowly I have found my way in' (2011, 105) in order to highlight the unhurried pace of entering the world. For instance, entering the wood, the spirit becomes 'responsive', there is an emphasis on the moment when it 'went out from her and was liberated'. There is a heightening of senses as hearing precedes sight: first the sound in 'the troubled hush of a thousand fir-trees' (2018, 6), then light, the transformation of which 'so changed, so subdued from its own lively ardour to the dark solemnity of that which it had entered' (2018, 6). This marks the birth of 'her perception of the world's beauty', when the 'quiet generosity of the visible and tangible world sank into her mind' (2018, 6). The world encroaches upon the embodied self, altering it. Yet the realisation that the world is not an object 'does not mean that there was a fusion or coinciding of me with it: on the contrary, this occurs because a sort of dehiscence opens my body in two, and because between my body looked at and my body looking, my body touched and my body touching', as Merleau-Ponty argues, explaining that 'there is overlapping or encroachment, so that we may say that the things pass into us, as well as we into the things' (1968, 123). As she walks deeper into the forest, the spirit of Martha, the protagonist of *The Quarry Wood*, resonates with the surrounding, gradually experiencing the encroachment of the world on her sense of hearing and sight. Becoming aware of the visible and tangible, her being is grounded in the flesh of the world, her perception based on a radical openness between the subject and object, resulting in the exchange between self and thing.

This moment when 'the things pass into us, as well as we into the things' (Merleau-Ponty 1968, 123) highlights the inseparability, the intertwining of inner and outer, an overlapping of one into another, making them subject to reciprocal openness. Shepherd demonstrates how centrifugal and centripetal forces govern the exchange as energy emanates from the interior of matter, 'lit up from within by contact with' the hill (2011, 14). The energy of the mountain enlivens its flesh, endowing it with agency embodied in 'the mountain's own doing' (2011, 98). For Shepherd, entering into the mountain resembles contact with 'another mind' (2011, 15). A being endowed with a mind, the mountain lives its own life, which Shepherd simply describes as 'the mountain's way of life' (2011, 50). The reference to the mountain's life recurs in expressions such as 'the very substance of the mountain is in its life' (2011, 51), glimpses of agency appearing in other forms of matter, for instance, 'living water' (2011, 23). Characterised with 'presence beyond representation', matter has 'an agency ordinarily attributed to human action and consciousness' (Allen 2014, 62).

There are instances of anthropomorphism in Shepherd's writing, particularly when she describes the seasons: spring depicted as a 'lady' (2017, 83), aurorae as the Merry Dancers (2018, 20), or when she attributes human features to the land, writing about 'a hardening of the whole temper of the land' (2018, 164). Yet Shepherd points out that she does not 'ascribe sentience to the mountain' (2011, 91). Through phrases such as water '[f]lowing from granite' (2011, 24), Shepherd shows the manner in which matter mingles in all its forms in a constant exchange. The changeability of the observed phenomena and things is inevitable, inherent to matter, or 'in plain fact', as Shepherd has it, just as '[t]he speed, the whorls and torrents of movement' are 'the mountain's own necessity' (2011, 64). Never inert but vibrant, to employ Jane Bennett's term, the world of matter is in a dynamic exchange with the embodied consciousness. For instance, the night brings serenity and radiance when paradoxically 'nothing moved, yet all was moving, eternally sustained by flight' (2017, 118). Material vibrancy is manifest in the depictions of entanglement between various forms. For instance, in Chapter 5 of *The Living Mountain*, 'Frost and Snow', she depicts an interaction between water and frost: '[e]ach is an interplay between two movements in simultaneous action, the freezing of frost and the running of water' (2011, 31); it is a 'materialisation of wind and frost' (2011, 33). As Shepherd puts it, 'static things may be caught in the very act of becoming' (2011, 10). Sleep affects consciousness so that '[o]ne is as tranquil as the stones, rooted far down in their immobility' (2011, 92). In the process, the soil ceases to be of the earth, becoming one flesh with the embodied self. The process of transformation continues when one wakes up, 'ceasing to be a stone, to be the soil of the earth, opening eyes that have human cognisance behind them upon what one has been profoundly a part of' (2011, 92). Shepherd concludes the description with two short sentences: 'That is all. One has been in' (2011, 92), as if the sensation of sinking into the earth, becoming one with stone and earth, when one form of matter momentarily dissolves into another. Similarly, identities permeate one another as species overlap: '[b]ird, animal and reptile – there is something of them all in the deer' (2011, 72); a flock of wild geese resemble 'the movement of a fish under water' (2011, 70); deer necks are 'like swaying snakes' (2011, 71). The process of momentary encroachment occurs when an object fuses with the surrounding: '[r]oes melt into the wood' (2011, 72), the earth 'seems to re-absorb' a doe disappearing into birches, 'this creature of air and light' (2011, 72). At another time, a tawny owl emerges from the dark only to be 'melted down into the air' (2011, 97) and a bird is a 'flake' of the 'earth that had escaped, far out into the blue air' (2017, 114). Towards the end of *The Living Mountain*, the realisation of the interrelated nature of the world intensifies, as Shepherd stresses being entangled with plants and non-human animals: 'I am a manifestation of its total life, as is the starry saxifrage or the white-winged ptarmigan' (2011, 106).

The interpenetration of matter, this deep entanglement, at times may lead to a total disintegration of self, becoming apparent in the momentary dissolution of the body into the surrounding world. For instance, the submergence occurs in *The Quarry Wood* as Martha experiences 'steeping herself in the life of earth and air' (2018, 204). Submerging herself into the landscape, 'sunk quite so deep into its life', Shepherd confesses in *The Living Mountain*, 'I have let go my self' (2011, 91). Shedding the ego is a moment when 'the mind grows limpid; the body melts; perception alone remains'. Through the separation of perception from mind and body, perception is distilled, which enables the perceiver to eliminate the intellect: '[o]ne neither thinks, nor desires, nor remembers, but dwells in pure intimacy with the tangible world' (2011, 90). The choice of the verb – 'to dwell' – to indicate the state of absolute perception suggests a slow, extended process, focused on being still, remaining in one place in opposition to the restless activity of the desiring body and the mind, constantly reasoning, remembering, wanting. Abolishing them, 'uncoupling the mind' (2011, 91) and releasing the body, the perceiver experiences an unmediated closeness with the physical world, becoming 'caught up in the tissue of the things' (Merleau-Ponty 1968, 135). Consciousness conjoins the two hemispheres, the complementary sky–earth. As Shepherd declares, 'there is nothing between me and the earth and sky' (2011, 90) ('nothing', that is air, to which I will return later in the chapter). The above passages echo a passage cited above in which Shepherd writes of 'a life of the senses so pure, so untouched by any mode of apprehension' (2011, 105). The embodied self incorporates what resides outside: it senses and communicates, and identity is 'for the time being merged in that of the mountains' (2011, 14). The experience of sinking far into the inner landscape of the mountain is accompanied by the sensation of shedding the physical body, of having 'walked out of the body and into the mountain' (2011, 106), becoming one with it, or even becoming it. In the above passages the opposition between self and other momentarily disappears in a shift beyond subjectivity. Thus Shepherd signals a radical openness to transcendence. Commenting on Merleau-Ponty's concept of flesh, 'the originary unity of the own and the non-own', Renaud Barbaras writes about 'a consciousness which sustains itself only by transgressing its own limits, by opening itself to another' (2004, 30). The ending of the penultimate chapter entitled 'The Senses' offers another image of the disintegration of self during an immersion in a mountain pool, which 'seems for a brief moment to disintegrate the very self': 'it is not to be borne: one is lost: stricken: annihilated'. 'Then life pours back' (2011, 104). The final statement reveals a paradox whereby being fully immersed in the world means in the outpouring of consciousness, there takes place a reduction of the sphere of self, that is or becomes an experience of a pre-cognitive, even pre-existent state. The unconventional punctuation emphasises the difficulty in capturing the sensation, the effect strengthened with the verb forms following one another 'lost: stricken: annihilated', as the passive form reflects the rendering of the self and an originary dimension of experience is revealed.

Touch and Texture

Admitting that 'eye and touch have the greatest potency' (2011, 98) for her, Shepherd reveals a deep connection between the sense of sight and touch in her work. The intertwining between vision and tactility occurs as the eye touches the world: 'like the exploratory gaze of true vision, the "knowing touch" projects us outside our body through movement' (Merleau-Ponty 2002, 367). We are transported outside our bodies, and in a reversible relation, the flesh of the world enters our selves. Shepherd calls touch 'the most intimate sense of all' (2011, 102), noting the versatility with which it activates the embodied self: 'The whole sensitive skin is played upon, the whole body, braced, resistant, poised, relaxed, answers to the thrust of forces incomparably stronger than itself' (2011, 102). Starting from the surface sensation, Shepherd then moves to the body conceived of as a totality. The attributes of the body are listed closely one by one, separated only by commas, thus denoting various, at times mutually exclusive states – both braced *and* resistant, both poised *and* relaxed – which the body undergoes and which begins always with touch. Touch may be external yet it is the most intimate, conveying 'an infinity of pleasure' (2011, 102) as well as essential knowledge. The point of direct contact between the embodied self and the world, touch plays an exploratory role. Similar to sight and hearing, touch is the portal through which the world enters: picking stagmoss equals gathering knowledge as it offers an opportunity to learn 'my way in, through my own fingers, to the secret of growth' (2011, 58).

Through parallelism, Shepherd emphasises the interchangeability of touch and vision – 'the freshness of the water slides over the skin like shadow' (2011, 104), and when submerged, the skin feels 'the glow that releases one's entire cosmos, running to the ends of the body as the spent wave runs out upon the sand' (2011, 104). The exchangeable nature of senses also includes touch akin to taste in a passage describing the sensation of feet meeting the long grass in the morning, 'like food melting to a new flavour in the mouth' (2011, 104). There are a number of descriptions of the tactile sensation of water throughout *The Living Mountain*. When the body meets 'the pouring strength of the water against one's limbs', the sensation of the stream's power emphasises 'this simple act of walking through running water' (2011, 104). At the coldness of water, 'the whole being retracts itself' (2011, 104), simultaneously presenting an 'icy delight' (2011, 104). At the source water contains a 'sting of life', which is 'in its touch' (2011, 26), and when it comes into contact with the palate or when it is poured down the throat, it 'stings' and 'tingles' (2011, 102).

Shepherd operates economically through taxonomical lists, enumerating different ways in which the world touches us, at times adding a modifier to make the description more precise: 'The feel of things, textures, surfaces, rough things like cones and bark, smooth things like stalks and feathers and pebbles rounded by water, the teasing of gossamers, the delicate tickle of a crawling caterpillar, the scratchiness or lichen, the warmth of the sun, the sting of hail, the blunt blow of tumbling water, the flow of wind' (2011, 103). Points of contact with surfaces of the world, hands and feet possess great sensitivity, sensing the touch of droplets of water from juniper and birches on the palms, and wet heather on bare feet. Shepherd relishes in coming in contact with various textures such as parts of plants: a flower stalk caught between her toes appears to be 'a small enchantment' (2011, 104); variable sensations of mud flats have 'a delicious touch, cushioned and smooth' (2011, 103); the skin 'feels the sun, it feels the wind running inside one's garment, it feels water closing on it as one slips under' (2011, 104). Through syntactic repetition in the latter citation, Shepherd emphasises the versatility of tactile sensations, the intimately sensitive nature of touch. Perception is both reversible – 'I can touch or that touches me' (2011, 103) – and exchangeable: as the eye touches the world, the world touches the eye. The body touches things around it, with the touching becoming plant, becoming bird, becoming stone, other identities spilling one into another. Attempting to transcend one's own perceptual frame leads Shepherd to wonder about other possibilities of being: 'If I had other senses, there are other things I should know' (2011, 105), which in turn suggests a move away from anthropocentric perspectives and an acknowledgment of other beings' *Umwelt*. Limitations in human perception stop us from knowing 'many exciting properties of matter', which cannot be accessed 'because we have no way to know them' (2011, 105). Realising that perception affects our knowledge of the world – just as the sense of smell contributes to our full perception of a flower – Shepherd recognises that 'other modes of perception' (2011, 105) would enable her to perceive things differently.

Vision and touch combine as the eye and foot relate in walking, their interconnectedness bypassing conscious thought as they 'acquire in rough walking a co-ordination that makes one distinctly aware of where the next step is to fall, even while watching sky and land' (2011, 13). Even if in her walks Shepherd returns to the same places, she sees them anew every time she goes to the mountain, the experience is incremental, growing with each visit, saturated moments when the embodied consciousness accesses Being. In such purity of experience the minute elements of the landscape 'come for a moment into perfect focus, and one can read at last the word that has been from the beginning' (2011, 106). Moments arrive when she is 'gazing tranced at the running water and listening to its song' (2011, 106) or walking for hours, 'the long rhythm of motion sustained until motion is felt, not merely known by the brain, as the "still centre" of being' (2011, 106). At times, the rhythm of walking resembles poetry ('she tramped the Quarry Wood beating out the metre' [2018, 89]); at other times it is akin to yogic breathing (2011, 106), a trance-like state bringing awareness to the present moment. The mind becomes embedded in the body, both welded with the world.

Yet something else occurs during the extended walks, as depicted in the following excerpt from *The Living Mountain*: 'Walking thus, hour after hour, the senses keyed, one walks the flesh transparent . . . The body is not made negligible, but paramount. Flesh is not annihilated but fulfilled. One is not bodiless, but essential body' (2011, 106). The above passage echoes Merleau-Ponty's statement that the body is one with the world but does not disappear in it, is not fused with it. Fusion with the existent world cannot occur as 'the visible things about us rest in themselves, and their natural being is so full that it seems to envelop their perceived being, as if our perception of them were formed within them' (1968, 122). The experience of the visible is not an experience of fusion as a real fusion, 'as of two positive terms or two elements of an alloyage', is impossible but 'an overlaying, as of a hollow and a relief which remain distinct' (1968, 123) occurs, thus rejecting the possibility of fusion with things as the 'sheath of non-being' inherent to subjectivity separates us from it (1968, 127). The seemingly paradoxical effect of walking occurs when consciousness is firmly embodied, in the mind. Extended walking reveals a direct connection between mind, foot and ground ('the grey-brown earth our minds had stood on' [2011, 17]) yet walking at night, under a moonless sky during a blackout, Shepherd finds with astonishment that her 'memory was so much in the eye and so little in the feet' (2011, 46), thus noting that the connection between the feet touching the ground must be supported by the relation between the mind through the eye.

Mind and Eye

When the embodied self perceives another, when a gaze falls upon an object, or 'stumbles against certain sights . . . and is thwarted by them' (1964, 94), 'intentional transgression' takes place, as Merleau-Ponty puts it. Following Husserl, who calls the event or experience as a 'pairing' or 'mating' phenomenon, Merleau-Ponty writes of 'paradoxically interchanged' (1964, 94) intentionality between viewer and object: 'The scene invites me to become its adequate viewer, as if a different mind than my own suddenly came to dwell in my body, or rather as if my mind were drawn out there and emigrated into the scene' (1964, 94). In Shepherd's work, pairing through vision is a fundamental perceptual activity. Viewing the world, she contemplates things and phenomena as well as the effect they exert on her vision (and therefore her self), her writing self-consciously coiling upon itself. Writing of eye accommodation, Shepherd employs a wording indicative of the separation of self from its senses, as if they were not one and the same thing. 'My eyes came closer and closer to myself' (2011, 66), she writes. Before pairing phenomenon occurs, a gap may open between the eye and mind, which augurs deception. From a claim that she believed her 'eyesight' (2011, 100) only when seeing a peregrine from a short distance, Shepherd moves to 'the illusions of the eye' (2011, 100), which are corrected by mist. A cloud may seem 'thick and threatening' (2011, 18) as it approaches, yet 'within it, it was neither tangible nor visible' (2011, 17).

Other illusions which are 'deceptive to the eye' (2011, 100) include distance and height. The reflection (or, one might say, self-reflection) leads Shepherd to conclude that such illusions of the eye, which may depend on a vantage point and experience, 'drive home the truth that our habitual vision of things is not necessarily right'; but, as Shepherd suggests, 'it is only one of an infinite number' (2011, 101). When we glimpse an unfamiliar object, it 'unmakes us, but steadies us again' (2011, 101), which suggests that, even though the pairing phenomenon lasts only momentarily, it may shake the perceiver. The self is solicited, and must respond. A sustained gaze may yield a deep, long-lasting result as it is one of the sensual means to uncover 'the essential nature' of the world, as Shepherd puts it. The phrase opens 'The Plateau', returning immediately in the next sentence as the author's statement of intent. As Shepherd declares, 'it is to know its essential nature that I am seeking here' (2011, 1). After announcing that she 'is seeking . . . [t]o know . . . with the knowledge that is a process of living', Shepherd admonishes her own 'glib assessment', proclaiming that it is impossible to know the mountain completely as it is impossible to know oneself in relation to the mountain. Through the circular language, Shepherd emphasises the importance of slow knowledge. Frequently, she enumerates things seen as if in an attempt to capture 'life in so many guises' (2011, 74), simultaneously recognising the limitations of this exercise as she asks, 'But why should I make a list? It serves no purpose, and they are all in the books. But they are not in the books for me – they are in living encounters, moments of their life that have crossed moments of mine' (2011, 67).

Foregrounding the importance of phenomenological experience as opposed to scientific descriptions of the world, to some extent Shepherd also questions the possibility of representation. These 'living encounters' when the embodied consciousness, focused on relational living, realises the entanglement with other beings and things, cannot be recorded in any form. Highlighting the brevity of these momentary crossings, Shepherd emphasises the subject's immersion in temporality. Once again she employs the words, which are 'living' and 'life' indicative of vital being, existence on the earth, the embodied consciousness entangled with things. The eye catches the dazzling plurality around, which the mind cannot comprehend and the tongue cannot express: 'How can I number the worlds to which the eye gives me entry? – the world of light, of colour, of shape, of shadow: of mathematical precision in the snowflake, the ice formation, the quartz crystal, the patterns of stamen and petal: of rhythm in the fluid curve and plunging line of the mountain faces' (2011, 101). In its insufficiency, language responds to that which the eye 'gives entry', to the directly felt experience of things which cannot be explained but may only be described through an approximation. There are always things and phenomena, which the eye grasps but language fails to express. (Briefly, Shepherd notes a glimpse of language in the coupling of poetry and the natural world when she admits to understanding poetry as she cites Gerard Manley Hopkins on sighting an eagle [2011, 100].) In *The Weatherhouse*, Lindsay acutely feels her inability to name the world: birds that she sees escape identification: 'by her untaught efforts it was hard to identify these moving flakes of life and the bright, multitudinous flowers' (2017, 183). She becomes obsessed with identifying them, determined to 'discover their identity' (2017, 183) as she realises that names hold a meaningful role: 'She had never valued accurate information, holding that only the spirit signified, externals were an accident; yet when she found that by noting external details she could identify a passing bird or a growing plant, a thrill of joy passed through her heart. She was no longer captive within her single self' (2017, 183). Spotting birds causes excitement, which grows after she learns what the birds are, two exclamation marks and the repetition highlighting her eagerness: 'Wild geese, wild geese! How wonderful the country is!' (2017, 47).

What follows is a succinct constatation: '"Names – they're like songs." And she chants in a singing voice, "Wild duck, wild duck, kingfisher, curlew. Their names are part of themselves' (2017, 47). Lindsay loves 'all beauty', which she considers to be a part of her 'undying self, possessed eternally, the kingdom within my soul' (2017, 181). 'Yet because she could not name the bird that flew up and hopped in front of her, a miserable sense of failure came across her spirit' (181). Such crushing sense of failure in the inability to name birds returns in the novel when Miss Annie asks Ellen what bird it was and she finds she is not only unable to name it but also say anything about its distinctive features. As she reflects on it, she realises that her ignorance extends further, onto 'the whole world outside herself' (2017, 182). As in the opening to *The Living Mountain*, the awareness of the lack of knowledge combined with the insufficient observational skills is a source of shame and failure. Not knowing a bird's name, not remembering the colour of its plumage or the shape of its beak seems 'absurd' yet the experience brings a realisation of a greater problem: 'she saw all at once that it was not only the bird's name of which she was ignorant: it was the whole world outside herself' (2017, 182). Not knowing the birds' characteristics means ignoring 'their real selves' (2017, 182), or even more, it is to despise them:

> She had never felt so much abased, so lonely in the multitude of living things. It was spring, they were around her in myriads; but she did not know them. They had their own nature. Even the number of spots upon an egg, the sheen on wing or tail, was part of their identity. And that, she saw, was holy. They were themselves. She could not enter into their life save by respecting their real nature. Not to know was to despise them. (2017, 182)

Knowledge of the natural world is synonymous with respect, as Lindsay feels that she owes it to birds to be able to distinguish and name them. She perceives them with reverence as each separate identity is 'holy': not paying attention to them individually, not knowing 'their real nature' means not valuing them. To perceive is precisely to 'regard', or respect, look with attention and take notice of things and phenomena.

Yet even being able to name is not always sufficient as language proves inadequate when sensual contact with the world is involved, as the taste of berries, which proves indescribable, the knowledge of their taste intersubjective, verifiable by the taste buds on one's tongue. Equally, the complex scent of the wood eludes verbal representation:

'All the aromatic and heady fragrances – pine and birch, bog myrtle, the spicy juniper, heather and the honey-sweet orchis, and the clean smell of wild thyme – mean nothing at all in words' (2011, 97–8). The list of various tree and plant species in the above passage, the aroma of which surrounds the embodied self, foregrounds the abundance of sensual stimuli surrounding one in the natural world which may only be experienced and not represented.

Reaching beyond the surface of things, describing them slowly and carefully, Shepherd offers an in-depth view. Even when she looks at an object, moving over its surface, she emphasises the deepening of one's experience, or, as she writes, 'one's sense of outer reality' (2011, 10). On numerous occasions, she stresses the significance of time in the act of looking as quick, careless survey yields nothing but the 'innermost inaccessibility' (2011, 11) of objects. For instance, after the initial moment in which she is 'mad to recover the tang of height' (2011, 9), she learns that time is needed to explore the complexity of Coire an Lochain, highlighting the multifaceted nature of the view, which proves 'incredible' (2011, 9) with every single climb. Observing the plateau is 'gazing into its depths, one loses all sense of time' (2011, 3) as if the space of the landscape extending before the observer stretched the temporal frame. Spatial relations are represented in terms of interiority rather than external dimensions. For instance, the ascent gives 'an interior' instead of the expected 'spaciousness' (2011, 16). Only when the perceiving I contemplates it slowly may its profundity appear. In moments when the self is all perception, 'not bedevilled with thought, but living in the clear simplicity of the senses' (2011, 93), it becomes momentarily fused with the world. Then, as Shepherd writes, '[n]othing has reference to me, the looker' (2011, 11), leading her to reach an insight that '[t]his is how the earth must see itself' (2011, 11). Such glimpses of perceptual lived experience occur when she gazes at the landscape for an extended period, becoming the landscape as she recognises that the observer is one and the same with the world, that the visible and seer are made from 'one sole tissue' (Merleau-Ponty 1968, 262).

The spatiality of vision is also foregrounded, whether the eye stretches towards the horizon or focuses on the nearby. Perception involves the depth of perspective, thus writing becomes a trompe l'œil. When Shepherd writes that she 'can see to the ends of the earth and far up into the sky' (2011, 22), vision extends horizontally and vertically, unhindered. At other times, the focus is on what is near, as in the following passage from *The Quarry Wood*: 'Midsummer: at their feet the sweet pink orchises, the waxen pale catheather, butterwort:

the drone and shimmer of dragon-flies around them: and everywhere the call of water' (2018, 114). The movement of the eyeball is traced through the adverbs: down, around and everywhere. The near focus closeness of the seen objects, which are 'at their feet' (2018, 114). The enumeration of wildflowers creates a sense of vibrancy, foregrounded by the splashes of colour. The passage is characteristic of Shepherd's style, which favours the interconnectedness of senses, whereby, as we can see once more, vision ('shimmer') combines with sound ('drone' and 'call') and possibly touch ('at their feet'). As already acknowledged, Shepherd's depictions of the landscape frequently suggest the interrelatedness of senses. It may be a relation between touch and vision as floating on air and 'tantalizing the face', gossamers are 'invisible, but flaring as they caught the sun like burnished ropes of light' (2018, 124). It may be a connection of other senses too, as in passages in which Shepherd moves from sight to the sense of smell to hearing, as light, scent and sound intertwine (see, e.g., 1928, 124–5).

A sense of sublimity appears fleetingly, as if in passing, in phrases recording astonishment at the surrounding landscape. On several occasions Shepherd notes something 'with amazement' or is 'amazed' at something. Being astonished, or an overwhelming sense of wonder, is a recurrent state, signalled by a cessation of faculties suggesting sublimity. The emotion starts at the visual level when a plant 'amazes the eye' (2011, 50) and when writing is an attempt to 'recapture some pristine amazement' (2011, 91). Reflecting on the essential, unfathomable mystery of elements, Shepherd touches upon the profundity of mysteries, which has the power to frighten – inspire awe – with their elemental simplicity (2011, 23). For instance, writing of water and its strength, she admits, 'I don't understand it. I cannot fathom its power' (2011, 27), or there is '[t]he secret the mountain never quite gives away' (2011, 58). Learning to read the landscape, Shepherd discovers a paradox which governs it: 'The more one learns of this intricate interplay . . . (an intricacy that has its astonishing moments, as when sundew and butterwort eat the insect), the more the mystery deepens', only to conclude that '[k]nowledge does not dispel mystery' (2011, 59). The plants which survived the ice age remain a mystery, inexplicable even to scientists, rendering 'the antiquity of a living flower' (2011, 59) unimaginable. This power affects the aesthetic sense, doubtless heightened by the unfathomable nature of the phenomena, which dominate the experience of the landscape.

Throughout Shepherd's writing there are references to the role of language in knowing the world, as has already been intimated; with this comes a divergence between what there is and what can be represented, thus emphasising linguistic inadequacy in capturing the nature of phenomena. For instance, when Shepherd writes about the interplay of water and ice, she admits that she does not know 'if description can describe these delicate manifestations' (2011, 31). On a few occasions, in search for an accurate manner in which to write about the world, she resorts to the register of optical and visual, often painterly aesthetics, for instance when comparing a pattern of a frozen burn with an artwork: 'the subtle shift of emphasis and superimposed design that occurs between a painting and the landscape it represents' (2011, 32) or when describing a view without depth, which appears as 'a painting without perspective' (2011, 98). Not eschewing evaluative language, Shepherd underlines the aesthetic pleasure of the landscape, employing phrases such as 'a stark splendour of line etched and impeccable' (2011, 25), 'majestic' (2011, 20, 21), 'a dream-like loveliness' (2011, 21). Words such as 'lovely' (2011, 25, twice on 32) and 'exquisite' (2011, 25, 43, 45, 51, and twice on 105) appear repeatedly. The landscape contains 'the sharpest beauty' (2011, 25) or 'a tenuous and ghost-like beauty' (2011, 44). The concept of the beautiful functions in Shepherd's texts as an aesthetic experience engendering Epicurean pleasure (see 2011, 67), yet rather than being superficial, it originates from the interplay between the mountain and the mind. 'Beauty is not adventitious but essential' (2011, 64), claims Shepherd, thus suggesting that the category does not arrive from the outside, that it is not something extraneous (in both senses of the word: external and irrelevant), but that beauty is an inherent attribute residing in the landscape.

Yet beauty is also something that is made by vision. In an attempt to eliminate 'confusion' and comprehend various elements of the landscape, the eye 'imposes its own rhythm' (2011, 101), which enables it to 'look creatively to see this mass of rock as more than jag and pinnacle – as beauty' (2011, 102). The moment of its revelation shakes the perceiver as the always unexpected onslaught of beauty touching the eye becomes palpable in the moments when 'the eye may suddenly perceive a miracle of beauty' (2011, 45). Recurring in Shepherd's texts, the word 'miracle' highlights the permanent unpreparedness of the perceiver for the singular event[5] – for instance in the expression 'a miracle of exact detail' (2011, 41), since in the rarefied air the shapes are sharper and the beauty of flowers enhanced, or in the phrase 'some rare miracle' (2017, 112) when the land is transfigured by light. Framing phenomena as miracles, or 'the whole wild enchantment' (2011, 3), Shepherd accepts the inexplicability of phenomena, which provokes moments of sublimity and highlights the purposelessness of things as well as their self-containment, as, for instance, the river, which 'does nothing, absolutely nothing, but be itself' (2011, 23). Similar to Norman MacCaig, Shepherd's appreciation of the landscape is not teleological, but is a response to the world as it is, for itself. When depicting Loch Coire an Lochain, or 'Loch of the Corrie of the Loch', she appreciates its anonymity. Despite expecting 'an idiosyncrasy', the loch appears to be 'a tarn like any other' (2011, 10). The paradox of the singular nature of the experience at the sight of a loch which is same but different from other lochs, makes Shepherd ask, 'what could there be there?' (2011, 10). Accompanied by astonishment, Shepherd finds there 'this distillation of loveliness' (2011, 10), whereby the word 'this', modifying the noun, emphasises what is being referred to and indicates a specific thing as if unable to name the thing. This specificity, or haecceity, highlights particular properties that make a thing what it is, bringing into relief the individualising difference, which emerges through vision as elemental presences foreground the phenomenological experience of a thing as such, drawing the essence of a thing to light.

Light and Colour

In *The Living Mountain*, light is mentioned around ninety times: it occupies the pages of the book just as it fills the landscape to the rim so that at times there is nothing but light. The emphasis that Shepherd places on light is revealed in recurrent words such as 'lucent', 'translucent', 'brilliant', 'brilliance', 'radiant' and 'radiance', while visibility is further stressed in words such as 'crystal clear' and 'limpid'. Shepherd spends a good deal of time watching and pondering on the properties of light, and depicting them (e.g. 2011, 91). Seeing the world in its graspable form momentarily revealed, otherwise obscure and unintelligible as objects intertwine with light, the perceiving subject observes an abstract quality become endowed with life and manifest its interactions through the medium of the body. Light touches the self, enveloping the skin and penetrating through the eyeball, creating the sensation of immersion as the body is 'bathed in the afterglow' (2011, 100). There is registered the impression of the insubstantiality of the world, 'hazed upon its edges, unstable where the hot air shook' (2018, 114), created by air and light challenges vision. As a result of an optical illusion, the heat moves the landscape, 'in a shimmering haze' (2018, 113), '[t]he hills trembled, so liquid a blue that they seemed at point of dissolution; and clouds like silver thistle-down floated and hovered above them' (2018, 113). On the other hand, Shepherd's texts also depict instances of the palpability of light, or 'a set of colors and surfaces inhabited by a touch, a vision' (Merleau-Ponty 1968, 135), whereby tactility and sight are interchangeable.

Light inundates the embodied consciousness, immersing it in the world as the radiance of the surrounding world permeates through the body, suffusing the incarnate self. In an interchangeable transfer, luminosity makes the outside and inside indistinguishable: it radiates from the self, endowing it with vitality 'too radiant to suffer from the privation' (Shepherd 2018, 113) of physiological functions. Penetrating through matter, light transforms its form and texture, as in the image of 'the fugitive spindrift feather' that light 'blows through', making it transparent (2011, 45). The transformative qualities of light, or 'the mystery of light', as Shepherd has it, under which the earth experiences 'the endless changes' (2011, 98). Suffusing matter, light makes it akin to itself, as is demonstrated in the depiction of a tree, which has 'no seeming substance', becoming 'like a lofty jet of essential light' (2017, 59), while catkins appear 'insubstantial', with 'the golden essence of its life escaping to the liberty of air' (2017, 59). The transmogrifying property of light is a recurrent motif in Shepherd's writing. A doe disappearing into birches is 'this creature of air and light' (2011, 72); in spring, light transforms trees out of all resemblance, making them 'little earthly' (2017, 176) and adding an ethereal element so that, Shepherd concludes. '[m]ere vegetable matter they are not' (2017, 176). Describing spring woods, she writes that they are 'flaming', with a flame 'strong and pure', as the trees 'not now by accident of light but in themselves' become 'etherealised' (2017, 176). This phenomenon occurs in spring when 'life in trees is like a pure and subtle fire in buds and boughs', light affecting how various trees appear: willows are compared to 'yellow rods of fire', while the sycamore contains 'blood-red burns' (2017, 176). The recurrent insistence on light already appears in Shepherd poems, for instance 'Fires' (2014, 4–5) and 'Lux perpetua' (2014, 12–13), in which the dual power of light and darkness is foregrounded, the latter poem ending with the lines: 'New revelations of the only Light, / Illuminating awhile, again returning / Within the unbroken splendour infinite, / The always burning' (2014, 13, ll. 33–6).

Shepherd devotes space to the description of beeches, elms, birches, ensuring that the effect of light is depicted differently. A walk through the wood at night brings paradoxes: the twilight 'luminous', the sky 'glowed like some enormous jewel' filled with fire 'diffuse within itself', its concentration 'focussed in leaping stars' (2017, 74). The transfiguration resides in the power of light to affect deeply sight, taking it 'without interruption to the rims of the world' (2017, 29). Vision may be carried through the air as 'if the winds have unhindered range, so has the eye' (2011, 2). In Chapter 6 of *The Living Mountain* entitled 'Air and Light', Shepherd reflects on the relativity of vision recording instances of visual illusion (see, e.g., 2011, 78), and the motif already occurs in Shepherd's novels (see, e.g., 2017, 46). The effect of the surrounding luminosity disrupts other senses as exemplified in the following passage from *The Weatherhouse*:

> The matted snow and grass were solid enough beneath her feet, but when she looked beyond she felt that she must topple over into that reverberation of light. . . . She was lost in light and space. When she moved on it surprised her that she stumbled with the rough going. She ought to have glided like light over in earth so insubstantial. (2017, 29)

Such is the energy of light that it permeates and saturates Lindsay, dissolving her identity and enveloping it within itself. Light creates an uncanny effect, heightened by the sense of stillness, 'part of the magic of the place and hour' (2018, 74), as Shepherd writes in *The Quarry Wood*.

Watching the sky change, Martha experiences the *Unheimlich* in the landscape as 'the familiar line of hills grow strange in the dusky pallor of a summer midnight' (2018, 113). The space of the field becomes her 'cubicle', which gives her privacy, paradoxically shrinking its vastness. Similarly, the paradox is there when, overwhelmed with air and light after climbing a mountain, Garry feels that space 'encompassed him' (2017, 112), made him become 'rapt up into the infinitudes around, lost for awhile the limitations of himself' (2017, 112). The sense of being held within the boundaries of space brings a paradoxical realisation of a limitlessness, which in turn provokes a reflection on the interconnectedness as exemplified in the words: 'the shimmer of light, a breath, a passing air' (2017, 112). Coming closely one after another, interlinked with commas, the three elements are enclosed in the phrase suggesting togetherness. Light itself suffices to transform the hard land of stone, gorse and heather. For instance, the trees and hills appear to 'float', suddenly insubstantial, 'like a distillation that light had set free from the earth', thus essentialised 'like flakes of green fire, floated too, the wild burning life of spring loosened from earth's control' (2017, 112). Appearing five times in the passage, the verb 'float' also refers to scent and 'song' suggests the interplay between matter, air and light, transforming one another. The embodied perceiver, for whom sight, scent and hearing intertwine, experiences a spectacle of transfigured substance, moving softly on the surface of air, 'the subtle life released from earth and assailing the pulses' (2017, 112). Resembling a spirit-filled fairyland, the earth becomes 'transmuted' (2017, 112), changing 'before one's eyes', and turning into 'an elfin and enchanted radiance', revealing the possibility of the world to 'look, by some rare miracle of light or moisture, essentialised' (2017, 112).

As well as transform, light can momentarily uncover the inherent nature of things and phenomena, which otherwise remain obfuscated. Couched in religious terms, the depicted change of an anthropomorphised land resembles transubstantiation: '[a] measure of her life this morning had gone up in sacrifice' as '[h]er substance had become spirit' (2017, 112–13). Solid matter turns insubstantial, the land appears to be on the verge of 'dissolution into light', and together with it the people, 'shaped from a stuff as hard and intractable as their rock, through weathers as rude as stormed upon their heights' become 'dissolved in light' during 'their hours of transfiguration' (2017, 113). This recalls the passage above, in which light distils the features of the earth unveiling 'life essentialised' (2017, 113) which resides in people. In that moment of illumination, substance becomes pure energy: 'All was life. Life pulsed in the clods of earth that the ploughshares were breaking, in the shares, the men. Substance, no matter what its form, was rare and fine' (2017, 175). The brief moment of perception passes, yet it reveals that each substance is governed by individual properties, possessing 'its own secret nature, exquisite, mysterious' (2017, 175), which suggests the revelation of enchantment, of becoming enchanted. Shepherd's preoccupation with the essence of vibrant matter occurs in her poetry. For instance, in 'The hill burns' (2014, 8–9), Shepherd evokes 'living water' (2014, 9; l. 47), which is 'fiercely pure' (l. 3), the adjective recurring in the closing lines of the poem: 'pure essence of being / invisible in itself, / Seen only by its movement' (2014, 9, ll. 48–50). The new theories in science and philosophy concerning the nature of physical matter learned at the university become real in front of the character's eyes, there in the countryside, which ceases to be 'the agglomeration of woods, fields, roads, farms' (2017, 176). The landscape, 'mysterious as a star at dusk', momentarily assumes a different form, becoming 'visible as an entity', it *takes form*, 'form from the dark, solid, crass, mere bulk', yet imbued – 'irradiated' – with light 'until its substance all but vanished'; it is stripped of its physical properties, becoming insubstantial. The land appears 'neither crass nor rare, but both in one'. So much that is 'fine' coming 'from coarse plain earth' (2017, 176). Suffusing the air, light yields itself to the appearance of the place, which 'has as many aspects as there are gradations in the light' (2011, 2). The distinctive atmosphere of the mountain transforms the light. The variable nature of the landscape is evoked in the repeated 'now', recurring five times over several lines (2011, 98), which emphasises the dynamism of changes and grounds the embodied consciousness in the present. The volatility of matter is evoked through analogies. For instance, a swift, first a dark shape, becomes transformed in 'a jet of water' (2011, 60), a burn has 'the effect of sunshine' (2011, 43), the stones retain their intensity 'as though the water itself held radiance' (2011, 43). The landscape gains a shimmering texture as illuminating the place, light unearths its variable features to the perceiving self. The shimmer, the glister, is the spirit of place, perceived by the subject entwined in the event of the world.

Profound reverence given to light is epitomised in the frequency with which it is mentioned as well as the phrases employed to depict it. Shepherd herself and her characters do not walk through a place but they pilgrimage 'in the growing and waning light' (2018, 204), the expression stressing the bodily immersion in the insubstantial landscape created by light itself. For instance, in *The Living Mountain*, Shepherd writes of walking 'in cloud', before it 'dissolved into the air', leaving 'nothing in all the sky but light' (2011, 22). The phrase 'nothing but light' already appears in *The Quarry Wood*, emphasising a marked feature of the Scottish landscape, namely openness. Pouring into the open space, light stresses the near borderless aspect of the landscape. As Martha, Geordie and Dussie 'stood on Scotland', Shepherd writes, 'there was nothing north of them but light' (2018, 20). The light extending far towards the horizon makes Dussie wonder 'what bounded Scotland when the Aurora was not there', to which the reply comes: 'Eternity. That's fat wast o'Scotland. I mind it noo' (2018, 20):

> Scotland is bounded on the south by England, on the east by the rising sun, on the north by the Arory-bory-Alice, and on the west by Eternity.
> Eternity did not seem to be in any of her maps: but neither was the Aurora. She accepted that negligence of the map-makers as she accepted so much else in life. She had enough to occupy her meanwhile in discovering what life held, without concerning herself as to what it lacked. (2018, 20)

The above passage suggests a boundless aspect to the Scottish landscape. In *The Weatherhouse* the power to release the embodied self through its vastness is emphasised yet again: 'It was a country that liberated' as '[m]ore than half the world was sky. The coastline vanished at one of the four corners of the earth' (2017, 9–10). The passages suggest that Scotland has an infinite plasticity, which expands and grows 'wider' as the north comes 'alive' (2018, 54), as Shepherd writes elsewhere. The effect the landscape exerts on Ellen, who 'lost herself in its immensity', is abandoned as she feels that '[i]t wiled her from thought' (2017, 10), a dissolution of mind, a state similar to the one described in *The Living Mountain*. The boundless space lures her from the separateness of body and mind, melting the distinction and thus 'restor[ing]' her. Elsewhere Shepherd writes of the 'vast north' and 'the enormous heaven' (2018, 18). Despite its vastness – or thanks to it – the land provides a foundation and footing. Surrounding the embodied self, the earth – 'primitive, shapeless, intractable' – offers stability, which the sea cannot as it is 'after all, not so very wide', as opposed to the earth, which is 'everywhere about one, and could not be ignored' (2017, 161), as Shepherd concludes. More importantly, it is the earth which is the repository of roots, hidden from sight and often forgotten.

Light is inevitably present in the recurrent depictions of northern midsummer and its night-long twilight, which affects the perceiver as '[w]atching it, the mind grows incandescent and its glow burns down into deep and tranquil sleep' (2011, 91), the prepositions once again indicating a move into the depths. Yet the northerly condition of the landscape is emphasised in the lingering light or by the spectacle created by aurorae when the night is paradoxically 'sheeted in light' (2018, 18). In *The Quarry Wood*, as the characters walk out of a firelit house during 'a bewildering January dark', they observe 'the north on fire'. It astonishes them as the night is not 'really dark' but rather a darkness 'that glowed' (2018, 18). The uncanny effect proves to be the result of the Merry Dancers. In the description of the Northern Lights, Shepherd extends the anthropomorphism of the Scottish name to create a dynamic image as the light 'danced in storm' while the elements are endowed with human-like abilities and characteristics: the sun 'crept doubtfully back to silence' (2018, 20); the winds are 'shifty' or 'unvarying' (2018, 20); 'Tongues of flame ran up the sky, flickered, fell back in the unstable pools of flame that gathered on the horizon, rose to crests again and broke into flying jets' (2018, 18). The above passages brim with verbs, animating the image and creating an impression of vibrancy, complete with the depiction of sky, which, through a reversal, becomes the sea as clouds resemble proud galleons, 'their white sails billowing on the north horizon' (2018, 21).

The hint of light in darkness is a common motif in Shepherd's writing, who underlines the manner in which light and darkness intermingle. Liminal phenomena, both light and crepuscularity are a condition of the 'character' of the Scottish landscape. It is depicted when, stepping into the night a character paradoxically experiences an overwhelming luminosity: 'The night astonished her, so huge it was. She had the sense of escaping from the lit room into light itself. Light was everywhere: it gleamed from the whole surface of the earth, the moon poured it to the farthest quarters of heaven, round a third of the horizon the sea shimmered' (2017, 29). In that moment of sublimity, Lindsay experiences an all-encompassing force of light as she leaves the room to be submerged into 'light itself' (2017, 29), or light which absorbs all the other elements of the landscape. As she walks into the landscape, she watches various textures of solid matter until 'that reverberation of light' dissolves her body into an insubstantial form and she is lost, '[h]er identity vanished' (2017, 29). For another character, the night opens up to reveal things about the land inhabited by 'old wives and ploughmen' (2017, 56). Walking at night-time, the landscape resembles a climb into the mountain, and going deep *into* the dark begins to affect consciousness: 'as he mounted farther into the night, the night, growing upon his consciousness, was a dark hole no longer. The sky, still dark, brooded upon a darker earth, but with no sense of oppression. Rather both sky and earth rolled away, were lost in a primordial darkness whence they had but half emerged' (2017, 56). During a walk into the vastness of the nocturnal landscape, darkness enters consciousness and the self becomes saturated with the outside.

There are recurrent suggestions of the ancient nature of the dark, exemplified in the expressions 'a primordial darkness' and 'primordial dark' (2017, 113): watching 'the land emerge and take form slowly from primordial dark' (2017, 113), the world 'takes form from primordial dark' (2017, 85), while a character becomes 'a creature only half set free from the primordial dark' (2017, 56). Endowed with enormous power, its ancient energy forged before the earth came into existence, self-emanating, self-originating, dark emerges from non-living matter. During such a night, astonished 'at the vastness which this familiar country had assumed', Gary notices the '[w]idth and spaciousness it always had, long clear lines, a far horizon, height of sky' (2017, 56). The properties of the landscape – 'spaciousness', 'width', 'vastness' – open up to reveal the depths of time, as the experience makes the character contemplate the turbulent history made by 'Picts and Celtic clansmen, raiders and Jacobites' (2017, 56) in the landscape of stone circles, forts, castles. All these, along with wall remnants blend with cairns, glens and recesses, crags, ledges and caves. If, before, Scotland had appeared to him 'a small land; poor; ill to harvest, its fields ringed about with dykes of stone laboriously gathered from the soil' (2017, 56), he begins to notice its vastness, both in spatial and temporal terms. In Shepherd's writing darkness does not appear as a void but a creative force from which things emerge:

> the darkness, to his accustomed eyes, was no longer a covering, but a quality of what he looked upon. Waste land and the fields, in common with the arch of sky, and now a grandeur unsuspected in the day. Light showed them as they were at a moment of time, but the dark revealed their timeless attributes . . . hinting at a sublime truth than the eye could distinguish. (2017, 57)

In the face of the dark vastness, time dissolves as Garry feels 'for a moment as though he had ceased to live at the point in time where all his experience had hitherto been amassed' (2017, 57). The self momentarily disintegrates, fused with the flesh of the world, becoming one: 'time and the individual had ceased to matter' (2017, 58), the state engendered not so much by the diminished capacity of vision as a glimpse into the timelessness of the landscape, uncovered by 'a sublime truth'. The defamiliarising effect of night is experienced by another character who notices an uncanny lack of darkness but replaced by 'the diffusion of light', which is 'strange and troubling' (2018, 116). In the small hours in the wood the light is 'stranger still', creating the sense of the uncanny, a place 'from another world; as though someone had enclosed it long ago in a volatile spirit, through which as through a subtly altering medium one saw its boughs and boles' (2018, 116). The eerie effect made by light – 'the glimmering gloom', 'a swift glimpse of fire' – engenders disquietude in Martha who experiences 'an undefined terror' (2018, 116).

The references to the uncanny aspect of light return in phrases such as 'the strange shimmering night' (2018, 116) and 'a ghost of light' (2018, 120), the latter recurring in Luke's rendition of his encounter in the woods with Martha:

> 'Ghost of light, not of darkness. You never saw such a night! Moon up and the whole sky like silk – gleamed. So did the earth. You felt

like – or at least I felt like – a stitch or two of Chinese embroidery. You know – as though you were on a panel of silk. Unreal. I went as far as Martha's wood – the Quarry Wood . . . You know that thing – Rosetti's – about going down to the deep wells of light and bathing. It was like that. Only it was like an ocean, not a well. Submarine. Seas of light washing over you, far up above your head, and all the boughs and things were like the sea-blooms and the oozy woods that wear – you know. It was like being dissolved in a Shelley ode. Your body hadn't substance – it was all dissolved away except its shape. You walked about among shapes that hadn't substance, unreal shapes like things under the sea. . . . You forgot ugly everything, and when Marty came walking through the wood you knew she wasn't real – just a ghost of light.' (2018, 119–20)

Filled with affected expressions such as the exclamation mark, ellipses and dashes, Luke's enthused account mediates a sense of enlightenment that he experienced on the encounter in the woods. The expression 'a ghost of light' frames the passage, highlighting the eerie, paradoxical aspect of the nocturnal encounter. A haunting which shakes the self, light assumes a form of an apparition in the land. Hauntings return in the local lore. For instance, sleet resembles 'sheered ghosts', part of a ploughman's story in Deeside, who, 'bewildered in an April dusk, saw white showers walk the land, larger than human, driven on the wind' (2017, 83).

It is April light which returns in Shepherd's writing most insistently as she frequently returns to the aspects of northern light after the spring equinox. Even though the image of light and darkness as a dichotomy appears in Shepherd's work, it is not a prevalent view. There are Christian echoes, as in the poem 'Lux perpetua' (2014, 12), where she writes of the 'strange darknesses' of the soul (2014, 14), illuminating the mind.[6] More frequent are the references to light in Celtic mythology, as, for instance, in 'a tree hung in light' (2011, 45), which echoes the Silver Bough in the sacred apple tree, a symbol of the connection between this world and the world beyond. This may suggest that ancient beliefs lie closer to the land.

The description of the transformative effect of light and water is captured as a hand becomes a tree becomes a plant becomes a bird. There appears a protective 'film of light' (2011, 45) between a dipper and the stream as it plunges into the water. The plateau is 'glittering white . . . an immaculate vision against, sun-struck, lifting against a sky of dazzling blue' (2011, 107). Colour assumes a material, almost palpable form as vision is 'within reach of my fingers' (2011, 107). It is colour that draws and binds Shepherd so forcefully to the mountain. As she recalls, as a child she gazed at 'the stormy violet of a gully' (2011, 106–7) and 'its almost tangible ultramarine' (2011, 107), which filled her dreams. It is that 'stormy violet' that '*thirled* me for life to the mountain' (2011, 107). Touching the eye, colour has the power to move: 'the violet range of colours can trouble the mind like music' (2011, 42), 'the colour seemed to live its own life, to have body and resilience, as though we were not looking at it, but were inside its substance' (2011, 30). 'An object is an organism of colours, smells, sounds and tactile appearances which symbolize, modify and accord with each other' (Merleau-Ponty 2002, 45). Water appears in various shades of green, changing with light, 'now aquamarine, now Verdigris, but it is always pure green, metallic rather than vegetable' (2011, 25), lochs can be 'black by place and not by nature' (2011, 25), the sky and the mountain the same 'deep slate blue' (2011, 34), as the black 'belongs' to the boulder. Capturing the sensation of colour in its overspill reinforces the entanglement of matter, whereby one object affects another through the 'play of colours' filling the field of perception (Merleau-Ponty 2002, xi). As if endowed with a life of its own, colour 'spurts upwards through all the creeping and inconspicuous growths that live among the heather roots – mosses that are lush green, or oak-brow, or scarlet, and the berried plants, blaeberry, cranberry, crowberry and the rest' (2011, 54). It emanates into the air becoming fire – 'flaming crimson', 'a multitude of pointed flames seem to burn upwards all over the moor' (2011, 54) – one element turning into another, contradictory and yet, paradoxically, complementary. Shepherd demonstrates how the perception of colour is affected by the embodied consciousness as, for instance, in the description of a midsummer twilight, when Martha and Luke, 'drowsed with happiness', watch the shadows on the hills, the 'darknesses' of which appear 'tender purple, and stars, too soft to shine', the sky 'dust-of-gold' (2018, 114). The phrasing – 'tender', 'too soft' – suggesting gentleness and enchantment, reflects their emotional state and affects their vision, further confirmed in the hyperbolic statement which follows: 'There were no stars too soft, no purple too tender, no dust-of-gold too paradisal, for their mood' (2018, 114). In Shepherd's writing, vitality is embodied in the shades of blue that suffuse the land. As a 'flood of new life . . . welled up within her', the character has the sense that 'the world for her was azure' (2017, 103). Various shades of blue – from indigo, to 'the clear enamelled blue', to hyacinth, to 'the unfathomable gulfs of blue' (2018, 80) – appear in following description of the land:

> The country was indigo, its austere line running out against a burnished sky to the clear enamelled blue of the mountains. Rain at sea, a soft trail of it like grey gauze blowing in the wind. And an enormous sky, where clouds of shadowed ivory and lustrous hyacinth filed by in vast processional; yet were no more than swayed in the wash of shallows when the eye plunged past them to the unfathomable gulfs of blue beyond. (2018, 80)

The view over the land is dominated by the vast sky into which the eye 'plunges', going deep beyond. It appears as if saturated with hues of blue; the sky colours everything around it with its enormity, as if it engulfs the mountains and the sea. At another time, when Martha watches the play of light on the land – 'those infinitudes of light' (2018, 80) – the ploughed land catches the afterglow, the soil and light intertwine, appearing 'to focus for her the life of the soil' (2018, 204). The phrase foregrounds the intertwining of light and matter, the former powerfully affecting the physical world. It is also colour which connects Shepherd's characters with the world of nature. After Martha gazes at the clouds, which appear 'like green glass curving upward from the east horizon', she looks in the mirror to discover that her eyes contain the same greens as well as a blend of other colours: 'She could not even tell their colour exactly: they had something in them of Nature's greens that have gone brown, of grassfields before the freshening of spring' (2018, 79). In the above passage, vision is affected by the view: as they touch the outside, the eyes assume the shades of the surrounding, they acquire the features of the outside, the indeterminacy of colour indicating the momentary crossover.

Elemental Being

Shepherd never ceased knowing 'that earth, air, fire, and water move, rebel, ally, crush, and desire' (Cohen and Duckert 2015, 5). The depictions of the elemental world in her work reflect the contrasting complementarity of elements and matter. This is, for instance, captured in Shepherd's depiction of snow: when still falling, it floats through the air, assuming its qualities, becoming air, then becoming plant, becoming animal, its delicate form resembling parts of a plant or secretions of an animal: 'the wind sailed minute thistledowns of snow, mere gossamers' (2011, 37). Fragile and delicate, snowflakes already contain the future form – 'presaged' – the nucleolus of the thing to come, revealing its future 'weight and solidity' (2011, 37).

A recurrent motif in Shepherd's writing, an interchangeability of faculties and spheres, is indicated through parallelism. For example, the sound of water in a stream is 'as integral to the mountain as pollen to the flower' (2011, 26). The sonic effect is apperceived, appearing in our line of hearing 'without listening[,] as one breathes without thinking' (2011, 26). Once active listening begins, the sound 'disintegrates into many different notes' (2011, 26), the ear reads different notes, recognising different forms of moving water, whether it is loch, rivulet or creek. During her walk to the source of the River Dee – 'the Wells of Dee' – Shepherd describes a feeling of sublimity that she experiences, comparing it to 'all profound mysteries' – the mystery of water (also 'the eternal mystery of moving water' [2017, 57]), 'one of the four elemental mysteries' (2011, 23), which appears 'so simple that it frightens' (2011, 23) for '[i]t does nothing, absolutely nothing, but be itself' (2011, 23). A simple mystery may seem oxymoronic yet it expresses the illuminating realisation of the elemental self-containment: enclosed within itself, water reveals its essential nature, which resides in its completeness. Where complexity already begins decipherability, simplicity suggests profundity, a *mysterium tremendum*, or an awe-inspiring mystery. Its elemental energy overflows onto objects which come in contact with it. Falling on the skin, water transfigures the embodied self, exemplified in the following passage from *The Quarry Wood*: 'She felt light, as though her body were seawrack floating in the deluge of waters; or as though an energy too exorbitant for her frame, coursing through her, had whipped her into foam' (2018, 102). The body becomes seaweed, becomes the surf of the sea as '[w]ashed by the rain she felt strong and large, like a wind that tosses the Atlantic or a tide at flood' (2018, 102–3). Being soaked with rain gives one a '[g]ood elemental feel' (2018, 102), as Shepherd puts it. The word 'elemental' reverberates throughout the passage, as the character realises the nature of her experience: 'Elemental! – That was it' (2018, 102–3). The use of the word resonates with the elemental as described by Stacey Alaimo, who argues that it is 'not bare life but something more denuded ... something not stripped at all but always only and ever itself, deep down' (2015, 298), thus referring to Agamben's *Homo Sacer* and his concept of bare life in relation to the elemental, which highlights the biological fact of life prioritised before its possibilities and potentialities.

The transformation of matter reflects the essential substance, its constant presence. The infinity of air, constituting 'part of the mountain, which does not come to an end with its rock and its soil' (2011, 41). The air is presented as a connective element, binding the earth and sky as, for instance, in the depiction of an eagle's flight (2011, 62), whereby the simile suggests that all is one, inextricably bound. A similar scene appears in *The Weatherhouse* where the open is suggested by bird flight (see 2017, 46), the lines of the wings marking the sky and connecting it with the earth through the air. As Luce Irigaray notices, '[n]o other element is in this way space prior to all localization, and a substratum both immobile and mobile, permanent and flowing' (Irigaray 1999, 8). The categories such as here or there cease to matter; the concept of presence is challenged. Air is 'impossible to appropriate' (Irigaray 2002, 79) as it is shared and exchanged. Breath is 'the first and last gesture of natural and spiritual life' (Irigaray 2002, 5); it reconnects the body and spirit, healing the split. Writing of autonomy when breathing by oneself – 'To discover that I can live in an autonomous manner, that no one is absolutely necessary for me' (Irigaray 2002, 5) – Irigaray ignores the connective aspect of breath: air connects through breath which is a trace of others – breath is the ghost of touch – human as well as non-human beings dwelling in a shared space. If the vital function of air with which 'the outside enters' the human body 'limitlessly' (Irigaray 1999, 41) is acknowledged, it emphasises relatedness, which begins with breathing 'before perceiving and awakening to relational living, belonging to colours and lights through sight, to sounds through hearing' (Merleau-Ponty 2002, 185). For Shepherd, the catch in the breath resembles 'a wave held back' (2011, 104), 'the glow that releases one's entire cosmos, running to the ends of the body as the spent wave runs out upon the sand' (2011, 104). The oceanic metaphor reinforces the interrelational nature of air. Matter becomes transmuted as water and air enter the body, exuded in the form of perspiration and breath. A 'primary process' of living (Merleau-Ponty 2002, 185), breathing relates the embodied self to the world. Bound up with breath (and aroma), scent is 'very much pertinent to the theme of life, for it is largely a by-product of the process of living' (2011, 51), as Shepherd puts it. Shepherd stresses this phenomenon, expanding on the description: 'I draw life in through the delicate hairs of my nostrils' (2011, 52). Penetrating the body, air as the scent of sap becomes breath becomes 'the very life itself' (2011, 52), which enters the lungs. Breath is the carrier of aroma, which is airborne. Scent activates the body, the process described in detail by Shepherd, even though its effect escapes definition: 'a tang that tautens the membranes of nose and throat' (2011, 52) and 'through the sensory nerves, it confuses the higher centres; one is excited, with no cause that the wit can define' (2011, 53). Entering the body, the fragrance suffuses it with the outside world, which becomes part of self. The embodied consciousness goes from one state into another, assuming other forms, as when it absorbs the attributes of the surrounding. The physical properties of air coming into contact with the inside of the body are highlighted by the use of the verb: the air 'smacks' the mouth as it enters it, filling the lungs with the wind and frost (2011, 102). But breath also frees the body, just as rain 'releases' the scent of birch (2011, 53). The word 'release' returns in the descriptions of being in the landscape, which yields 'that joyous release of the body' (2011, 6) and 'the joyous release of an exhausted body' (2011, 85), the altitudes 'released' the self (2011, 7). The depicted sense of abandon becomes thwarted when one walks through a field of fragrant heather, the intensity of which may have a stupefying effect on the body, which resembles 'too much incense in church' (2011, 51), stifling intellectual faculties. Thus, while air releases the body, its scent may overwhelm and dominate other senses.

Extensive passages devoted to the atmospherics emphasise the extent of the embodied self's immersion in the weathered landscape.[7] Frequently contradictory, the weather on the plateau may astonish with its dynamic changes as when summer months bring winter weather: 'cloud, mist, howling wind, hailstones, rain and even a blizzard' (2011, 60). At times 'a splash of radiant weather' (2011, 93) occurs, a phrase which underlines both the suddenness and briefness of sunshine. Suspended in the air, rain and haze trick vision, creating unexpected effects. Akin to a sea, the mist floods the land, obscuring and revealing, making the view disappear, only to make it reappear, released by the emergence of the sun (cf. 2011, 18). What appears is unveiled in the play of the visible and the invisible. This effect – 'the dim white ghostliness out of which stark shapes' emerge – deceives the mind, or, as Shepherd puts it, they 'batter at my brain ... [they have] overpowered my reason' (2011, 99). The physical aspect of the atmospherics may be overpowering, for instance when sleet creates a 'barricade' (2018, 36), preventing walkers from passing. The embodied experience entails an immersion in its elements, coming in contact with its textures. At times the elements combine – '[w]ind, water, earth, came with him' (2018, 37) – accompanying the walker and intertwining with the self, leaving traces. At other times the touch of the weather-world is insubstantial as when climbing, Shepherd walks 'out through the top of a cloud' (2011, 18). Sensation units may vary one from another: one time the cloud may be 'wet but not wetting' (2011, 17), while at another 'just dry-dull' (2011, 18).

The blending of elements, one into another, is emphasised through language, for instance in the interchangeable use of verbs denominating wind and rain in the following passage: 'The wind poured on – a south-wester like an elemental energy. Garry stood awhile in the fury. The shriek of wind' (2017, 171). The two nouns set together – 'fury' and 'shriek' – reinforce the elemental energy of the wind, its unharnessed energy. Thus depicted, the landscape loses its physical properties as substance becomes pure energy.

Life on the land, invariably lived according to seasonal rhythms, is highlighted in detailed descriptions as the characters experience the effects of the atmospherics and following the change of light. As Shepherd reminds her readers in her stories set in rural landscapes, spring is awaited impatiently, the wait which may only be accelerated in narrative terms as February rolls into March in the space of one paragraph:

> The sleet eased off, but the roads were like mortar and the land looked bleak. And empty land – he remembered his vision of it as taking form from primordial dark. Some human endeavour there must be: like Lindsay unaccustomed to a country year, he had hardly realised before today how much endeavour, skill and endurance went to the fashioning of food from earth in weathers such as these. His midsummer holidays had not told him of wet seed-times, of furious winds blowing the turnip seed across the moors, of snow blackening the stooks of corn. . . . He had never thought before of these things. There must be grit and strength in the men who sowed their turnips thrice and ploughed land that ran up into the encroaching heather. (2017, 85)

The above passage demonstrates another example of becoming: as day becomes night, winter becomes spring becomes summer. Noticing the harsh conditions on the land, Garry realises the effort required in growing anything 'in weathers such as these'. Only when he sees the country in extreme weathers, so frequent at that time of year, every year, does he realise that a summer tourist's glimpse obfuscates rather than reveals the true nature of the landscape, romanticising life and work in the country. It is in early spring that the hard, daily toil takes place. The closeness (intimate proximity even) of the people to the land is evoked in plant metaphors – for example 'like whin blossom on the cankered stem of her people', 'an antique pine, one side denuded, with gaunt arms flung along the tempest', or 'a bed of thyme' (2017, 85). These comparisons are followed by a withdrawal, reinforcing the anthropocentric view, when Garry dismisses the musings as merely 'pleasant fancies, dehumanising the land' (2017, 85). Thereby admonishing himself for making analogies between women and plants, the character reveals a human-centred opinion that the land is inextricably bound with people and that it is human activity which makes it 'useful'. Yet metaphors referring to the world of plants and non-human animals promptly return, emphasising the relation between different beings. Humans are connected by 'a teasing tangle' (2017, 85); the tension feels as if bound by 'nets of spider-web, or some dark stinging noxious weed from under ocean' (2017, 86). The oscillation between the human-centred vision of the land and a more inclusive one is swayed towards the latter. The former recurs in another form when, once again, Shepherd employs the convention of anthropomorphism in her depictions of spring, endowed with a 'temper', appearing as 'the lady', who may have a 'suave and gracious mood', yet as she 'had no more mind for honeyed promises', so she must be courted by 'those who would win her favours . . . must wrestle a fall with the insolent young Amazon' (2017, 83). Indeed, the difficult temper of spring is a recurrent motif. One must be prepared for sudden changes in the weather as '[a]ll spring' is comprised in one week: 'its tempestuous disinclinations, its cold withdrawals, its blaze of sun, its flowers, its earthy smell' (2017, 49). Spring is not the one imagined as the 'smooth security of seed and egg', made picturesque and sentimentalised, but instead appears as 'most terrible in all the cycle of the year, time of the dread spring deities' (2017, 49).

The depictions of spring involve the gods and heroes of Greek and Egyptian mythology – Dionysus and Osiris, Prometheus and Oedipus – as well as a Christian god – 'the risen Christ' – suggesting the continuity of European culture going back thousands of years to imagine these 'gods of growth and resurrection, whose worship has flowered in tragedy, superb and dark' as well as 'massacre and the stake' (2017, 49). The season's paradox – 'Life that comes again is hard: a jubilation and an agony' (2017, 49) – captures the contradiction of life on the land, in its joy, hardship and pain. The inherent violence, the brute force embedded in the landscape reveals itself through the ferocious phenomena of the weather-world. True to its title, *The Weatherhouse* abounds in descriptions of the effects of the atmospherics on the land. When a violent wind comes, nothing is 'at peace upon the earth' (2017, 160), bringing with it darkness so deep that it eliminates even the thought of light. The roughness of the wind spills onto things, transforming their form, from smooth, 'suave' things to those that are roughened, 'soiled', bringing 'the universal restlessness' (2017, 160). The force brings change in the prospect of things, transforming the garden. Paradoxically, silent and covered with snow, it appears more alive than 'when this frenzy of motion tormented it from end to end' (2017, 160). The energy of the wind is not 'the motion of life' (2017, 160) but instead it appears to be a 'wind of death' (2017, 160), its movement seeming aporetic and defying logic.

Decidedly different, the states which arrive after a long walk are bliss, and serenity, or 'the serene sublimity', steadying to the mind. To achieve the latter '[i]t is worth ascending unexciting heights' (2011, 19), as Shepherd notes. Another word indicating the condition of the embodied self is 'quiescence' (2011, 90, 92) and its variant 'quiescent', as in the phrase 'moments of quiescent perceptiveness' when there is 'nothing between me and the earth and the sky' (2011, 90), as the self 'entered into' quiescence of mind and body. In these expressions Shepherd records a paradox: through movement, during prolonged walking, the mind becomes still. This happens when, running 'before the wind', the self achieves 'the peace that is beyond understanding: she was at one with the motion of her universe' (2017, 161). Training the senses – 'the eye to look, the ear to listen' – is necessary in order to immerse itself in the quiescence, all the body needs to be 'trained and disciplined', as Shepherd puts it, 'to move with the right harmonies' (2011, 90). Quiescence brings a suspension of temporality, which leads to the suspension of selfhood as listening for silence 'one slips out of time' (2011, 96). The absolute silence, which resides in the landscape is not the reverse, obverse, or opposite of sound, but, as Shepherd insists, it is akin to 'a new element' (2011, 96). Silence connects us to sound as it 'keeps us in contact with the being of sound' (Merleau-Ponty 2002, 382). Understood as the absence of human speech, silence is essential to allow the embodied consciousness to become immersed in the surrounding. 'Mankind is sated with noise', Shepherd notes, 'but up here, this naked, this elemental savagery, this infinitesimal cross-section of sound from the energies that have been at work for aeons in the universe, exhilarates rather than destroys' (2011, 97).

The elemental energy which resides in the mountain has its place. Human speech is 'superfluous' (2011, 14) in a place filled with the sound of movement, with the call of the golden plover, or 'the boom of angry seas' (2011, 97). Hills may roar with the activity of stags, or melting snow, when 'cataracts sound in my ears all night, pouring through' (2011, 95), as water is 'speaking' (2011, 22).

The sounds of the world also appear in the yodelling song of stags (2011, 70–1), when 'the hill broke into a cantata' (2011, 71). In the world filled with speech and song, the stillness of a spring dawn appears uncanny, or even 'unearthly, as though the wind had blown itself out and with it all the accustomed sounds of earth' (2017, 172) as 'the normal world' returns in birdsong. Life begins anew with the return of sound, which sound enters the ears, penetrates the body. Through their openness, all of the senses let the world in, each 'a way in to what the mountain has to give' (2011, 97). The dual exchange occurring through sensual knowing is the constitution of the embodied self affected by reversibility, whereby '[i]nside and outside are inseparable', thus reaching a climax in the revelation that the world is 'wholly inside and I am wholly outside myself' (Merleau-Ponty 2002, 407). This reversible relation of the seeing and the seen, the touching and the touched mutually informing one another, impacts both as '[p]lace and a mind may interpenetrate till the nature of both is altered' (2011, 8), writes Shepherd. This unnameable force – 'something' – residing 'within the mountain' (2011, 8) is transferred from it to the embodied consciousness and back. In an exchange between the embodied consciousness and the world, the self becomes constituted, the mind and matter in dynamic transfer.

'This intricate play'

In Shepherd's texts, being-in-the-present is marked by moments of redoubling during which the self binds with the visible. Merleau-Ponty explains this phenomenon: 'What makes the weight, the thickness, the flesh of each color, of each sound, of each tactile texture, of the present, and of the world', he writes, 'is the fact that he who grasps them feels himself emerge from them by a sort of coiling up or redoubling, fundamentally homogeneous with them' (1968, 113–14). The embodied self sinks into the world, which absorbs it, consciousness becoming entwined with 'the ontological tissue' (1968, 253).

The sensation of becoming one with the world is evoked in a passage from *The Quarry Wood* when Martha spends late spring nights outside:

> The hushed world took her in. Tranquil, surrendered, she became one with the vast quiet night. A puddock sprawled noiselessly towards her, a bat swooped, tracing gigantic patterns upon the sky, a corncrake *skraighed*, on and on through the night, monotonous and

forgotten as one forgets the monotony of the sea's roar; and when the soft wind was in the south-west, the sound of the river, running among its stony rapids . . . floated up and over her like a tide. She fell asleep to its running and wakened to listen for it; and heard it as one hears the breathing of another. (2018, 114)

As stillness envelopes the embodied self in an extended fabric, everything intertwines, one being becoming another: a bird's call resembles the sound of the sea, as does the river, the rhythm of its tide like breath. The oscillation between nearness and distance – the toad moves 'towards' her, while the corncrake is heard 'away' – creates a sense of being surrounded by other beings. Similarly, the harmonic motion is there in the interchangeable rhythm of silence and sound. The sonic presence of other beings and phenomena is sensed, as is the rhythm of breath. The phrase 'the breathing of another' foregrounds the vitality of the living landscape, connecting its internal as well as external environment, the image of the breathing organism foregrounding the interconnectedness of various elements. The verbs of action associated with the world – 'sprawled', 'swooped', 'screeched', 'running' – demonstrate a place filled with movement, actively encompassing the embodied consciousness, which enfolds and contains it, the self sinking into the surroundings.

While the above passage is dominated by non-human animal presences, the plant world features prominently in Shepherd's texts. In her depictions of the landscape, she blends descriptions of the physical world with elements of Scottish folklore, which reappear in the references to the plant world. For example, rowan is considered to be 'the "blessed quicken wood", it has power against the spirits of evil' (2011, 54), as if unable to resist the bewitching properties of a charmed Scottish landscape. At times, folk beliefs interchange with references to evil from a Christian perspective, as, for instance, in the description of the alpine flora of the Scottish mountains, Arctic in origin, which, according to Shepherd, possess 'the angelic inflorescence and the devil in their roots' (2011, 59). The world of spells and magic, embedded in the Scottish landscape where everything is invested with magical properties and possibilities, is made manifest in the features of the plant world. For instance, the pines 'show the amazing adaptability' as they 'can change their form at need, like any wizard' (2011, 57). In a passage depicting 'a night of purest witchery', Shepherd concedes to the undeniable presence of the supernatural, admitting that the night makes one believe 'all the tales of *glamourie*' that may seem unlikely to be true and 'that Scotland tries so hard to refute and cannot' (2011, 93). Yet for Shepherd the concept of *glamourie* is simply an affected label which fails to address the real nature of things, as it 'interposes something artificial between the world, which is one reality, and the self, which is another reality, though overlaid with a good many crusts of falseness and convention' (2011, 93). She argues that only 'the fusion of these two realities . . . keeps life from corruption' (2011, 93) as, instead of separating the two realms, it is necessary to accept their coexistence.

Human presence marks the mountain in the form of paths, cairns, stepping-stones, the remains of huts, the sluices, the remnants of kilns, bothies; in the map and compass, and 'in the names recorded in the map, ancient Gaelic names . . . show how old is man's association with scaur and corrie' (2011, 77), as elements of the material culture combine with non-material culture, both present in an incomplete, or even vestigial form. Shepherd feels 'touched at many points' (2011, 77) by this presence, which provokes ambivalent feelings during her walks. One sign of this presence, however, is unambiguously unsettling, or, as Shepherd puts it, 'disturbingly evident' (2011, 77), and these are the wrecks of planes. Reminding walkers of a war which was taking place as Shepherd wrote *The Living Mountain*, the metal debris scattered around stands out from the landscape, drawing the perceiving I into the present of military action.

Another sign of human presence is the disappearance of ecosystems, which Shepherd notices and deplores, expressing dismay in a characteristically succinct style, gathering the effect in one paragraph, or using a phrase '[m]an's touch' (2011, 80), containing a terse rebuke of actions leading to the erasure of forests and loss of habitats. The destructive effect of human activity occupies Shepherd's mind as she notices the changes which have undergone in the several decades of her walking through the landscape, adding a foreword to *The Living Mountain*, published over thirty years after it was written. The Rothiemurchus Forest, the remnant of the ancient Caledonian pine forest which covered much of the uplands of Scotland, remains the most important native pinewood remnants in Scotland. Shepherd's note is an expression of sadness at the disappearance of the pine forest, mostly felled and destroyed. What remains are 'a scatter of enormous venerable Scots firs' (2011, 54), roots, 'twisted and intertwined' (2011, 55), half-submerged, 'the roots of trees long perished' (2011, 55). The changing landscape of the modern world included the appearance of sawmills when 'the timber was first realised to be a source of wealth' (2011, 55); yet, as Shepherd points out, it is the wars – first the Napoleonic Wars, the First World War, the Second World War – which dramatically affected forestation. 'It will grow again', writes Shepherd, 'but for a while the land will be scarred and the living things – the crested tits, the shy roe deer – will flee' (2011, 56).

Irreversible anthropogenic change includes loss of habitats; yet, writing in the first half of the twentieth century, Shepherd did not yet experience the accelerated disappearance of many species of 'our animal other' (Krell 2013, 1). The landscape abounds in traces of presence, left behind, imprinted or, as with swifts or the eagle, momentarily apperceived. Animal tracks on the snow suggest a more-than-human presence which, even if it is not co-temporal, offers company, gives a sense of living in shared worlds, of being 'companioned, though not in time' (2011, 30). Shepherd records encounters with swifts, eagles, dotterel, ptarmigan, snow buntings, dippers, golden plover, grouse, kestrels, blackcocks, wagtails, reed buntings, seagulls, oyster catchers, crossbills, 'capercailzie', peregrine, red deer, wild cat, finches, wild geese, a curlew, tits, wrens. Revealing ecological kinship, the author's gaze is tender, her language endearing, as, for instance, when she writes of small birds as 'morsels' (2011, 95). She notes the contrast between the harshness of the environment and the frailty of its inhabitants, as in the example of snow buntings, whose 'delicate perfection' appears to be 'enhanced by the savagery of their home' (2011, 67) – environment and inhabitants thus complementary, like ducks, who are 'two halves of one organism' and 'each following every modulation of the other' (2011, 69). Shepherd's texts abound in observations that are a blend of singular events, which, unfolding before her eyes, create associations which concern the philosophical aspects of vision. For, as Shepherd observes, the swifts' flight and high-pitched cries 'seem to make visible and audible some essence of the free, wild spirit of the mountain' (2011, 61). Through its unharnessed energy, the eagle's flight 'enthrals the eye' (2011, 62) as its power 'binds the strength of the wind to its own purpose' (2011, 62), making it 'intimately' entwined in the landscape. This observation leads to a comparison between the eagle and moss campion, both 'integral to the mountain' (2011, 62). Joining the two hemispheres – the earth and the sky, as well as the animal, the vegetable, and the mineral – the bird's flight performs the biocentric interconnectedness, or 'this intricate interplay', which constitutes the foundation of Shepherd's worldview. It is this worldview in its movement between distance and intimacy, which offers us a bridge to our next writer.

Notes

1. More information is available on the project's site: http://www.intothemountain.co.uk/about/
2. The biocentric preoccupations of Scottish rural modernism have yet to be explored.
3. The verb 'penetrate' recurs regularly – six times – in Chapters 1, 2, 10, 11 (twice) and 12: Chapter 1: 'Place and a mind may interpenetrate until the nature of both is altered' (2011, 8); Chapter 2: The sun 'penetrated directly into the water' (2011, 12); Chapter 10: The sun 'penetrates a red cloud of twigs and picks out vividly the white trunks, as though the cloud of red were behind the trunks' (2011, 99); Chapter 11: Look at the mountain with 'the love that penetrates to its essence is to widen the domain of being' (2011, 102); Chapter 12 (already cited above), the final paragraph in the book: 'It is a journey into Being; for as I penetrate more deeply into the mountain's life, I penetrate also into my own' (2011, 108).
4. Charlotte Peacock interprets such moments as instances of *satori*, or the 'flash of intuitive insight in Zen Buddhism' (2017, 27). Peacock reads a number of excerpts in *The Living Mountain* as indicative of Zen, confirmed by a passage from 'Nirvana' in Lafcadio Hearn's *Gleanings in Buddha Fields* found in Shepherd's commonplace books (2017, 30). Another Eastern text, which, according to Peacock, exerted influence on Shepherd was *Tao Te Ching* (2017, 259), which proved important during the Second World War.
5. Cf. Kant on singularity, aporia and the event of the sublime in the Third Critique.
6. In her essay 'Reading the Word: Spirit Materiality in the Mountain Landscapes of Nan Shepherd', Rachel Gilman proposes a wholly religious reading of Shepherd's work.
7. For instance, *The Weatherhouse* (2017, 160–1); the chapter in *The Quarry Wood* entitled 'Sundry Weathers' (2018, 58–65).

Chapter 2

'Where are your dictionaries of the wind, the grasses?': Logos of the Landscape in Norman MacCaig's Poetry

Entwined between the leaves of the world, the subject of Norman MacCaig's poems oscillates between distance and poetic consciousness welded with that world. His fertile lyrical imagination explores the manner in which the inner world connects to the world outside, as the poet emphasises being-through-attunement based on seeing openly and speaking plainly. Many of MacCaig's poems explore the possibility of the landscape to cause in the subject a sense of transcendence, and the manner in which it connects and mediates human experience whereby embodied consciousness immerses itself in the comforting familiarity of landscape. Even though MacCaig returns repeatedly to the same places – Assynt in the West Highlands, Scalpay on the Isle of Harris – and to the same subjects and motifs, he avoids monotony, as reiteration highlights the singularity of each experience of the landscape. His lifetime acquaintance with the area allows him to examine its varied constitution. At times the poems break the dichotomy and immerse the subject in the world, foregrounding a sense of harmony between embodied mind and world; at other times, the absolute otherness of beings and things is emphasised, in the examination of the relationship between human and non-human subjectivity and exemplification of the biosemiotic focus through the ecocentric imaginary. In the earth-centred approach, MacCaig explores the relation between poetry and the environment in ecologically minded poetic structures. The principal source of contact with the world, the body, experiences this world sensually as, through the embodied consciousness, humans relate, acquire knowledge, and so create meaning: through the body, the material landscape connects with the inner phenomenal landscape, establishing reversible correspondences between the physical world and the self in various modes of perception. Many aspects of MacCaig's poetry – the sense of temporality, a penchant for animism, lack of hierarchy between human and non-human relations, and 'the sense of the whole nature as a living entity' (Bateman 2018, 14)[1] – originate from a Gaelic aesthetic.

With only the most minimal colouring, and with a stringent limitation of emotions or ego, MacCaig evokes the landscape, ceaselessly exploring the spirit-world, in a form of celebration and affirmation of the immediate, while resisting the impulse to romanticise or sentimentalise. The abiding relationship with place is manifested in his careful attention to language through his endless striving for exactitude and precision. 'Landscape . . . is my religion' (Taylor 2005, xxxiii), declares MacCaig. Demonstrably dismissing organised religion as a form of institutionalised authority, MacCaig nonetheless practises secular reverence as spirituality animates his poetry, which constitutes 'a theology of a most sentient kind' (O'Gorman 1958, 268). A similar 'metaphysical combination of earthy and Eastern' (McGuire 2009, 153), self and mountain, may be found in Nan Shepherd's and Kathleen Jamie's work.

Commenting on MacCaig's jocular declaration that he was a 'Zen Calvinist', Douglas Dunn writes that it was 'a sect with no priesthood', 'a congregation of one', with a 'secular understanding of what he believes to be sacred, as well as the ethical, rational tug of his poetry while surrounded by detailed, natural epiphanies' (Dunn 1990, 67). Relating to Celtic praise poetry, MacCaig's poems explore quotidian wonder, drawing intimate pleasure from the beauty of the landscape. His conception of beauty as aesthetic value defies the teleological principle: it is there without a purpose, unclaimed, its ungraspability emphasising the singularity of every experience. To cite Alan Riach, MacCaig is 'a great love poet of the natural world' (2018, n.p.).

For MacCaig 'the natural world' is contained in one region of Scotland – Assynt in the south-west of Sutherland – which recurs in his poetry. Celebratory, the poems stem from his affectionate approach, as the poet explains: '[i]f you love something, surely it gives you an entry into their nature' (MacCaig 2005, xlix). Returning to the same place repeatedly, MacCaig grounds his poems in a regional, local landscape. As he admits, travels abroad never presented an attraction for him (Walker 1981, 34). Underlining the significance of his West Highland and Hebridean heritage, MacCaig affirms the affinity with 'the Gaelic side of Scotland' as manifested in several elements: 'landscape, the language, the music, the people and their dying culture' (MacCaig cit. Board of Regents 1979, 641), which constituted an unrelentingly powerful magnet, for many years drawing him to the region every summer. The oral culture of the Gaels, with the unique engagement between song and place present in Scottish-Gaelic psalmody, informs MacCaig's evocation of the landscape. The surging, dissonant harmonics of Gaelic psalms form part of the Sunday soundscape entwined with acoustic environment of the everyday life, with its ebb and flow of daily rituals. Living in Edinburgh all his life, MacCaig rarely wrote about it; while Edinburgh was 'an old coat . . . taken for granted' (Walker 1981, 34), the Lochinver area in Assynt was a place to which he would return for forty years every summer:

> a landscape which is so beautiful. And it's linear. The mountains are small, but you see them from their ankles to the tops of their skulls, so they look about three times their cheating, conning height. And you only have to walk two hundred yards and you get a new view . . . If you are in the Cairngorms you walk four miles, but up there you just turn the corner . . . My ideal . . . would be to spend the six winter months in Edinburgh and the six summer months up there. Because I need both. I love both. (Walker 1981, 34)

MacCaig's abiding love for the West Highlands – 'this corner' of the landscape – is closely reflected in his poetry, resulting in hundreds of poems which evoke its geological and organic features. Now, at the foot of one of the poet's beloved hills in the Scottish Highlands, Stac Pollaidh, is a bench with the carved line 'I took my mind a walk' from his poem 'An Ordinary Day', reminding passers-by of MacCaig's attachment to that place and his fondness for the intimately known landscapes of Assynt.

This chapter examines the relation between self and landscape through a selection of MacCaig's poems. It discusses MacCaig's evocations of place and the manner in which they reveal a world filled with speech, through a poetry 'concerned with giving voice to the experience of the world' (Merleau-Ponty 1991, 28). It analyses the manner in which the poems offer (and frequently resist) a translation of meanings revealed by the world, or the logos of the landscape. Informed by a phenomenology of embodied consciousness, the readings examine various modes of perception as present in MacCaig's poetry, which combine to overcome the divergence in self, matter and time, mediated and attuned, providing the essential basis for the creation of meaning and communication, the primordial source of enworlding.

Having written about 3,900 poems over forty-five years, MacCaig was a ruthless editor of his own work, destroying the poems which did not pass muster.[2] *The Poems of Norman MacCaig*, 'the definitive (though not complete) MacCaig' (E. MacCaig 2005, xix), contains 797 poems, including ninety-nine previously unpublished. The number of published poems – over 1000 poems exist – is comparable with Thomas Hardy, leaving anyone who wishes to discuss MacCaig's oeuvre overwhelmed with its vastness. As Robin Fulton notices, 'the critic's difficulty lies in the wealth of illustrative material to hand' (Fulton 1977, 486).[3] Barry Cole observes wittily that MacCaig's 'apparent prolixity' makes him 'someone who throws his generous talent about us like an intellectual Father Christmas' (1974, 24). In the light of vastness and complexity of MacCaig's work, Marjory McNeill's sea metaphor appears particularly apt:

> Trying to discuss his work is rather like trying to discuss the sea. One can put a small amount of MacCaig onto a page or one can observe the sea on a calm day from the shore, then say 'that is MacCaig' or 'that is sea water.' There is no way, however, that one can accurately measure and indicate the turbulence, the varying aspects, the storms, the cruel wit, the subtle jokes, the moments of depression, the visions of love, the everyday clarity or the mysterious depths of his poetry. Like the changes in the moods of the sea, it defies description. (McNeill 1996, 125)

This may explain the relatively small number of critical studies of MacCaig's poetry despite his reputation as 'Scotland's most popular poet for over 30 years' (Thornton et al. 2012, n.p.). Being confronted with a poetic oeuvre of such an extent and breadth may pose difficulties in presenting constructive interpretations and conclusions.

When the world experiences a rapid, irreversible erosion, art attentive to the natural world merits special attention, with ocular as well as aural perception, and through reflection on the experience of the lived body, corporeal experience. MacCaig's poems possess an 'undated freshness' and that many years after the publication 'everything about them [was] as alive, as new and essential, as ever', as Ted Hughes argues (Hughes in Pow and Hendry 1995, n.p.).[4] The sustained power of MacCaig's poems lies in their universal sweep; rereading them 'after a long time, poems you had thought were the last word in beauty, skill and efficiency have that startling knack of seeming even better than you remember them'; this in turn may suggest that 'their career is only just beginning' (Hughes in Pow and Hendry 1995, n.p.). In the age when the negative consequences of anthropogenic activity can no longer be ignored, MacCaig's poetry, with its attentive focus on the natural world, appears particularly needed, more than ever before.

Seeing the world requires exactitude and clarity, which may only be rendered in a direct, precise language, without unnecessary embellishments, which would falsify the image. Achieving such a stripped-down style took MacCaig years of work. Having disavowed his early poems, MacCaig was unforgiving about his early writing, calling his first volume a 'collection of terrible poems – semi-surrealistic' and describing them as a 'vomitorium of unrelated images ... which nobody could understand' (Nicholson 1992, 40). He expressed a profound dislike for obscure poems ('what can you communicate in gobbledygook?' [MacCaig 1979, 86]) and relished repeating a self-deprecating anecdote about his friend's reaction who, after reading the volume, asked 'When are you publishing the answers?' This reaction helped MacCaig realise that 'a poem is a form of communication' (MacCaig 1979, 86), as a result changing his style in order to communicate more directly. MacCaig's 'obsession with the world of ideas' originates in the early period when the poet experienced 'hesitation and discomfort' as he attempted to find 'a sense of place' (Kindrick 1998, 835).[5] As he immersed himself in the Assynt landscape, his style became increasingly pure and lucid, even bare. MacCaig developed a poetic language stripped of decorative flourishes, a language that does not flaunt itself or advertise its own presence, the early stylistic density yielding to an entirely different style: minimalistic and pared down.[6] The change includes metre and rhyme, regular in MacCaig's earlier poems, which was replaced by free verse. The departure from iambic pentameter was an attempt to 'rescue' the metre from 'a rocking-horse humpty-dumpty by using off-beat stresses – but not so off-beat that the ghostly paradigm of the iambic pentameter (for instance) was not to be noticed behind the frailer metrics' (MacCaig 1979, 82) in which MacCaig still wrote. Experimentation involved MacCaig 'indulging', as he puts it, in 'the ancient practice' of 'sprung rhythm' (used, for instance, by Gerard Manley Hopkins), based on 'taking liberties with the number of syllables in the foot – but, again, still preserving the fundamental iambic movement of the line' (MacCaig 1979, 82). Even though metre, rhyme and structure may appear to be a 'restricting straitjacket', MacCaig sees their importance in preventing the poet 'from flailing [their] arms about in meaningless, shapeless gestures' (MacCaig 1979, 83).

Declaring an abiding affection for Assynt, MacCaig underscores the intimacy of the human relationship with a familiar landscape, suggesting that experimentation with different rhyme patterns is an influence of Gaelic poetry, 'assonantal for centuries' (MacCaig 1979, 82), thus foregrounding his connection with the land, culture and tradition of Gaels. MacCaig's conscious exploration of formal possibilities of verse coincides with his sustained immersion in the Highland landscape with its rhythm of gneissian rock and lochs. Through his deep attachment to that part of the world, articulated in the poems overtly referring to particular places, such as 'Culag Pier', 'Looking down on Glen Canisp', 'Above Inverkirkaig' or 'Loch Sionascaig', MacCaig's created work radiates far beyond that 'corner' of the land.[7] Despite a marked preference for the local landscape, MacCaig's work confirms that poetry – if it is to go beyond current affairs – is unbounded and universal, transcending locality in spatial as well as temporal aspects. Calling MacCaig a 'peripheral nationalist' (Duncan 2007, n.p.) suggests a complete misreading of his poetry. Among the great number of poems written by MacCaig, many do not include even the slightest mention of Scotland. Even so, specific geographical references do not confine an author to one place, and certainly do not make him or her a nationalist.

As is known, MacCaig distanced himself from political matters, carefully avoiding touching upon these subjects and refraining from taking a stance in interviews. In effect, this consistent attitude of non-engagement has been perceived as a weakness by some critics. What they ignore or fail to notice is that there are many ways in which political views may manifest themselves. They appear to confuse the political with the nationalistic, narrowing down its scope. MacCaig's engagement manifests itself in his belief that art's purpose is not to be entangled in debates about the so-called 'big' themes, which are in effect void and futile. Poetry that is embroiled in current political debates fades before long. The universalising quality of MacCaig's work transcends local strife, both in a geographical and temporal sense. Donald Davie, who believes the measure of a great poet is his or her engagement with grand themes, argues that MacCaig's 'consistent refusal ... to engage himself cannot but count against him' (Davie 1989, 20).[8] MacCaig provided an emphatic retort to such accusations, ending his essay 'My Way of It' with the following words:

> Poetry teaches a man to do more than observe merely factual errors and measurable truths. It trains him to have a shrewd nose for the

fake, the inflated, the imprecise and the dishonest. So, it compels him to resist stock responses, because it compels him to examine the emotional significance, as well as the rational significance, of whatever comes under his notice. To have unexamined emotional responses is as immature, as dangerous as to have unexamined beliefs. And what proportion, I wonder, of the misunderstandings and miseries in the world are due to no more than the stock use of big words – liberty, patriotism, democracy and all their dreary clan – and the stock response to them? (MacCaig 1979, 88)

Considering 'big words', belonging to the 'dreary clan' of other lofty concepts, a sign of immaturity, MacCaig dismissed timeworn, oft-repeated, vague terms, which are mostly used unreflectively, placing poetry on the other end, in opposition to stereotypical responses, in search of precision, authenticity and truth.

A constant preoccupation with truth marks MacCaig's work, whose understanding of the concept was influenced by his attitude to representation. In a seminal essay, 'Neoclassical MacCaig', Mary Jane Scott situates MacCaig in a broader literary tradition, searching for the links between MacCaig and other poets and thinkers.[9] While there is little doubt about MacCaig's metaphysical correspondences, it appears that links with Romanticism, suggested by some critics, are misplaced.[10] For a poet dedicated to truth, seeking to challenge representation, and withdrawing as far as possible his ego from his evocations of the natural world, the Romantic approach appeared unacceptable. Emphasising the value of truth, MacCaig openly dismisses Romantic poetry for its 'falsity' and 'sentimentality' (MacCaig 2005, xlviii). He believes that it offers an 'overblown rhetoric for feelings that are trifling in the first place' (MacCaig 2005, xlviii), which demonstrates his strong preference for the impersonal over the sentimental in art (Morgan 1990, 246). Being 'especially attracted by the honesty and truthfulness of seeing things as they are—and he doesn't care whether they are small or not' (Morgan 1990, 241), MacCaig's investment in the truth or authenticity of representation caused him to reject the Romantic vision, which to him appeared 'too far removed from reality' (MacCaig 2005, xlviii). The dislike also of sentimentality in poetry includes MacCaig's withdrawal of the personal, declaring: 'I don't like burdening other people with your own fascinating interests' (Walker 1981, 35). This extends to other forms of confessional poetry: 'I also detest the notion that *all* art is a therapeutic expression of inner, psychological tensions, of the quarrel with ourselves' (MacCaig 1979, 84). For MacCaig, poetry is not a form of psychotherapy, a place for a poet to 'put my feelings onto it, or extract new feelings from it' (Nicholson 1992, 46). Striving for precision of language, he refrains from stifling descriptions with his emotions. A staunch opponent of the pathetic fallacy, MacCaig demonstrates intense dislike for, again, inundating poetry with one's ego, and this is made visible in a number of poems which oscillate between concealing and revealing the perceiving I. MacCaig believed in the commonality of pleasure in making things, which includes making poetry, or craftmanship, which resembles making functional objects such as a table or a boat (MacCaig 1979, 87–8). For 'a great deal' of art the 'cause, purpose and effect is pure celebration' (MacCaig 1979, 84) of the other, of an object or a landscape. 'Are we to dismiss these as trivial? If so, I have written a good many trivial poems' (MacCaig 1979, 84). In a 1973 interview, MacCaig believed that 'it is all the more important in this sad world to notice, record and praise the good things that are still there' (cit. Morgan 1990, 241). Commenting on MacCaig's words, Morgan suggests of MacCaig's poetry that 'the modesty of its claim for art, [is that] it sees art mainly as a corrective, a chastener, a reminder, a test for false ideas and unexamined ideals' (Morgan 1990, 242). Rejecting an auratic, exceptionalist vision, MacCaig believes poetry should celebrate small, 'trivial', seemingly insignificant things.

MacCaig's disinclination towards Romanticism includes rejection of a romanticised image of Gaelic culture, whereby Gaels are represented as 'chaps twangling harps while their ladies are away marrying seals' (MacCaig cit. McNeill 1996, 8). Emphasising the connection between his Gaelic heritage and Classical culture, he notices how the formality of the Gaelic language bears resemblance to Latin and Greek, which explains a distinct predilection for the Classical manifestly present in his work, which is associated with his Gaelic ancestry. In 'My Way of It', MacCaig writes that for 'a three-quarter Gael' such as himself:

> Celtic art is not at all the romantic, not to say sentimental thing of popular belief. Its extreme formality is to be seen in all the forms it takes . . . All those genes I carry about, therefore, incline me strongly towards the classical rather than the romantic, the Apollonian rather than the Dionysian, and this inclination was both revealed and supported by the fact that I took a degree in Classics. (MacCaig 1979, 81)

The emphasis on form and structure already mentioned above in art are essential for MacCaig, who believes deeply that 'poetry involves order' (MacCaig 1979, 85). In that, it is necessary to control the making of poetry by 'the rational mind'. As he puts it, 'it's not enough to lift the trap-door to the subconscious and lasso whatever crawls out' (MacCaig 1979, 85). In an attempt to banish the messiness of consciousness and find an appropriate response to the logos of the landscape, MacCaig searches for the most suitable means of expression, carefully seeking to eliminate emotional and intellectual overflow. Emphasising the significance of form, MacCaig says that:

> art, whatever else it may be or do, is concerned with form, and that's to say, with order. I don't know whether artists see an order in the chaos of experience that other people don't or whether they impose an order on that chaos. But that order must be there. To defend formless and chaotic writing on ground that it's an enactment of the chaotic times we live in is to commit that aesthetic sin, the fallacy of imitative form, and to renege from the primary duty of any artist, in whatever mode he is operating. (MacCaig 1979, 83)

In these words, as well as through his poetry, MacCaig stresses the responsibility of the poet, which is to create form, acting against imitation and rejecting poor mimesis as it offers false promise, and a fallacious delusion of representation, thereby rendering a poem invalid or inauthentic.

The label 'descriptive' returns in many reviews of MacCaig's poetry (cf. Johnson 1965; Morse 1963, 332; Wakeman 1979, 641). At times it appears to be a mild dismissal of his work, but there are also critics who openly admire MacCaig's 'power of description' (Johnson 1965, 45). Questioning the label 'our best descriptive poet' given to MacCaig by 'the usual clump of journalists', B. S. Johnson considers it is 'as fatuous a useless distinction as they have ever produced: for what poet does not describe?' (1965, 45). According to Johnson, 'the title bears too a hardly hidden diminution: the adjective "mere" hovers all too closely to their "description"', adding that 'MacCaig rarely describes anything without relating it very closely and pointedly to some wider and often more personal theme: he employs the objective correlative, in fact, with great assurance and success' (Johnson 1965, 45).[11] The objective correlative, or 'a set of objects, a situation, a chain of events which shall be the formula of that *particular* emotion' that the poet feels (Eliot 1950, 100), requires a connection between the emotion expressed by the poet and the image or event in the poem aiming to evoke that emotion in the reader. Occurring in MacCaig's early poetry, objective correlative yields to a more impersonal style, whereby description is a way to erase the ego from the poems, appearing only as a perceiving I. Invariably demonstrating that 'a poem is a form of communication' (MacCaig 1979, 86), MacCaig seeks various means to communicate, all the while striving to avoid false representation. Responding to place by stating what he sees, MacCaig proves what it means to engage truly – and truthfully – with the landscape.

'A small oasis of order and happiness and beauty'

In MacCaig's poetry, evocations of the Scottish landscape function as aide-memoires, emphasising the relation between self and world, sustaining connections over time. The landscape exists through the perceiving I. In order to avoid pathos, MacCaig deflates elevated emotions when speaking of Suilven, which is 'only a lump of sandstone' and 'a most beautiful lump of sandstone' (Nicholson 1992, 46), as MacCaig repeats, resisting the appropriating impulse and evading lofty declarations, at the same time attributing singular beauty to the landscape. Yet, it does not mean that the landscape, in all its distinctiveness, cannot be admired: it may be (and often is) pleasing aesthetically, in the manner of seventeenth-century pictorial representations which served the pleasure of the view. Whenever MacCaig speaks of the region, the adjective 'beautiful' returns, often with added emphasis, as, for instance, when he says that Sutherland is 'a beautiful, beautiful countryside' (Nicholson 1992, 54).

It is worth considering at this point what the use of aesthetic value entails in MacCaig's poetry by looking briefly at the concept of beauty from a theoretical perspective. While philosophers have been concerned with the experience of the beautiful since the antiquity, Immanuel Kant doubtless exerted the greatest influence on the understanding of the concept in the modern era.[12] Stressing the human urge for a purpose which nonetheless shifts as the subject experiences beauty, he argues, 'surrounded by the beautiful nature, he [man] finds himself calmly and serenely enjoying his existence' (Kant 1987, 335), thus the purposiveness of the beautiful becomes a 'purposiveness without a purpose'. Governed by a peculiar form of teleology, '[b]eauty is an object's form of purposiveness insofar as it is perceived in the object without the presentation of a purpose' (§17, 84). Without carrying any purpose, the beautiful engenders pleasure in the human subject. Resisting conceptual reduction, beauty cannot be curtailed by the intellect. The play of the faculties remains outside the mind's grasp, eluding explanation and making beauty irreducible. Yet, playful harmony creates pleasure in the subject: we experience pleasure at the sight of free play (§12, 68) as an object 'is given to us' (§11, 66). Instead of focusing on abstract concepts, MacCaig turns to tiny beings, things and phenomena. Challenging the classic Kantian theory of the sublime, MacCaig finds the sublime in that which is small-scale, which is endowed with the transcendent power to move. In 'Small round loch' (MacCaig 2005, 209–10), it is not the vastness of the landscape or the dramatic weather but a 'minuscule' (l. 9), jewel-like body of water. Admiration does not require 'the vulgarity of crashing waves' (l. 3), subtle transformations of the weather-world suffice, causing ripples on the surface of the loch in its 'inextinguishable preciosity' (l. 6). Through his aesthetic formalism, MacCaig finds pleasure in the beautiful landscape and all its elements, celebrating their lack of purposiveness. Intrinsically, purposive nature occupies the inaccessible noumenal realm, a poem accessing the intangible, salvaging beauty and harmony which reside in the landscape.

Yet MacCaig is also aware of the ambivalence of beauty. In 'A.K. MacLeod' (MacCaig 2005, 334) the word 'beautiful' recurs three times, every time gaining a distinct meaning: made beautiful by the presence of a friend – 'the man who was its meaning and added to it' (l. 2) – only to obtain a different dimension with his passing. Not an impersonal, aesthetic value, the concept of beauty may be coloured by finality as the landscape becomes marked by personal loss with time. Similarly, the question of the purposiveness of beauty is challenged in 'Highland funeral' (MacCaig 2005, 335), where death and grief mark the landscape, which belongs to the dead man, which is 'his' (l. 1). Ugliness coexists with beauty: while the timelessly beautiful sea is 'boring' (l. 8), there is no beauty in grief even if it, too, is boring. The indifference of the beautiful landscape highlights the sense of every biological life's finitude. Through the use of parallelism, MacCaig highlights differences between various aspects of the landscape: the recurring preposition 'over' draws attention to the religious functions of space. The words of prayer uttered by the minister are an intrusion, polluting the landscape which is inherently sacred, its air 'a scrawny psalm' (l. 2). Only after the minister's voice falls silent, 'the pagan / landscape is sacred in a new way' (ll. 15–16). Such secular reverence stresses the self-contained nature of the landscape, which does not require human intervention.

As Edwin Morgan points out, MacCaig perceived a work of art 'as a small oasis of order and happiness and beauty against the dark chaotic background of ultrasound reality' (1990, 240). The Assynt appears to be such a sanctuary, imbued with all-encompassing transcendent divinity, lifted from the surrounding chaos. Pantheistic elements, which pervade MacCaig's poetry, reveal the presence of logos governed by the forces beyond human comprehension. Ancient echoes appear in a number of poems, such as 'Notations of ten summer minutes' (MacCaig 2005, 342–3), where Latin and Greek coexist with Gaelic. The patron god of Arcadia, Pan, appears in the hills around Lochinver: he 'cocks a hairy ear' (l. 15), then returns to sleep. The anthropomorphised embodiment of Nature, Pan listens to the music coming from the boat, which blends with other natural sounds. Belonging to that place, a boat is a Gaelic element, yet its name – *Arcadia* – suggests a fusion of traditions. The name creates an image of peace, adding to the glimpses of bucolic village life, which moves at a slow, orderly pace, the setting seemingly perfect for naively innocent poetry. Yet the unspoiled wilderness is there in name only as the utopian idyll may only exist as a signifier: a label of a functional object. This figure enables MacCaig to distance himself from pastoralism and avoid imposing a falsely idealised image of place. Such ironic distancing, characteristic of MacCaig's style, prevents making claims on place, imposing an idealised vision.

The lively dance tune heard from the deck bodies forth an image of harmony with the natural world. The whole landscape is filled with music, which resonates long after the speaker leaves the place. The last stanza freezes time as the eponymous ten minutes do not end, the speaker never leaves the place, silence never falls. Where each line is a paradox, the triple 'except' reverts the statements it introduces: time becomes suspended, the music continues to reverberate, the speaker remains there indefinitely. The event becomes etched in the poet's consciousness and recorded in the poem. Gathered in the space of ten minutes, the scene is carved in high relief from the background of the flow of time.

A classical ideal among other transcendentals, beauty is inextricably connected with truth, both forming an essential part of MacCaig's poetry, whereby the aesthetic experience is the embodiment of truth. This aspect of aesthetics, combined with phenomenology, is explored by Mikel Dufrenne in *The Phenomenology of Aesthetic Experience* (1973), who considers the aesthetic experience to be a fundamental aspect of human existence, valuable in itself precisely because it conveys truth. Dufrenne argues that through the aesthetic experience the subject contemplates the expressed meaning of an aesthetic object, which is felt through a sensuous sphere and apprehended bodily, thus constituting a meaning. The aesthetic object does not appear to the observer as his/her projection but is the expression of the aesthetic object itself:

> It is primarily our body that is moved by rhythm and that resonates with harmony. It is through the body that the aesthetic object is first taken up and assumed in order to pass from potentiality to act ... The unity which is in the object and which is ... the unity of its expression can be grasped only if the diversity of the sensuous is first gathered together in a *sensorium commune*. (Dufrenne 1973, 339)

The object or phenomenon attracts the body, offering it aesthetic pleasure and unveiling the real. Our bodies exist in the world and are formed by it as the embodied consciousness is firmly rooted in space and time. This is the sphere where the visible and the invisible cross, where seeing is corporeal, and perception phenomenological.

The Small Scale

The scene evoked in 'Notations of ten summer minutes' is one example, among many, of MacCaig's predilection for the small, the momentary, the elusive. Suspicious of grand claims, MacCaig frequently emphasises the significance of the small-scale. The 'miniaturist MacCaig', as Alan Riach calls the poet (1998, n.p.), often shows affection for the close-at-hand, which contrasts with his aversion towards grand ideas. While Robin Fulton perceives MacCaig's 'caustic attitude to Big Themes' to be 'a way of celebrating the human-sized' (1980, 684), Edwin Morgan remarks that, in his evocations of the non-human animals, 'MacCaig the misanthropist reveals himself' (Morgan 1990, 245). MacCaig himself declares:

> I don't like big mouths, I don't like Big Business, I don't like Big Brother. Except in my more athletic moments, which may be my best, I prefer small pictures, short poems, the Chaconne in D minor to the Mass in E minor. In a big-scale country you walk your legs off for a trifling re-arrangement of the scenery. Around Lochinver a couple of hundred yards means a split new view. And I have often seen a little hill in Harris collapse to half its size when a cow appeared on the top of it. It needed the intrusion of the known, ordinary object to show the hill at its proper height. I think it is a part of patriotism to stare at the hill till there's a cow on it. (MacCaig cit. Morgan 1990, 240–1)

The appearance of the cow suddenly diminishes the scale of a seemingly high hill, making it appear as it is. As Morgan suggests, 'the small poem' responds to the smallness of Scotland 'as a country, the small scale of its landscapes (as compared with those of, say, America or Russia)' (Morgan 1990, 241).13 Inflated out of all proportion, patriotism needs a cow, or another 'ordinary object', to deflate its grand claims and help people see properly.

MacCaig's fondness for the small-scale is most pronounced in poems focusing on the biosemiotic sphere and evoking small animals such as blue tits, long-tailed tits, sparrows, stonechats, greenfinches, wagtails, dippers, corncrakes, lizards, caterpillars, earwigs, toads and frogs, to name just a few.[14] Through the use of metaphors, MacCaig constructs connective bridges between human perception and non-human otherness, which creates a sense of both alterity and *rapprochement* with the world. Focusing on non-human subjectivity, MacCaig strives to find similarities with the human world but demonstrates difference through analogy. 'Abstract concepts are largely metaphorical,' argue Mark Johnson and George Lakoff (1999, 3). Humans create primary metaphors because we are bodily creatures, immersed in a world, where intimacy arises from proximity, 'affection with warmth, and achieving purposes with destinations' (1999, 59). In MacCaig's poetry, the metaphor does not serve the purpose of exploring the kinship between non-human and human animals but underlines the distinctiveness of the latter. The exploration of non-human agency lies at the centre of his animal poems.

As Bryan Walpert proclaims, poems are 'almost never truly about animals' (2017, 38).[15] In 'Caterpillar going somewhere', the eponymous caterpillar is anthropomorphised 'Its green face looks as if / it were about to spit – pft' (ll. 1–2). The combination of the pronoun 'its' with the noun 'face' alerts the reader's attention from the very first line, as it paradoxically links an impersonal pronoun with an anthropomorphic feature. The accumulation of sibilants in the first line provides contrast for the consonantal cluster combined with strong plosive, fricative and dental sounds that fall onto the end of the second line. The three-letter sound remains unuttered: the onomatopoeia resides in the realm of imagination suggested by the conjunction 'as if', which creates a possibility, conjuring a sense of presence. In 'Swimming lizard' (MacCaig 2005, 33), the eponymous creature is presented in movement, as he unhurriedly swims without a clear purpose. The detailed description and the affectionate analogies aggrandise the creature. MacCaig thus marks the distance between human speech and the language produced by the non-human environment.

Visible on the lizard's back, the pattern forms a text belonging to the grammar of the living world that we cannot decipher: 'He twinkled his brief text through the brown and still' (l. 9). The verbs 'glitter' and 'twinkle' in the second and third stanza point back to 'the brightness' in the opening verse, suggesting that the quality does not reside outside but is in effect inherent in the lizard. The shimmering illumination on the lizard's back, a fragment of the Merleau-Pontian luminous field to which the speaker is not given access, the text too brief, unreadable. The glimpse caught by the speaker is a flash of logos, understood here as the authentic speech of the living world, the invisible principle of order which brightens the speaker's perception for a brief moment. Standing by the lizard, the speaker may catch only a glimpse of the brightness radiating from it. The air of perfect self-containment emanating from 'the tiny monster' emphasises its completeness. Deftly patterned, the rhyme scheme did/lid/still/will; down/brown/Cause/was (abc/abc/def/def), with its regularity and strong, masculine rhyme, introduces order which responds to the rhythm of the world. The speaker-observer is revealed only in the last stanza, comparable in size to 'the Cause' and just as insignificant. Suggesting that the speaker is 'too big to be noticed', MacCaig reverts to the conventional understanding of size and scale with an appreciation of smallness. The tiny lizard, which occupies the whole poem, stands in contrast with 'the Cause', with the capital 'c' which makes it appear big and grave (and pompous), but merits little attention. The conjunction 'as though' in the second line offers the speaker's imagination of the lizard the lack of a sense of direction. Yet direction does not seem to concern the lizard; the sole thing he does is swim. His 'beingness' is in his motion. The verb in a different grammatical form returns five times in the first three stanzas (six, if we include the title). The poem plays with scale: from the depiction of the lizard as '[t]he tiny monster, the alligator / A finger long' (ll. 4–5), the capital letter in the phrase 'an unknown Cause' (l. 8), to the speaker 'too big to be noticed' (l. 10), his pace 'unhurried' (ll. 5, 8). The subject's distance emphasises the respected difference, despite shared space, without assuming the sameness of *Umwelt*. Beings are what they are, each being identical with itself; they merely present themselves to the perceiving I. The use of the gerund 'swimming' in the title gives to the lizard, and thereby reveals to the reader the being of the creature, in a movement that summarises, without offering a greater meaning: to swim in the instant of this recognition is what for that instant the lizard 'is'. It may be other things at other times, but this just is at this very moment, and the gerund does not suggest a greater 'swimmingness' but rather that the lizard is 'becoming-swimming' in its being observed neutrally, with the minimum of interpretation.

In poems such as 'Swimming lizard' or 'Caterpillar going somewhere', MacCaig proves that not only humans are decision-making animals. Through democratic inclusiveness, he emphasises the shared ability to experience the world, observing detail without the speciesist assumption of superiority, engaging with the possibilities of non-human consciousness. MacCaig believed that every animal and thing has its own identity, which, even if unknowable, resides in it: 'I don't know what their identities are, of course, but I'm aware that they have them and I hate intruding on their identity. I loathe the pathetic fallacy . . . I loathe burdening outside objects with human feelings, making them some kind of sympathetic translator for my tiny small self' (MacCaig 2005, xlix). By employing the phrase 'tiny small self', MacCaig once again deflates the human ego, making room for non-human identities. Challenging human scale, MacCaig demonstrates a stark difference between what is perceived as significant and insignificant, thus piercing the bubble of the anthropocentric self-importance. A short poem of twelve lines, 'Compare and contrast' (MacCaig 2005, 432–3) exemplifies the focus of MacCaig's poetry by juxtaposing a 'great' man, an intellectual, with a hen. While the man spent his life 'poking about' (l. 2), ill-equipped with only a mind 'in the dark forest of ideas, / in the bright glare of perception' (ll. 4–5), the hen 'sauntered unerringly' (ll. 10–11). The thinker's meandering walk through the thicket is placed aside the hen's unfailing sense of purpose. The world from the inflated anthropocentric perspective suddenly appears insignificant, even ridiculous. As Edwin Morgan points out, the animal poems 'simply use the world of nature to give man a jolt, to make him think, make him ask questions' (Morgan 1990, 246). Aware of the limits of anthropomorphic thinking, MacCaig nonetheless avoids objectifying or idealising non-human beings through poetic representations of the non-human. Additionally, animal alterity is foregrounded formally through a number devices such as analogy, metaphor and parallelism. The relativisation of the human perspective prevents non-human animals from being reduced to objects existing as a pretext for spreading the poet's ego and instead stand against human exceptionalism.

Time Embedded in the Landscape

As he encounters place in its actuality (inevitably marked by the past), MacCaig juxtaposes the changeability and fleetingness of perceived moments, when permanence underpins geological time. In his poetry, perception of the present prevails over narratives of the past, yet Highland hauntings, with which we are already familiar from the work of Nan Shepherd, nonetheless recur in many poems.

Both blending with the landscape and separate from it, proper names present a fascinating resource for MacCaig in the exploration of the nature of things. These are the names which 'come out of geography but emerge, too, / from myth' (MacCaig 2005, 269; ll. 27–8). Every place name echoes the poet's Gaelic ancestry and links his present moment with the distant time when the inhabitants of that land thought of terms which later became familiar. It demonstrates MacCaig's relationship to language, to the texture of words, which goes beneath their surface, revealing layers of meaning. Resisting the appropriating impulse, MacCaig's use of Gaelic names reflects an engagement with language and aesthetics. As Alan Riach points out, MacCaig's 'poems are . . . quizzical about the inadequacy, uncertainty, inefficiency, unreliability and limits of language itself, the borders of what language permits us to understand' (2018, n.p.). These aspects of the language are examined in 'The Loch of the Peevish Creek' (MacCaig 2005, 488–9), where the name in the title is also the reason to write about the place, which unleashes in the poet an irresistible urge to create: 'A name like that – how can I not / write about you?' (ll. 1–2). The name proves to match the place when the loch does not yield much than a few small trout. The loch, likened to 'the metaphorical waters of poetry' (l. 10), becomes the text in which the poet fishes, at times proving acrimonious, every poem a catch fished from 'peevish waters' (l. 18).

Marco Fazzini claims that the poet's 'insights into the deceitful nature of language as it describes the world' is aggravated by the conflicted nature of the English–Scottish relationship (2016, 51).[16] While Fazzini's reading may appear attractive from a limited and limiting postcolonial perspective, it should be pointed out that MacCaig's perspective is not constrained by, nor that much engaged with, national interests, if at all. The landscape remains unreadable not, as Fazzini claims, because it 'suffers the naming imposed by a colonizing language' (2016, 51); it remains unreadable regardless of human history or language, regardless of political or social conflicts. None of these events affect the immanence of the landscape which exists through and within it, and which cannot be comprehended. If MacCaig 'betrayed his strong sense of dislocation and regret', as Fazzini suggests, it would be false to claim that these emotions could be attributed solely to the specific situation of the West Highlands

(2016, 51). Constraining MacCaig's interest in the natural world to Scottish nationality is a limited – and limiting – reading of his work. What drew MacCaig was the beauty of the landscape, which he highlighted in interviews. Thus it is difficult to agree with Fazzini's generalising statement that '[t]he sense of a disappearing Gaelic society is always present in MacCaig's poetry, as well as the disruptive historical references to the Clearances and their consequences' (2016, 51). While the references appear in some poems, most notably in 'A Man in Assynt' (MacCaig 2005, 221–9), which arguably offers the strongest expression of the historical and social injustice, MacCaig's 'only openly politically committed work' (Greig 2010, 179), it may hardly be said that they are 'always present'. The oft-quoted lines reveal broad concerns with land use which still sound pertinent:

> Who owns this landscape? –
> The millionaire who bought it or
> the poacher staggering downhill in the early morning
> with a deer on his back?
>
> Who possesses this landscape? –
> The man who bought it or
> I who am possessed by it? (ll. 32–8)[17]

Reversing the relation between humans and the land, MacCaig offers a consideration of the structures of power prevailing in modernity, enshrined in landownership and the hunting of animals by those who claim them as their possession. He answers these '[f]alse' (l. 39) questions, stating that the landscape cannot be owned as it is 'masterless' (l. 41), 'intractable in any terms/that are human' (ll. 42–3). Refuting the post-Enlightenment belief of the human mastery over all the world, MacCaig underlines the futility of the illusion of control and possession of the land.

Despite his regular visits to Sutherland, year after year for over four decades, MacCaig remained an outsider to the landscape, with an awareness of the past rooted in the place yet unable to read it in Gaelic place names which speak eloquently of history. MacCaig's Highlands decidedly do not resemble the Highlands evoked in Macpherson's *Ossian* where the romanticised landscape is swathed in mystery, thus 'glamourising its mists and peopling it with shadows' (Morgan 1990, 241). History is nonetheless embedded in the landscape, present in proper names, the abandoned crofts and the remaining Gaelic population. MacCaig was outspoken about the Clearances, which affected Sutherland, 'the most shamefully treated' region:

> you keep coming across ruins of what used to be crofts, in the most unlikely places, from a time when the population was much bigger than it now is. So it's a sad landscape, in that way. You can walk for miles and miles and miles and miles and never see a house, let alone a person. It's got that sadness in it, and you can't help being afflicted by that history in that landscape, because there it is under your very eyes. (Nicholson 1992, 54)

The powerful sway of history outpouring from the landscape overwhelms the poetic subject, who is 'watching / the landscape pouring away out of my eyes' (ll. 1–2), which also highlights the idealist tendency in MacCaig's writing: the world is created as it is being perceived. The above line comes from 'Crossing the border' (MacCaig 2005, 203–4), which underlines the power of contested history over the observer's perception. Being 'lugged backwards / through the Debatable Lands of history' (ll. 14–15), the speaker is 'watching / time pouring away into the past' (ll. 12–13). The historic formation of the land dominates the experience of Assynt, sparsely populated since the Clearances. Inevitably affected by painful historical events, the actuality of landscape, with its present desolateness, reminds the observer of the past strife. The stark nature of the Highland landscape is also evoked in 'Crofter' (MacCaig 2005, 452), in which history is embodied in one man, whose life remained unnoticed, recorded only by the poet. In its anonymity, the nameless crofter becomes synecdoche of all the inhabitants of that part of Scotland, over time. The complex present of the landscape is also explored in such poems as 'Wester Ross, West Sutherland' (MacCaig 2005, 473), where the memory of local heroes – the people inhabiting 'this hard landscape' (l. 8) – is ingrained in the mountains and passed down by streams and lochs, carrying the 'thin threads' (l. 12), connecting the past with the present. Similarly, in 'High mountain loch' (MacCaig 2005, 486–7), it is the present moment which remains: from the perspective of the loch, which talks to the speaker, history 'lies in ruins' (l. 5); there is no past or future, only now. History has no pattern and offers nothing for the present or future; what matters is the elemental aspect of the landscape. While the genealogical links to the land and the ancestral pull of Gaelic names constitute the bearers of memory for MacCaig, there also exists a geological bond, or '[m]emory of the world' (Merleau-Ponty 2003, 120; cit.

Toadvine 2014, 266). Exploring Merleau-Ponty's remarks on time, 'the absolute past of nature, as a past that has never been present' (Toadvine 2014, 266), Ted Toadvine compellingly develops the idea of the phenomenology of the 'elemental' past (2014, 262). As he poetically puts it, 'our embodied immersion in the Memory of the world tears us apart, scattering us across an incommensurable multiplicity of temporal flows and eddies', adding that this is when we encounter 'an asubjective time, a time without a world, at the heart of lived time', to conclude that '[t]his worldless prehistorical time, independent of any subject, is precisely the time of the elements, of ashes and dust' (Toadvine 2014, 266). Citing Merleau-Ponty, Toadvine argues that this is the experience of 'time before time' (1968, 163, cit. Toadvine 2014, 266), one that 'remembers an impossible past' and 'anticipates an impossible future' (1968, 123, cit. Toadvine 2014, 266). The observations of the paradoxical nature of time, both fleeting and eternal, occupy an important part of MacCaig's poetry, fulfilling one of the most fundamental functions of art according to the poet; 'what the devil is Time anyway' (MacCaig 1979, 84), he asks dismissively. In 'Two skulls' (MacCaig 2005, 392) the image functions as a material reminder, a memento mori. Biological time often contrasts with deep, geological time. As 'a crofter in the landscape of time' ('Processes', l. 13; MacCaig 2005, 507), MacCaig accepts the eroding temporal processes, yet is continuously mending the wall. Poetry, made of words, is a discursive 'wall', each word a stone or brick, being used so as to halt temporal depredations and erasure. There is thus, in the register of the crofter against the landscape of time, the image of a work being done in relation to the landscape – of shoring it up, keeping it in place, maintaining a human relationship over time with a non-human environment.

Birds' skulls appear in the work of Scottish poets such as Hugh MacDiarmid and Kathleen Jamie. In Jamie's essay 'Findings', she finds a gannet head on a beach (alongside a plastic doll's head) and uses it as a paper weight. MacDiarmid's poem 'Perfect (On the western seaboard of South Uist)' (Armitage and Dee 2011, 249–50) in which the speaker finds a pigeon's skull on the Atlantic shore, is preceded by an epigraph from a Spanish play: 'Los Muertos abren los ojos a los que viven' (Horozco 2005, 354). Using a line from a sixteenth-century poet, Sebastián de Horozco of Toledo, MacDiarmid plays with the ambivalence: the dead open the eyes of the living or on the living. Similarly, life's inevitable finitude is evoked in 'Treeless landscape' (MacCaig 2005, 80–1), starkly contrasted with the seemingly unchangeable nature of 'a bald, bare land' (l. 2), reinforced by the impression of stillness pervading the image, as if time stopped. In this image, the land itself becomes a skull. Temporal processes are manifest in the weathering and erosion of the surface, revealing time in its underdetermination – there are a 'million shapes of time' (l. 7) – dominates the image, affecting everything as '[t]ime's no procrastinator' (l. 17). The landscape is 'weathered half away' (l. 2, l. 16), slowly being eroded as a result of wind and rain. In this image the paradox of time is revealed: nothing changes for the observer, as whatever takes place falls outside of the human temporal frame as the changes in the formation of the landscape can rarely be observed during human lifetime. Similarly to Thomas Hardy's prose and poetry, MacCaig is a poet of the small, the microcosmic, which constantly informs his work. Placed in-between the currents of time, human experience is inevitably paradoxical. Yet time is also present in what happens there and then, in front of the speaker's eyes as an event or encounter. In this still landscape, an event takes place when a buzzard catches a vole; even if the change is minimal, constrained to the two beings, the dynamic alters. The radical singularity of the event remains beyond representation and against the appropriative impulse. The space of the event exists in relation to activity which is not limited to the human, and what is more, is often unachievable to humans, as the speaker's expressed desire to be 'a buzzard and create a sky' (l. 20) demonstrates.

In a number of poems the terrain's elements are anthropomorphised. In 'Treeless landscape' the whole land is depicted as a set of human bodily parts: 'armpits of hills' (l. 1), a 'rotting elbow' (l. 18) and 'bony blades' (l. 3), which stick through the 'skin' (l. 3) of the land. Thanks to this device, the geological changes which take place, though extended in time, resemble biological finitude. Yet MacCaig is also keen to demonstrate the limits of anthropomorphism. 'Humanism' (MacCaig 2005, 184) opens with an anthropomorphic image of a glacier 'defeated / In the siege of Suilven' (ll. 1–2), further emphasised by such phrases as 'limped off' (l. 2) and 'left behind' (l. 3). The passive aspect of the first verb denies the glacier agency, a view which is reversed at the end of the poem. The military language transforms the glacier into an army, imposing a human interpretation on geological processes; it humanises and domesticates them, offering a familiar perspective that denies the landscape any alterity. The urge to anthropomorphise is promptly undermined in the next stanza in a statement which admonishes the 'greed' (l. 8) and 'arrogance' (l. 9) of humans who do 'not allow the glacier to be glacier' (ll. 9–10).

MacCaig mocks the self-centredness governing human perception, juxtaposing the grand war image with that of a Cinderella who lost her shoe as she fled at midnight. The contrast highlights the absurdity of humanising metaphors employed eagerly in order to narrate the natural world. The final stanza presents a strong personal declaration, the speaker's voice sounding boldly: 'I defend the glacier' (l. 18). The line is followed by another mockery of the self-aggrandising tendency of humans to create a precious self-image. The title is thus an ironic comment on what truly represents the lofty values of humanism: an incorrigible anthropocentrism which arrogantly places our species at the pinnacle of creation and causes humans to view the surrounding world with hubris. The ending of the poem reverses the order of significance by placing the glacier as an active agent, which eventually 'absorbs' (l. 19) humans as if to prove the falsity of the dreams of omnipotence.

Eye and Mind

MacCaig's engagement with place relies on the exploration of various perceptual modes of presence. The descriptive form foregrounds the reliance on sight as the evocations strive for clarity of vision and language. As MacCaig says, his mother 'thought in images' (McNeill 1996, 1), which might explain why a great number of poems, which MacCaig calls 'snapshot poems' (MacCaig 1979, 85), evoke a scene, a momentary glimpse, capture an event or, more often, non-event. Employing description is a way to comprehend the world as through corporeal perception that the poet or subject partakes in. Through the precision of language and exactitude of description, MacCaig pays attention to the physical world, in a form of 'constant notice, respectful looking, the spotting of unlikely material significance', to cite David Matless (2015, 9). Highlighting the relation between the observer and the observed, connected through the eye, MacCaig explores visual forms of being-in-the-world. In the first lines of 'Instrument and agent' (MacCaig 2005, 4), the poem opening *Riding Lights*, the speaker expresses a democratically inclusive attitude: 'In my eye I've no apple; every object / Enters in there with hands in pocket' (ll. 1–2). In the active, ever-changing, constantly ongoing process through which the eye and mind see, imagine and create, the selection and interpretation involved in their functioning underpins the elusive ability to perceive things, which 'merely are'. The ontological primacy of the perceived world is emphasised in a number of poems such as, for instance, 'Signs and signals' (MacCaig 2005, 130), in which the components of the landscape – the Loch of the Wolf's Pass, the Loch of the Green Corrie, '[r]ock, sphagnum and grass' (l. 4) intertwine with deer, eagle, ptarmigan – all suspended in space, 'hung high in the air' (l. 3). Through the use of parallelism, MacCaig emphasises the perceptual exchange between human subjectivity and the world. These same components are 'hung there in my mind / drenched with meaning' (ll. 16–17). The emergence of meaning occurs in the reversible nature of perception where the seer is also the seen, the touching, the touched in the constantly ongoing relational process, as reversibility is 'always imminent and never realized in fact' (Merleau-Ponty 1968, 147), but rather encountering *un écart*, or a divergence. In the profound exchange, the evoked landscape is endowed with a sacred dimension, as the air is 'the tall cathedral' (l. 26), open into '[t]he altar of everywhere' (l. 28), the latter phrase ending the poem, but also expanding it further through the openness of the vowels. In 'Looking down on Glen Canisp' (MacCaig 2005, 181), the texture of the air affects the colours, turning them into 'their cloudier selves' (l. 4), the scent, sights and sounds; walking, the mind starts to 'fuzz into the air' (l. 16), joining Suilven and the ravens, all fused with the surroundings. Substance undergoes a transformation: through the fuzziness of matter the stags create 'antlers of water' (l. 21) as the organic entwines with the inorganic. The landscape becomes a cathedral, suggested by a reference to a stained-glass window at the end of the first stanza. The self is at times occluded and disclosed, creating ironic distance, and highlighting the complex nature of the self, with all its paradoxes: its fickle, unstable, shimmering nature as well as its permanence. The speaker is revealed only in the middle of the last stanza, five lines from the end of the poem, through aural perception: 'till I hear' (l. 17). In a number of poems, the superiority of the sense of sight is dismissed, as, for instance, in 'Inverkirkaig Bay', where 'the lust of looking' (l. 3) ruled by 'the cheating eye' (l. 1) must be discarded. While vision dominates, aurality occupies a significant place, the poet listening to the world, detecting different languages, yet aware of the limitations imposed by the human *Umwelt* preventing him from apprehending speech. Such poems as 'Sound of the sea on a still evening' (MacCaig 2005, 91–2), 'Sounds of the day' (MacCaig 2005, 182), 'Sounds and silences' (MacCaig 2005, 453) or 'Looking down on Glen Canisp' (MacCaig 2005, 181), explore varied modes of attention, including, again, ocular and aural forms. In a process of exchange, the sea becomes the light through associations of the ear, with the onomatopoeia '[t]he sea goes flick-flack or the light does' (l. 1), as, in listening, the perceiving I becomes the landscape (MacCaig 2005, 136–7). Perceiving 'is a keeping-in-touch with the world, an experiencing of things rather than a having of experiences' (Gibson 2015, 228), as James Gibson argues; thus, [t]o perceive is to be aware of the surfaces of the environment and of oneself in it. The interchange between hidden and unhidden surfaces is essential to this awareness' (Gibson 2015, 244).

Predominantly inhabiting the open, MacCaig's poetic subject enters the landscape, aware of its surfaces and self-reflective, aware of the occurring exchange through which their true nature manifest itself. Placed between engagement and withdrawal, the observer self-consciously takes part in the ambivalence of perception, at times unveiling and at others obscuring. The whole body is involved in perceptual activities, being in direct corporeal contact with the environment as the world enters the self sensually, through 'five ports of knowledge' carrying 'many cargoes' (MacCaig 1979, 84). As the signs of the outside world are transmitted through the embodied consciousness and translated, the poet's role is to 'unship the lot' (MacCaig 1979, 84). Even when they are speculative, the poems nonetheless maintain clear focus on the perceived objects, avoiding abstraction and aiming to define with precision the emergence of the world through an active exchange with the embodied self. This is not an authoritative, imperial consciousness from which the world is derived, but a dynamic emergence through an exchange between the embodied self and the world.

A Physical Metaphysical

As a Scottish poet, MacCaig could not avoid becoming 'profoundly affected ... by the metaphysical bent of Scotland as a whole' (Hendry 1990, 63). Arguing that MacCaig is not a Romantic, 'who joyfully obliterates himself in the thing seen' (Ascherson 1981, 21), Neal Ascherson confirms that there exist metaphysical connections in the poet's work. In writing 'from the impulse of the physical thing seen—mountain and loch—with a metaphysical response', MacCaig resembles Andrew Young, 'a poet who owed nothing to the Scottish Renaissance' (1981, 21). This unique intertwining of the physical world with the metaphysical confirms MacCaig's description as 'a physical metaphysical', to use Louis MacNeice's phrase (cit. McNeill 1996, 31), which succinctly evokes the paradox ever-present in

MacCaig's work and describe his oscillation between materiality and transcendence. From observer to participant, phenomenological reflection experiences the landscape through the body and senses. Permeating the poems, sensuality stems from MacCaig's reliance on sensuous perception, constructing the relationship with the world through its material substance. 'The physical world keeps bumping gently into him' (Ascherson 1981, 19). Joined with the intellectual and conceptual, the sensuous intertwines with the abstract, presenting yet another paradox and reinforcing the physical/metaphysical coalescence in his poetry. This is paired with the withdrawal of the ego, already mentioned, and demonstrated in a many poems, which evokes the world whereby thought is entangled in matter. Existing outside the self, the physical world intertwines with it, thus creating a becoming-entangled. Things change through a becoming which transcends the self, simultaneously absorbed by, and absorbing it. The landscape performs actions, alive with all beings and things, participating in a dynamic, mutual exchange.

Always standing firmly grounded in real place, MacCaig celebrates it in its multifariousness. Formed of Torridonian sandstone millions of years ago, MacCaig's beloved Suilven represents the world of substance reflecting the depth of time, whereby substance and light delineate the experience of place. When speaking of Assynt, the poet foregrounds the combination of its material composition, deep time, and the physicality of light: 'The groundwork on which the mountains there stand are made of a hard, hard, hard rock: I'm told it's one of the oldest rocks on the earth's surface – Lewisian gneiss. It's all over the Hebrides, the west coast, the Highlands. Very hard, comes in different colours, grey, greenish, purplish, that change with the light' (MacCaig in Nicholson 1992, 53). The solidity of stone combined with flickering light and colour, bouncing off its surface affects the intensity of perception, when the mind transforms the thing seen through association and analogy. Nested together, physical objects manifest themselves in different forms and sizes as the poetic imagination attempts to gather them in their interdependence.

MacCaig's focus on the material aspects of reality, filtered through intellect and imagination, has merited him comparisons with Wallace Stevens (cf. Scott 1972–3; Nicholson 1992). The poet himself admits to 'a sort of affinity' with Stevens, with 'his persistent . . . talk about the difference between reality and imagination, and what imagination does to reality. He was all for what the imagination does to it. I don't go that far; in fact rather the opposite. But I felt this interest of his in reality and imagination, and his notion that everything has to be a fiction' (Nicholson 1992, 47). Where Stevens favours abstract speculation, MacCaig's sharp focus remains on the observed object. He emphasises the experience of the world through a continuous exchange with the physical substance of reality. As Peter-Paul Verbeek argues, '[m]aterial things are, in philosophical terms, understood to mediate the internal and external world of human beings' (2005, 168). Hugh MacDiarmid, writing perceptively and persuasively on MacCaig, observes that, 'Instead of giving the object an individual existence based on its being, he conceives things of the exterior as an aspect of his soul, as a sensible "complex" of himself. This progressive, ambiguous fusion of the spirit and the world presupposes a certain faculty in the poet for sensing the most delicate reciprocities between the interior and the exterior' (MacDiarmid 1955, 20). In MacCaig's poetry, the engagement with the physical world coexists with the metaphysical realm, emphasising the occurrence of the undecidable. Consciousness enters the solidity of matter, as, for instance, in 'On the north side of Suilven' (MacCaig 2005, 438), where language and water interweave, reversibly present in the streamlet and the rivers, and in the speaker's throat, filling the body. Water connects the subject with the world, as does the air, entering the body in the process of breathing.

'Landscape outside and in'

MacCaig's poems frequently explore the constant exchange between the interiority of the subject and the landscape outside. The world enters the embodied consciousness in the interplay of the self and the landscape, as interiority becomes deeply affected by place. What occurs then, as Husserl explains, is the proper, or primary, enworlding (*Verweltlichung*), which involves 'the constituting I' actively participating in self-apperception, which equals self-enworlding 'world-constitution' (Fink 1995, 108). As the world gives itself to the speaker, the speaker reciprocates in the interrelationship between the sky, the self and the stone, the poetic language providing a connective thread. Enworlding happens sensually as the speaker demonstrates in 'Centre of centres' (MacCaig 2005, 269–72):

> I name myself, I name this place, I say
> *I am here*; and the immediacies
> of the flesh and of the reports
> of its five senses (I welcome them)

make their customary
miraculous declarations, from which
all else falls away. The landscapes
and histories of memory
disappear (ll. 55–63)

Naming the self is inextricably related to naming the world as the realisation of spatial relations occurs through sensual perception, reminding the reader of Merleau-Ponty's concept of the 'flesh of the world' where the body is an open system embedded in the surrounding. Enworlding is a recurrent preoccupation of MacCaig's poetry, returning for instance in 'Landscape and I' (MacCaig 2005, 286), where the elemental world interpenetrates the embodied consciousness. Schiehallion enters the speaker's mind to yield a meaning, which becomes '[t]he meaning of the meaning, no less', carried everywhere. Similarly, in 'Landscape outside and in' (MacCaig 2005, 412), the world and the embodied consciousness interweave in a reversible exchange. Perpendicular and horizontal lines cross to combine all the components of the landscape, which branches out to all singing birds, 'all my selves / sing together' (ll. 12–13). Through parallelism, MacCaig foregrounds the analogy 'all my selves / are still singing' (ll. 18–19). Introducing a micro-pause, the enjambement separates and joins 'selves' and 'sing'. As the landscape sings, it enters the speaker, creating inner resonances. Thus the outside becomes the inside, chiasmically intertwined in all its forms as the plural 'selves', recurring in stanzas 3 and 5, highlight the multifarious identity of the landscape, the motif already there in early poems such as 'Summer farm' (MacCaig 2005, 34): '[s]elf under self, a pile of selves I stand' (l. 13). As the speaker leaves the place, the bluebells and the loch water are not left behind but are carried within. 'On the pier at Kinlochbervie' (MacCaig 2005, 446) explores the recurrent theme of distance and proximity. In an attempt to diminish the gap, the poet plays with scale, creating an analogy between stars and peanuts, while he admitting that it is a 'ludicrous image, I know' (l. 4). Such self-conscious awareness of the limitations of associative language recurs in other poems, for instance, 'Estuary' (MacCaig 2005, 194), where the poet reproaches himself: 'I make / horrible correspondences' (ll. 13–14). In 'On the pier at Kinlochbervie', the speaker longs for closeness as the mind is 'struggling with itself' (l. 8), yearning for nearness yet incapable of achieving it as the sense of *écart* is particularly powerful.

MacCaig is fascinated in the constant oscillating motion of the landscape. Expressing his deep affection for the West Highlands in general and for Suilven in particular, MacCaig admits, 'I love Suilven, because from the West it looks like the top joint of your thumb. But he cons you: there's a ridge and there's a pinky at the far end, so that he is infinitely variable. And he spouts cool clear water from innumerable springs' (Walker 1981, 34). The deceptive nature of the hill, its shimmering appearance and its apparently protean ability to change forms, which change depending on the viewer's perspective, appeals strongly to the poet (as this suggests that meaning is never fixed, but of the moment, singular, provisional). As the observer's position changes, it changes shape, morphing into different forms. This 'infinite variability', the potential to transform itself in front of his eyes, fertilises MacCaig's imagination. The hill comes alive, resembling part of a giant hand, at times flat and sturdy as a thumb, then a little finger. Limitless, impossible to apprehend, 'infinite' and 'innumerable', manifold, a rock which produces water. The urge to climb the local hills – 'these miniature Alps' (Walker 1981, 34) – resided in him. The frequent reiteration of the same viewpoints allows MacCaig to explore the manifold relation between the world, the eye and the mind, accentuating the boundlessness of the landscape, which remains impossible to grasp. Movement is for MacCaig 'an elementary thing' (MacCaig 2005, xlix). As he says, 'I find myself to be fascinated by movement. I love the movement of creatures and grasses, anything. And I think I'm sometimes not bad at describing things in movement. I'm not a static writer in spite of these snapshots' (MacCaig 2005, xlix). While it may be 'despite' the phatic nature of MacCaig's poems, such snapshots only prove how things move and are constantly on the move. Despite the fact that many of his poems have 'rather painterly titles' (Watson 2018, xviii), MacCaig's poems are often dominated by movement: the movement of the eye following the image and the mind making connections, emphasising the interplay between stillness and motion. Extensive walking around Assynt, climbing the mountains and cycling inform MacCaig's poetry, as the reiterated vantage points yield singular perspectives every time. In 'Walking to Inveruplan' (MacCaig 2005, 216), the regular rhyming pattern marks a rhythm of the speaker's steps, resounding with the beat of answers. The swaying motion of problem and answer is emphasised in the parallel structure of the poem: the last line of the first stanza, 'under the final problem of lit skies' (l. 3), is structurally echoed in the words ending the poem, 'above the final problem of my feet' (l. 18). Complementary, the two prepositions strengthen the connecting bridge within the sky–earth. Walking and cycling enabled MacCaig to explore the landscape flatly as he often returned to the road along the coast, cycling up to the lighthouse at Stoer Point with the North Sea to the west, and Suilven, Cùl Mòr, Cùl Beag and Stac Pollaidh to the south (McNeill 1996, 21); yet it is particularly climbing, when 'suddenly you see miles and miles instead of just what was under you' (MacCaig in Walker 1981, 34), that nourishes many poems. For instance, in 'Climbing Suilven' (MacCaig 2005, 46), the rhythm of steps is evoked in the repetitive phrases such as 'I nod and nod' (l. 1), 'down and down' (l. 2), 'down and down' (l. 6). 'my parish is / This stone, that tuft, this stone / And the cramped quarters of my flesh and bone' (ll. 7–9). Through walking, MacCaig's poetic self connects the two planes: vertical and horizontal, the ground and the atmosphere in a Merleau-Pontian intercorporeality of humans and the world. According to James Gibson's ecological approach to perception, two hemispheres brought together, the sky–earth complement each other. The space of air is the medium

> in which animals can move about (and in which objects can *be* moved about) is at the same time the medium for light, sound, and odor coming from sources in the environment. An enclosed medium can be 'filled' with light, with sound, and even with odor. Any point in the medium is a possible point of observation for any observer who can look, listen, or sniff. And these points of observation are continuously connected to one another by paths of possible locomotion ... As the observer moves from point to point, the optical information, the acoustic information, and the chemical information change accordingly. Each potential point of observation in the medium is unique in this respect. (Gibson 2015, 13)

Perceiving bodies in space are affected by the changing medium of air. In 'High up on Suilven' (MacCaig 2005, 103), the self is immersed in the open, the substances of the atmosphere are entangled, bound together with the speaker's corporality, who is surrounded by '[g]ulfs of blue air' (l. 1); the speaker gazes at the lochs in the distance with the near presence of a frog. From that viewpoint, the sky–earth become one, and the Isle of Harris appears 'in the sky' (l. 2). Fused with the wind, ravens glide, making dynamic the image and connecting the embodied consciousness with the elements in a perceptual exchange. The openness of the landscape is foregrounded by vast horizons, the sea, the mountain ranges and the plateaus stretching far ahead as well as the birds and other non-human animals inhabiting that land, creating the open world where all beings and things relate, immersed in the same weather-world.

In the ecological optics, animal movement braids the ground with the space of air. In 'Ringed Plover by a Water's Edge' (MacCaig 2005, 292), motion is rendered through formal devices such as line breaks, enjambments and dashes. The poem is composed of very short lines of varied length, from eight syllables to one. The suddenness of the birds' movement is evoked in one-syllable words, prevailing throughout the poem, particularly in the first stanza where all the lines but one end in a one-syllable word. The monosyllable further reinforces the fleeting moment, thus having paradoxically a sense of motion, underlining the question of temporality and singularity. The repetition of the phrase 'like that' (of that nature, effortlessly) expresses the indescribability of the birds' manner, which may only be contained in a general statement which attempts to encompass their nature. With a hint of admiration, the phrase also emphasises the effortlessness with which the ringed plover change pace. The verb 'to be' appears three times: twice in the second stanza when they are likened to life itself, and at the end of the poem, when they turn to gravel; they simply are. When they move, they form a single file and 'parallel the parallel ripples' (l. 14), analogous to the sea. As soon as they stop, they change into the background, or rather into the ground, becoming gravel. Blending with the elements, ringed plover become indistinguishable, difficult to notice, fitting, creating correspondences. They focus life as if through a 'burning-glass', intensifying it, converging it. Part of 'the world of delicate clockwork' (l. 11), the birds are inextricably connected with the subtle inner workings of their surroundings – moving in brief, irregular bursts, in a series of small waves, the feeling that spreads around increasing then dwindling. Brief and fitful, the ripples of bird movement emphasise the temporal flow as the plovers interweave intermittently with the landscape – presence and absence – and, through analogy, juxtapose the recursive nature of the tidal sea with the immobility of the mountains.

'A text composed of earth and sky'

Through the poet's response to the landscape unfolding in front of his eyes, the interplay between poetic language and world is created. 'The philosophy of Nature needs a language that can take up Nature in its least human aspect, and which thereby would be close to poetry' (2003, 45), Merleau-Ponty tells us. MacCaig's search for such a language is visible in his gradual move away from rhyme, which departure thereby highlights its artifice, as he moves towards the subtle rhythms of the landscape, affording it a voice of its own. Theodor Adorno's assumption that 'the language of nature is mute' and the role of art is 'to make this muteness eloquent' (Adorno 1997, 101) is disproved by MacCaig, whose poetry reflects a belief that the living and non-living world produces speech, even if it remains inaccessible to human comprehension. In an early poem, 'Dying landscape' (MacCaig 2005, 48), human feeling does not affect the land, leaving no mark as it 'makes no water speak' (l. 1) or 'hoists no hill' (l. 4). Aware of the power dynamics, MacCaig attempts to erase the perceiving subject, tucking it away in order to eliminate the ego scrupulously. Through these images, the elusive power of pathetic fallacy as a device to represent the landscape is undermined. The phrase 'Recalcitrance of tree and hill and bird' (l. 14), added in parenthesis, as if observed from the corner of an eye, stresses the resistance of the surrounding to yield 'to a listening ear' (l. 3). The final stanza introduces Christian echoes in the reference to Christ's descent from the cross, further strengthened in the lines: 'The limiting differences / Making their huge withdrawal, selves away, / Behind the first simplicity of the Word' (ll. 16–18), which suggest that the textual origins of the world may be unveiled only if false distinctions are abolished purifying speech, peeling away the layers of constraining selves. In 'By the Graveyard, Luskentyre' (MacCaig 2005, 434–5), there are '[m]essages everywhere' (l. 6), yet few are decipherable. While death's messages are clear, there are no 'dictionaries of the wind, the grasses' (l. 7).

Scholars who wish to explicate everything nonetheless often lack the instruments to read the messages sent 'in a foreign language' (l. 8) emitted by the natural world. Scientific observation is just that, taking notes on the field, drawing conclusions, labelling, ordering. Mistrustful of the grand claims and ambitions of scientific method in mining knowledge about the natural world, MacCaig gestures to the limitations of science. There are things that elude scientists, things which form 'a volume beyond the wit of scholars' (l. 16), as the last line of the poem announces. The languages of the natural world do not 'unlock' the mystery, as humans lack the key. Rhetorical questions reverberate throughout, highlighting the variety of forms of speech filling the landscape: 'who can interpret the blue-green waves / That never stop talking, shouting, wheedling?' (ll. 3–4). There are languages everywhere. The larks are singing 'Four larks are singing in a showering sprinkle / bright testaments: in a foreign language' (ll. 7–8). The alliteration composed of sibilants which follow the four larks reimagines aurally the moment when they burst in song. The word 'testament' originating from *testis*, 'a witness', as speech, in its various forms bears witness to the surrounding world. The use of verbs emphasises the active function of the landscape and its participants, the accumulation of gerunds evokes the traffic of speech in the landscape, which is replete with language even if they cannot be deciphered. The beach is marked with bird alphabets, 'oghamed and cuneiformed' (l. 9) by a knot, a dunlin, a sandpiper. To cite Louise Westling, 'This is only the human translation or expression of the world's meanings, a second-order reference that makes sense of things from within our limited perceptions. The universe will always elude efforts to capture its full meaning, but from within its depths, language witnesses its revelations and questions its mysteries' (2011, 131). The elusiveness of various languages of the landscape is succinctly expressed in a line from 'A voice of summer' (MacCaig 2005, 128–9): 'Something that it could say cannot be spoken' (l. 14). In 'A man I agreed with' (MacCaig 2005, 414), the question of elusive meaning of the 'bright testaments' returns. At the centre of the poem is the attunement to the world demonstrated in man's embrace of the 'unfailing hospitality of five senses' (l. 4) and his acceptance of things and beings as they are, without trying to investigate, prod, dissect or drill in order to find answers. His curiosity is limited to wanting to know 'how they came to be what they are' (l. 8), as he realises that posing a direct question to a caterpillar or a loch as to 'what do you mean' (l. 10) would be an insult, an unnecessary questioning of their essence. In this approach – respecting their singularity – he resembles God, as the poet tells us. The expression '[i]n this respect' (l. 11), opening the fourth stanza gains a double meaning: the man's godlike bearing (in the atheist sense, as the poet assures us) opens a path to a respectful coexistence.

The question of undecipherable language is evoked in 'At the foot of Cul Mor' (MacCaig 2005, 493), as translation of coded messages from an unknown script into wordless emotions poses an insurmountable challenge in the world where stone, grass and water combine in one line of the poem, interlinked with a conjunction and followed by light, flooding the next line, all to itself. The speaker is situated amid these components of the earth, with their permission, sharing their purposelessness. The preposition 'among' emphasises the link between the surrounding and the self, mingling together: sensuous experience, bodily immersion, all elements 'gathered together in a *sensorium commune*' (Dufrenne 1973, 339). Established from the observer's vantage point by the distance of the mountain and the proximity of the bird, spatiality is reversed as the sole separate being there is the stonechat, marking its otherness with purposeful behaviour. Amid the unknowingness, despite lack of reference tools, the speaker attempts to transfer the components of the landscape in a lyric form, translating the meanings revealed by the world: 'Yet I'm translating / their language which has no dictionary / into feelings that have no words' (ll. 9–11). Communication ensues: a religious rite in a form of an exchange of blessings, which highlights the sacred nature of the landscape. Expressed openly, the speaker's paganism poses no obstacle to the secular reverence of the surrounding world. Similarly, the poem titled 'Illumination: on the track by Loch Fewin' (MacCaig 2005, 184) contains Christian allusions as, for instance, in a reference to the Book of Kells, an illuminated manuscript to which the blazing landscape is compared. The lovers walk 'in a medieval manuscript' (l. 10), among the mountains and water, which resembles a walk in Eden; biblical symbols are present: doves, the thorn, the serpent. The adverb 'suddenly', opening the poem introduces an event of the light appearing through a rip in the clouds, and becoming 'blazed on the eye' (l. 5), a phrase which highlights the moment of revelation. As the speaker climbs with a companion, the view reveals a text, spreading before their eyes. Suddenly they see: both in the literal and metaphorical sense. The title of the poem also plays with the double meaning, suggesting the medieval art of decorating a manuscript and a moment of epiphany, or spiritual enlightenment. In this form, the logos of the landscape does not require exegesis or explanation, it is made explicit in its revelation.

MacCaig's poetry is filled with languages produced by the living and non-living world. There is elemental speech, as in, for example, 'Sound of the sea on a still evening' (MacCaig 2005, 91–2), in which pebbles 'roar / At their harsh labour' (ll. 21–2) and waves 'run / Fawning on rocks and barking in the sun' (ll. 23–4). In 'Landscape outside and in', all the elements of the landscape sing together the selves in silent song as they 'make no sound / but you hear their every note' (ll. 19–20). At times, the deceptiveness of human language is contrasted with animal speech, as for instance in 'Sounds and silences' (MacCaig 2005, 453), as the river is 'gabbling' (l. 1), 'talking to itself' (l. 2) and the stone 'has / a language beyond our hearing' (ll. 10–11), all in the process of transforming, 'never silent' (l. 5). In 'Landscape and I', in an uneven exchange, the landscape communicates '[h]is symptoms of being' (l. 3) to the speaker. Language spills from the sun, in its 'hieroglyphs of light' (l. 6), as light constantly recreates itself, renews its message. Through his song, the lark soars 'in true / Translation' (l. 11), the sound left behind once he disappears. In 'Languages' (MacCaig 2005, 504), everything speaks: from the dragonfly to the streamlet, to the grasses, all in their own form, parts of speech, 'solemn paragraphs' (l. 11), depending on the matter, whether these are wings, water or hue, they talk, explain. The first line reveals the speaker spoken to: 'A dragonfly speaks to me' (l. 1). The stoical grasses are 'imperturbable philosophers' (l. 10). The speakers own a language, composed of 'sounds' and 'scribbles' form the word-hoard. The engagement with the landscape happens *through* language, despite its limitations and inadequacy. Poetry is a mode of bearing witness to, and affirming immanence in beauty, transforming and continuing the world where thought, matter and time are mediated and attuned, the body-subject becoming integrated with the world. It is through poetic expression that we may gain a glimpse of the meaning which goes beyond human language. It is that meaning beyond language which, we shall see, Kathleen Jamie finds in her temporal explorations.

Notes

1. Among ideas forming part of a Gaelic aesthetic, Meg Bateman enumerates 'the circularity of time', 'the non-hierarchical attitude to life forms' and animism (2018, 14).
2. As MacCaig maintained, writing a poem took him '[a]bout two cigarettes' (Stephen 2017, 7).
3. In a slim study published in 1977, Erik Frykman cites or refers to approximately 186 poems. In his book, entitled simply *Norman MacCaig* (2010), Alasdair Macrae does not devote much space to in-depth analysis of poems.
4. MacCaig's reputation grew steadily throughout his writing life. After the publication of *Measures*, he was considered 'certainly outstanding amongst poets writing today' (Johnson 1965, 45). Nominating MacCaig for the 1980 Neustadt Prize, Alexander Scott maintained that MacCaig is 'the most distinguished poet writing in English to emerge in Scotland since World War II' (Board of Regents 1979, 641). For some critics, MacCaig is '[n]ot only . . . one of the best Scottish poets of the last half-century, he is also the best known' (Roy 1980, 474) and 'deservedly one of the best known and most popular of contemporary Scottish poets' (Fulton 1986, 507). MacCaig's poems 'reveal mastery of style which sets him apart from many of his contemporaries' (Morse 1963, 332). A significant poetic voice, MacCaig inevitably influenced other Scottish poets, including Robin Fulton and Iain Crichton Smith

(Board of Regents 1979, 641). His pervasive influence extended to Ted Hughes, who admits that MacCaig's poetry exerted a powerful impact on him from the late 1950s, providing him with 'stylistic clues' (Hughes in Pow and Hendry 1995, n.p.).
5. When one critic dismisses MacCaig for 'his addiction to ideas' and 'intellectual speculation' (Kindrick 1998, 835), another considers him a 'contemplative poet' (Cole 1974, 24), and yet another accuses him of occasional bathos (Johnson 1965, 45). MacCaig's early poems were written in a style that was 'syntactically dense and quasi-surreal' (Thornton et al. 2012, n.p.) when he was part of the neo-Romantic movement of the New Apocalypse, which focused on myth, surreal imagery and the free flow of emotion, elements dominating MacCaig's first two collections. During that period MacCaig 'used words more splashingly', as Neal Ascherson puts it (1981, 21), while Alan Riach mentions the 'avalanching language' (Riach 2018, n.p.) which characterise the poems.
6. Starting with *Riding Lights* (1955), 'the scalpel has been at work, as Edwin Morgan observes, 'there is a progressive paring away of all excess' (Morgan 1990, 243). In *Measures* (1965), the style is already 'stripped and apparently casual' (Davie 1989, 19), marked by 'masterly' simplicity (Curry 1978, 63).
7. Edwin Morgan wonders if, after we 'strip away the props, the local speech, the language societies, the desideria', what would be the element which would enable us to identify whether an author was Scottish, 'and not an English or "British" writer', suggesting that it might be 'subject-matter or thematic interest' (1990, 23). Similarly to poets such as Allan Ramsay and Robert Burns, MacCaig's poems may be identified as Scottish 'only because of the idiom', as Ross G. Roy suggests, who also observes that '[s]uch a voice does not speak only to the countrymen, for art is bounded by neither time nor place' (Roy 1980, 474).
8. Comparisons with Hugh MacDiarmid are 'inevitable'. Donald Davie writes, 'If MacCaig feels like this about history, he has every right to say so. And it was refreshing to have it said in 1965, when poetry was becoming every day more politically inflamed. But if MacCaig's thoroughgoing scepticism about history has saved him from the self-contradictions, the absurdities and the duplicities that punctuated MacDiarmid's career, readers across the political spectrum may yet agree that MacDiarmid's engagement with history is one of the things we expect of a great poet, or of a poet ambitious to be great' (1989, 20). In turn, Colin Nicholson suggests, 'Rather than claim, oddly in my view, that Norman MacCaig "exhibits a feeling of frustration, of being imprisoned in language", it might be potentially more rewarding to consider why and how his close friendship with Hugh MacDiarmid – and in particular the latter's dominance in longer forms – kept MacCaig distant from political

commitment and engaged instead with tightly controlled lyric brevity until his delayed recovery of genealogical memory gave him what he called a "telephone wire" to the past and developing access to free verse' (Nicholson 2009, 104–5).

9. Critics tried to situate MacCaig's work in literary tradition, neoclassical, metaphysical, or even romantic. The attempts to place MacCaig in the philosophical context include parallels made between him and David Hume, both of whom consider self-knowledge to be the utmost form of study, which they 'pursue . . . throughout their works with a philosophy that can indeed be called humanistic in an Italian Renaissance sense – man-centred, ultimately self-centred and on an accessible human scale' (Scott 1972–3, 139). MacCaig has been compared to such Scottish poets as Andrew Young (Ascherson 1981, 21), Robert Garioch (with whom he shares 'a sense of the pathos of the epic effort', as Alan Riach argues [2018, n.p.]) and even Robert Burns (Kindrick 1998, 834). The comparisons extend beyond Scottish literature. Donald Davie suggests that MacCaig's poetry offers 'a series of perceptions such as it is hard to find precedents for in English', only found in 'foreign modernists such as the young Boris Pasternak' (Davie 1989, 19). A number of critics have pointed out the connections between MacCaig and the Metaphysical poets. For instance, John Donne – in MacCaig's 'skill in making abstracts tangible' and an 'acquired discipline over imagery' (Scott 1972–3, 140) – and George Herbert – in 'an elaborate baroque formality' (Davie 1989, 18) – present in some of MacCaig's poems. As Scott argues, the 'optimistic' version of humanism offered by the Augustans is equally rejected by Hume and MacCaig, both of whom 'hold great respect for reason and a realization of its limits, and both subject it to a skepticism which is undoubtedly strengthened by their Calvinist background' (1973, 139).

10. Frykman sees instances of 'truth revealed in a brief moment of grace and glory' in MacCaig's poetry as revealing an affinity with the Romantic movement' (1977, 26). O'Gorman notices similarities between MacCaig and Wordsworth, comparing 'The glass of summer' to the *Prelude* (958, 269), which is contained in its 'mightiness' (1958, 269).

11. As we learn from an anecdote told by Valerie Gillies and cited by Marjory McNeill (1996, 71), MacCaig expressed intense dislike of T. S. Eliot's poetry. Some critics notice the ambivalence of the term 'descriptive', arguing that MacCaig is a descriptive poet 'in the best sense of the word' because describing things he does not stop at their surface (Morse 1963, 332). The majority of MacCaig's poems are considered to be 'descriptions, the elements of which by witty wordplay become illuminating metaphors of multiple meanings' (Weston in Board of Regents 1979, 641).

12. See discussions on the subject, for instance, in Berleant 1992; Berleant and Carlson 2004; Brady 2003; Quigley and Slovic 2018.

13. Other critics argue that MacCaig's poems 'can do things which . . . we do not find too often in British poetry: they can make open and direct statements, say, of affection for the small creatures and objects of the world' (Fulton 1986, 507). The poems, 'often slight in their overt subject-matter . . . in other ways . . . are not . . . [T]hey . . . imply a metaphysic that makes minor events and objects as important, ultimately, as major ones' (Kell 1963, 73).
14. MacCaig's propensity to focus on small creatures manifests itself particularly intensively in the poems on frogs. 'Frogs' (MacCaig 2005, 180), 'Jumping toad' (MacCaig 2005, 372) 'My last word on frogs' (MacCaig 2005, 417). Marjory MacNeill cites an anecdote about MacCaig's conversation on his eightieth birthday about frogs: 'A lot of people rather like these poems and I can well imagine when I die and I am spoken about for a *fortnight* say, somebody will say, "Do you remember that fellow, MacCaig?" And the other would say, "Oh, aye, the frog poet?" And I did not want to be hurtling through that fortnight of immortality as "the frog poet", so I decided I would stop' (McNeill 1996, 121).
15. See Walpert's reading of MacCaig's poem 'Interruption to a journey' (2017, 37–9).
16. Alan Riach's suggestion that MacCaig's detection of 'the provisional' and 'sometimes duplicitous' in language was caused by the 'predominant ethos of the Cold War', with its accompanying apprehension (Riach 2018, n.p.), is more convincing than Fazzini's postcolonial reading.
17. Andrew Greig recalls that MacCaig did not consider 'A man in Assynt' 'a very good poem' (2010, 178).

Chapter 3

'A wing's beat and it's gone': Between Transience and Permanence in Kathleen Jamie's Writing

'You are placed in landscape, you are placed in time' (2012, 71). These words end 'A Woman in the Field', one of Kathleen Jamie's 'archaeological' essays, published in *Sightlines*. The statement echoes the work of a number of scholars concerned with the historicity of place who draw parallels between time and landscape (cf. Bender 2002; Ingold 1993; Tilley 1994; Toadvine 2014). Barbara Bender argues, for example, that 'landscape is time materialized' and 'landscape is time materializing' (2002, 103). Time is measured in embodied experience through movement, authenticity through presence and memory as represented in material artefacts and phenomena. Concerned with the manner in which former ways of life are embedded in landscapes, Jamie explores the past engagement with the land. Landscapes have '[d]ifferent needs for different eras', there is a 'gradual withdrawing, then an age of forgetting' (2012, 171). Thus understood, landscape is not a static entity but a dynamic processual space undergoing transformations; to understand this is to demonstrate the various ways in which spatial temporalities are inscribed within and upon the 'natural' material of the world. The discussion in this chapter focuses on Jamie's work through the understanding of landscape as temporal, representing it as a composite of the geological features of the land, vegetal and animal presence, and an assembly of material objects, created and jettisoned by humans, scattered around or buried in the ground, demonstrating that the transforming materials of the world are constantly in a state of becoming. Building on Barbara Bender's work on time and landscape, Jeff Malpas's work on place, Tim Ingold's notion of the weather-world, and Ted Toadvine's research on elemental time, as well as a number of critics (see Collins

2017; Falconer 2014; Gairn 2005; McGuire 2009; Marland 2015; Marland 2021), I consider a variety of aspects of temporality in the landscapes as they are manifested in essays from Jamie's three collections – *Findings*, *Sightlines* and *Surfacing* – namely notions of ephemerality and durability, the oscillating movement between distance and proximity, presence and absence, matter and the sublime; finally, the thickness and depth of time in light of the Anthropocene.[1] While these motifs may be found in Jamie's poems, this chapter focuses on her essayistic work, as I have already dealt with Jamie's poetry in some detail, in my previous book.

Provisionality, frequently formulated as a paradox, is a recurrent motif in Jamie's work. The time of biological life and the time of nature are incommensurate, brief life spans confronting immeasurable totalities. Thus it remains impossible to capture more than mere glimpses in momentary form; this is all that may be accessible to humans. Landscapes have always undergone changes, but the Anthropocene has brought a sense of urgency to the act of bearing witness. The publication of *Findings* in the first decade of the twenty-first century coincided with a rise of environmental consciousness as the realisation of biodiversity loss began surfacing ever more urgently. In the light of dominant anthropogenic biomes, bearing witness is an ethical necessity in late modernity. Concerned with what may last and what may vanish, Jamie considers our moral relations with the living and non-living world, interrogating at the same time teleological premises, reflecting on things that are 'brought to the surface' (2019, 180) through acts of attentive listening and looking.

Considering the ontology of the Anthropocene, Peter Sloterdijk notes that 'the human being plays the dramatic animal on stage before the backdrop of a mountain of nature, which can never be anything other than the inoperative scenery behind human operations' (Sloterdijk 2015, 334). However, Sloterdijk's magisterial critique of the post-Romantic human subject fails to grasp that, implicated in the transformation of geological formations as well as changing weather patterns, human exceptionalism brings an ethics of responsibility. In distinction to the problem Sloterdijk presents, we might note that it is important to see from any reading of Jamie that the senses in her writing are active. It is important to observe, from the outset, that while vision is an important faculty, it does not dominate Jamie's approach.[2] Even though Jamie stresses the need to 'keep a weather eye' on rare birds (2012, 186), the reader might also note how the faculty of listening is equally important, as, for instance, when she explores Rona with a Walkman to count Leach's fork-tailed petrels among rock crevices and burrows.³ The process of knowing the landscape is a multisensory experience concerned with exploring sensate, variegated matter; making sense of the world is slow and painstaking, as demonstrated by examples of archaeological work, whereby the retrieval of artefacts requires time and patience. The archaeological metaphor, suggesting an appropriate manner of engagement with the world,⁴ offers a reflection on human relations with the changing landscape.

The multisensorial aspect of Jamie's writing produces a poetics of environmental storytelling, which offers an appeal to the readers as all manner of engagements with the environment emerge through curiosity, which is propelled by the sense of otherness of things, affecting human life in terms of aesthetics and ethics. As in the eighteenth century, when (what Jamie reads as) the sense of embarrassment transpiring from Gilbert White's letter on bird migration might have constituted one of the motivations behind the Enlightenment, the urge of discovery and the new science may have been motivated 'not by the will to master and possess nature', Jamie suggests, 'but out of chagrin' (2012, 214).⁵ Chagrin continues to drive people concerned about the planet, but its shade has changed. In the first decades of the twenty-first century, the surges of glaciers and the calving of icebergs are regularly measured, the numbers compared, bringing 'worrisome news from the farthest remotes' (2012, 17). While distant from eco-eschatological perspectives, environmental prophesies and doomsday scenarios, Jamie's self-deprecating reaction to the news – 'I sail on the surface of understanding, a flicker here, a silence there' (2012, 17) – counters the manic activity of late modernity with deep melancholy, contemplation, and what appears to be acceptance of temporal effects. Her writing offers a recognition that we are beings immersed in time, through a simple phrase 'if we're spared' (2019, 188) expressing the conditional form of existence, allowing for hope while embracing the unknowable. What is more, by suggesting that she is an amateur, Jamie justifies her 'amateurish' intervention in the realm of experts, which serves as an important model for readers: we do not have to be experts to be attentive and therefore engaged in our world.

The Unseen Landscapes Within

As the recurring phrase 'the nature within' (2012, 36) demonstrates, Jamie's writing constantly plays on the figure of the inner subjective landscape as mediation of the external world, and she achieves this through troping between the natural world and human nature. Seen under a microscope, human tissue contains '[r]iver deltas and marshes, peninsulas and atolls', which form '[t]he unseen landscapes within' (2012, 34).[6] It is a 'countryside, a landscape', resembling an estuary, with 'wing-shaped river islands or sandbanks, as if it was low tide' (2012, 30). Even if it is 'a map of the familiar', the image appears 'astonishing', resembling a 'local river, as seen by a hawk' (2012, 30), containing features such as 'old field dykes, the marks of a long inhabitation of the land' (2012, 31). Bacteria appear to be 'grazing' (2012, 34) on the vast expanses of tissue resembling fields: 'an image you might find in a Sunday-night wildlife documentary. Pastoral, but wild, too. So close to home, but people had landed on the moon before these things were discovered, free in the wilderness of our stomachs' (2012, 35). It is not 'some mystical union between body and earth' (2012, 34), as Jamie insists, but a visual trick, an illusion created by a hunter-gatherer mind. The motif of a trick played by vision and imagination returns in *Surfacing* with an image of a bacteria colony which resembles a tundra landscape (2019, 237). Jamie metaphorises human biology and psychology to suggest an extension that traverses and so undoes figures of inner and outer, demonstrating that the natural world is not something 'out there' (2005, 141), as she puts it, but is everywhere, outside as well as inside, reminding us that nature is represented through our bodies, whose organs hide 'the intimate unknown' (2005, 141), permeating through the limmus of skin.[7] In this manner, Jamie shows the manner in which binaries deconstruct themselves through the tropological work that emphasises inner and outer continuities and the porosity of any subject/world border. In doing this, she models a different way of thinking about subject-world, jettisoning any 'either/or'. Jamie's landscapes are not external, static views but instead they scintillate with movement and change, encountered outside as well as inside, on the top of a hill in Perthshire and in 'the cave-uterus' (2012, 166), while looking at the painting of a horse that is 'walking in an unseen landscape' (2012, 169). Besides the play of reversibility, recurring in the essays, the above images emphasise the motifs of the shifting scale and the tension between proximity and distance.

A number of Jamie's essays are concerned with landscapes close to home – the River Tay, the fields of Perthshire, North Berwick, Orkney, Shetland, Rona, the Isle of Harris, St Kilda – but also farther afield, documenting foreign travels to the Arctic Circle, Norway or Alaska, which are motivated not by wanting to know what lies beyond the horizon but by an awareness of the briefness of human life cycle, a realisation enforced by the physical and temporal placement in proximity to the geological time of fjords and icebergs. Travelling to a number of Scottish islands, Jamie reflects on the ambivalence of the complex, fraught notion of remoteness and the shifting perception of the centre and the margins, inscribed in modern concepts of landscape which fetishise these places.[8] The concept of remoteness appears in the essays only to be challenged repeatedly, as nowadays 'our sense of centre is different', concludes Jamie (2012, 180). The use of inverted commas around the word 'remoteness' underlines the manner in which perception is embedded in language. An island appears remote solely for the metropolitan subject. Denoting a place as remote relegates it into the peripheries of significance, exoticising it and diminishing its value. And thus, St Kilda is 'like the Holy Grail', a myth and fable, a fixation, partly created by literary fantasies of Ossian and Scott, as Jamie suggests. Legends surrounding these places enhance the romantic, mysterious literariness of the landscape. Associated with the rise of tourism in the nineteenth century, the concept of remoteness involves romanticising such places as St Kilda and Rona, which provide 'something faraway and special' (2012, 184). Populated once, places such as Mingulay, Pabbay, Stroma, the Shiant Isles have 'long human histories', which, in a counter-Romantic reflex, makes Jamie dismiss concepts of wildness and remoteness as 'starry-eyed' (2012, 143), with 'the fabled outliers' such as St Kilda, North Rona and Sula Sgeir, known for their gannetries and puffin colonies as well as their bothies and brochs, becoming the subject of naive idealisations and travel dreams. The reader is reminded of the bird's-eye perspective when Jamie imagines the gulls' point of view from which humans are 'interlopers' (2012, 181), a change of perspective from the human to the non-human challenging the thought of remoteness. It may be said that nesting grounds have become invaded by humans, so, while birds may not have the word or concept of interloping, they nonetheless feel that. After all, human habitation on the island was but a brief moment, as if on borrowed time, and now sheep shelter in cleits: 'the island is returned to birds and seals' (2012, 182). Deemed 'exotic' and 'remote' by some, these islands are home to seabirds, including gannets. The passages describing their colonies demonstrate how pervasive is the idea of remoteness. Listed by name, 'wild and far-flung' gannetries titillate the imagination, 'facing down the wild sea'; similarly to lighthouses, they are '[r]omantic outposts' but 'without all that rugged manliness', having instead elements of homeliness, appearing 'domestic, ignoble, noisy, seasonal' (2012, 87). The anthropomorphising description sounds as if it could be a critique of tourist sites into which some of the Scottish islands convert in the summer season.

Humans continue to be drawn to these geographical sites in search of wildness, as these deserted or abandoned faraway places are expressions of the myth of the north, embodiments of northness in its liminality, which fills modern imaginary realms. The landscapes are still considered to be 'the edge of the world' (2012, 134), or 'Ultima Thule', which constituted the farthest north location according to ancient Greek and Roman literary and cartographic sources, in an extension of the mythical image of a remote place found in Virgil's *Georgics* (1:30).[9] Even if, for Jamie, St Kilda is one of 'the places that lay almost on my doorstep' (2012, 135), the deeply embedded concept of remoteness persists, as elsewhere she writes that going to St Kilda – '[w]ild, remote, famous, oft-imagined . . . so theatrically abandoned' (2012, 142) – seems like '[t]he last adventure', bringing images of '[s]ea-cliffs and abandonment' (2012, 134) and 'the breathtaking clifftop views' (2012, 141), admitting that 'the sea ramparts and tremendous sea-views attracted' her (2012, 152) as 'it must be pretty wild and remote out there' (2012, 135). St Kilda may only be seen 'fleetingly' (2012, 142), a remark which emphasises the sublime potential and captures the essence of the place resisting definition.

Attempting to capture the sense of place, Jamie employs phenomenal language, following a reaction that ascribes meaning, albeit a meaning suffused with unknowability, in phrases such as 'tall and mysterious, and capped in its own private cloud' (2012, 139), which in turn admits in the limits of language in representation. The far limits of the world can only be figured by the limits of language. Elsewhere Jamie offers a personified image, redolent of the opening lines in Eliot's 'The Love Song of J. Alfred Prufrock', in which the village is depicted as 'a chaos of stone', its view obscured, and the island appears to be 'semi-conscious under a peculiar, oppressive atmosphere; cloud like damp wool obscured its hills' (2012, 141). Throughout 'Three Ways of Looking at St Kilda', Jamie demonstrates how in the twenty-first century a fantasy about a 'remote' island clashes with modern reality all too frequently: Romantic wildness meets a radar base, missile tracking system and a souvenir shop,[10] as the notion of remoteness encompassing a pastoral view of unspoiled landscape is invaded by technology. There are other glimpses of technology affecting the manner in which humans inhabit the world. Some manifest themselves in how the sea is navigated: instead of gazing at the marinescape, skippers keep their eyes on digital charts. (Yet, despite technological progress, the weather still delineates the borders of possibilities, as the attempts to reach St Kilda are thwarted by the wind.) The old-fashioned ways of exploration remain available to amateurs, who still look intently at the sea. Sea charts and maps are still displayed on the walls, and before visiting the places, Jamie studiously learns about their history and geography in order to know the names of these places, which is a manner of domesticating and thereby controlling the landscape. These textual approaches demonstrate the extent to which the exploration of the landscape begins – and sometimes continues – in theory. Writing the world is always already textual, full of private and mysterious signs hinting at reading, but also it becomes an embodied practice as landscapes are experienced corporeally through multisensory engagement.

At the same time, Jamie reflects on modern practices, which reveal the shift in the ways in which landscapes are examined; the naked eye is contrasted with technology, the latter being 'strongboxes containing satellite receivers, laptops, batteries, chargers and digital cameras—the wherewithal of the scientific gaze' (2012, 148). The gaze never disappears, its ubiquity unsettling; or, in Jamie's words, its omnipresence is 'disquieting, to be aware all the time of satellites prowling unseen above the sky, while examining a landscape others had created and left behind' as nothing 'escaped notice—not a bird, not a stone, certainly not a person' (2012, 159). The scientific gaze prevails in the current exploration of certain landscapes. And so 'far from being an escape', St Kilda became 'instead a place of comment and note' (2012, 159). A dual World Heritage Site, preserved by the National Trust for Scotland, St Kilda is examined by surveyors from the Royal Commission on Ancient and Historical Monuments of Scotland as part of a project to investigate the 'cultural landscape' of the whole archipelago, that is to research the human-made constructions on the islands with the use of technology (GPS satellite). A 3D digital model of the island prepared by Historic Environment Scotland exists 'to allow visitors to voyage to St Kilda from the comfort of their own homes' (Campsie 2019, n.p.).

The phrase 'cultural landscape' returns in the essay, which, similar to 'remoteness', is enclosed in inverted commas to highlight its constructedness: 'A "cultural landscape" they called it, but up on the island's heights, giddied by the cloud shadows over the turf, and by sea and sky, and distracted everywhere by birds, you could be forgiven for asking where, in this wild place, was the culture?' (2012, 153). Bearing the memory of the 'ancient race' in the form of 'the relics of a lost intelligence, the long-forsaken fields', the remains of dwellings made in the earth can make a place 'homely and recognisable' (2012, 195). The remnants of former civilisation include buildings called 'cleits', or *cleitean* in Gaelic, used for storage of food, that lasted for centuries – demonstrating that the Stone Age continued until 1930, as one of archaeologist points out (2012, 150) – until their decline initiated in the nineteenth century by an Englishman, well-intentioned but ignorant of the conditions on the island, who, along with the minister and the laird, supported the plan to replace the blackhouses with modernised dwellings, which did not serve their purpose in those weathers. Thus began the depopulation of the island. Extending thousands of years into the past, cleits are 'a complete expression in stone of a unique way of life' (2012, 146), built in search of 'some seclusion, some corrective to the sky, the sea and wind' (2012, 160). Human culture is 'camouflaged by stone and turf' in the form of these constructions, which appear to be 'curious, half nature and half culture, with their stone walls and turf roofs that shivered in the breeze' (2012, 155), their sense of mystery not dispelled despite meticulous measurement.

The attempts to read the land yield contradictory results, as the island landscape appears both 'very recent and very ancient at once', the former expressed in stone, the latter the effect of modern media, beginning with film coverage from the evacuation (2012, 156). In the first decade of the twenty-first century remoteness is but a fantasy, as there is no escape from 'the modern world with all its technology', with data-loggers and satellites that form part of 'the cultural landscape of the heavens' (2012, 159). The inverted commas around 'the cultural landscape' used before are removed as soon as the linguistic convention of the institutional construct disappears. Despite the myth of remoteness, the island had already been made accessible by teletechnology in the 1960s. Thirty years separated the leaving of the inhabitants of St Kilda and the launch of Telstar, which was like 'moving between the Stone Age and the Age of Satellites' (2012, 159) in an instant, a time comparable to the span of a fulmar's life, as Jamie notices, shifting the perspective from technological to organic and from human to more-than-human. The experience of the island landscapes evoked by Jamie stretches between the reflections on time materialised in the weather-worn remains of ancient constructions and the immediacy of the phenomenological experience of open space. The former are material expressions of the phrase 'time taking its toll' (which, along with the expression 'nature takes its course', is a recurring phrase in Jamie's writing). The demise of cleits is witnessed by archaeologists whose surveying is the record of death, as they conduct a 'ritual', resemble 'priests, giving each of these little buildings the last rites'.

Yet the need to perform constant 'data recording against loss' (2012, 160) only demonstrates that fixing anything proves impossible as tidal waves move the land. '[Y]ou can only record what remains. What's gone is gone' (2012, 157).[11] Archival anxiety will not prevent the disappearance of all the traces:

> Everything will fall into the sea, so far as I could tell, looking at the archaeologists' reports in Stornoway Library. Does this matter? A team of archaeologists had walked and mapped all the features on that part of the coast and, with their expert eye, and by dint of asking local people, had measured and defined and assessed every human intervention in that landscape: illicit stills, sheep fanks, standing stones. Their anxiety was coastal erosion, things were in danger of slipping away forever. The report itself had been poorly bound, pages slithered out and fell on the library floor. (2005, 178–9)

Such precise, relentless surveying appears to confirm the truth of Jean-Luc Nancy's observation that '[n]o culture has lived as our modern culture has in the endless accumulation of archives and expectations. No culture has made present the past and the future to the point of removing the present from its own passage' (2015, 40). Yet, accompanying the surveyors in their painstaking job is a way of reading the land, which activity changes vision. As Jamie admits, this meticulous recording forms 'a wholly different way of looking at St Kilda': alone, she would have 'rushed around, thrilled but hampered by a kind of illiteracy, unable to read the land', omitting details such as 'a clump of tiny violets quivering on a cleit roof', or 'the cats'-paw pattern of lichen on a lintel-stone', which complements 'the patterns made by the wind on the surface of the sea below' (2012, 156).

Similarly to Alec Finlay, Jamie frequently explores landscapes accompanied by other people, learning from their knowledge and expertise. Such collaborations are typical in Scotland and are 'in the way of small countries' (2012, 143). Notes from various places are complemented by exchanges with archaeologists, surveyors, ornithologists, naturalists, boatmen, which reveal layers of landscape with stories of change over time. Even if, as Jamie reluctantly admits, she is not 'necessarily comfortable with having a place, a vast new landscape, mediated by guides' (2012, 17), she receives it with an expression of humility and acceptance of her limitations. Shifting perspectives yield different views of those pelagic landscapes: looking 'through the window', they are 'sea, wildness, distance, isolation', while looking at them directly reveals 'utility, food security, domestic management' (2012, 158). Jamie demonstrates how the landscape may be explored in at least two ways: from the height of a cliff and closely, on one's knees, whereby the former enables one to leave all the manifestations of civilization – both the modern and the ancient one – while the latter is a method to examine formations of the land and its vegetation. The remnants of human-induced transformations of the land are contrasted with the view unchanged by humanity on a promontory not found on any map. Yet, what is most striking about the landscape of St Kilda is the uncanny aspect of the cottages which 'didn't sing of a lost idyll': 'If the cottages spoke at all, it was to say—Look, they made their decision. They quit. They moved on' (2012, 162). The attitude towards a landscape alters, 'tempered by a particular piece of knowledge' (2012, 204) concerning the inhabitants of Rona. Unlike the inhabitants of St Kilda who, left to their own volition or the Gaels in the Highlands, were forced out of the land and their houses, Rona became depopulated suddenly in the seventeenth century with no one to bear witness.

As the evidence shows, the inhabitants died in around 1680, as accidentally discovered by a shipwrecked crew on their way from St Kilda to Harris who buried the corpses but did not learn what caused the deaths. What remains are the ruined dwellings made of stone and turf, habitations built upon other habitations between periods of abandonment, and the gravestones, which mark the lives of those people and now make their claim to the land, observing the shifting functions of the place. During the Cold War the island was turned into a military base. Similarly to St Kilda, Rona is undergoing intense scrutiny by environmental health officers in an attempt to protect the landscape with the use of modern technology, ensuring that nothing goes unnoticed: anything that resembles human-made structures such as cleits, turf dykes, enclosures is surveyed. This is a landscape where the remains of old dwellings contrast with such symptoms of modern culture as cruise liners and film crews, the old and the new unceasingly intertwining: sitting among the ruins, Jamie and her companions eat the products of capitalism – 'packet soups and tinned fruit' – food preserved using modern technologies and materials, plastic and steel.

Real Presences

The archipelagic landscapes in Jamie's essays are imbued with other presences; they are alive with other beings, emphasised by the realisation that '[y]ou just might be making the same journeys as these other creatures, all of us alive at the same time on the same planet' (2012, 209). These past and present forms of more-than-human consciousness create a sense of companionable fellowship as the presence of other animals such as seals, gannets, puffins, terns, crossbills and Risso's dolphins adds to the sense of not being 'truly alone in the ocean' (2012, 194). Similarly, the awareness of animal presence emerging from a drop into deep time during a visit to the cave reveals 'a new relationship, closer than ever', a relationship that Jamie sees as a form of travel through time as 'we'd all travelled together, separating and overlapping, out of a deep, shared evolutionary origin' (2012, 171). The embodied experience in the enclosed space of the cave is encompassed in the awareness of the touch and the organic rhythm of breath, which provokes a sense that these landscape formations were visited thousands of years ago, the breaths mingling in the intimacy of human involvement with the intertwining of flesh. This proximity also counteracts the separation between the viewer and the viewed, whereby distance signifies the remoteness of space manifested in re-presentation. In an imaginative leap, the interchange between the body and stone tells us of the sharing of space with other animals in the past which assumed more intimate forms. The cave representations of animals are a form of drawing – drawing in both senses of the word – '[c]oaxing animal presence out of the deep source, the cave-uterus', thus advancing the image of the body-world in which stone becomes flesh. The metaphor seems inevitable, as Jamie suggests that 'We are deep in a hall of similes' (2012, 166) and 'We are deep in metaphor, the membranes between body and stone, and cave and animal are dissolved: melded' (2012, 169), concluding that 'what drives us, what has brought us thus far ... to think in simile, in metaphor', the 'connective leaps, the careful taxonomies, how our minds work' (2012, 171). The metaphors that establish bridges between various ideas and objects help humans overcome the gap between the reality of late modernity and the real presence, as Paleolithic traces remind us of another dwelling in the landscape,

> a time—until very recently in the scheme of things—when there were no wild animals, because every animal was wild; and humans were few. Animals, and animal presence over us and around us. Over every horizon, animals. Their skins clothing our skins, their fats in our lamps, their bladders to carry water, meat when we could get it. (2012, 168)

Yet, 'Our Palaeolithic kinship with animals, with nature', Jamie writes, 'is over, broken, or so we say' (2012, 171), stating directly:

'We have a crisis because we have lost our ability to see the natural world, or find it meaningful. There had been a break-down in reciprocity. Humanity had taken a wrong path, had become destructive and insulated' (2012, 22).

In late modernity, for many people being in the landscape means hoping for a furtive glimpse of animal presence. When travelling to Quinhagak, Alaska, Jamie notes how, seen from the plane, the landscape is empty of animals, offering no caribou or wolves, despite her hopes of spotting them. The breakdown of kinship ushered in an era in which coexistence has been replaced by haunted presence. As Akira Mizuta Lippit puts it, 'Modernity can be defined by the disappearance of wildlife from humanity's habitat and by the reappearance of the same in humanity's reflection of itself: in philosophy, psychoanalysis, and technological media such as the telephone, film, and radio' (2000, 2–3). Writing of animal presence, Jamie moves towards a true engagement with other beings while distancing herself from constructed meanings, as the recurrent references to real presence suggest resistance to symbolic and metaphorical meanings imposed on the landscapes. The occasional allusions to whales as cultural symbols (e.g. 'through the jaws of Leviathan' [2012, 220]) appear deliberately self-conscious, and as such follow a deliberate projection of vacancy for poetic and political effect, highlighting the way in which such references affect our perception of the species and construct the whole cetacean iconography. Such cultural allusions are rare, however, as Jamie resists transforming animals into metaphors and other textual figures, focusing instead on writing presence and direct experience.

Presence, understood as 'a movement away from the notion of constructed meaning and towards an engagement with things (the past included) that actually exist', to cite Ethan Kleinberg (2013, 2), announces an attempt to re-join with the material. One might argue with such a definition of presence because, even if one engages with an other, the other never occupies the space of the one initiating or recording the engagement. There is always a gap, absence, differentiation, which the subject either side of that divide will read, and cannot but help interpret, even as the writing subject is interpellated by the apprehension of the call of the other, to which writing is a response. In late modernity, animal presence in the landscape tells of the consequences of their objectification, whereby the utilitarian purposes of more-than-human nature are a result of 'the anthropological machine', to use Giorgio Agamben's phrase, which distinguishes animals from the 'fully', 'properly' human and the 'less-than-fully-human' (Smith 2011, xii). The workings of the anthropological machine – or, more precisely, the capitalist machinery' – are most visible in the consequences of industrial whaling, mentioned in a number of essays (see 'Aurora' [2012, 1–19], 'Voyager, Chief' [2019, 237], 'The Hvalsalen' [2012, 95–119], 'Cetacean Disco' [2005, 185–90]). Whales have been killed for baleen, blubber, meat, bones, oil since the Stone Age, but whaling intensified in the eighteenth and nineteenth centuries, marking the period of insatiable, rapacious colonialist-capitalism; hunting stopped only when whales were markedly depleted. Perceived through their worth and value, whales were used for the sole purpose of human activity and profit, as industrial whaling obliterated the ethical concept of the equality of worth and proved indifferent to the inherent worth of all beings as it revealed a strong urge of domination over other animals and control of landscapes.[12] After a period of intensive whaling, the 'vast Atlantic domain' (2012, 200) has in effect been transformed into the 'ocean as endangered global commons' (Buell 2001, 29). Rendering these marine mammals to bones suggests an urge to 'leave some mark', almost as if it were a tree on which people would incise their initials, as if to stamp it with the 'I was here' sign, 'like everyone who encountered it had been challenged by it, had to leave some mark' (2012, 114). Being in close proximity with whalebones offers a chance to 'extend your sense of self'. Informed by the self's historical moment, being inside the skeleton of a blue whale in Hvalsalen offers Jamie both a physical and temporal perspective: looking back at the bones that made it, but also, one could say, looking back in time, turning the gaze to where we came from, imagining other animals inhabiting the sea: our ancestors. Jamie's invitation to 'begin to imagine what it might feel like, to be a blue whale', in an exchange of bodies and consciousness, echoes Thomas Nagel's oft-quoted thought experiment.[13]

Exemplified through the elegiac tone of the essays devoted to this exploited species, the loss of the whale stands for other animals which have disappeared and are disappearing from landscapes and seascapes, in turn ushering in the thought of other losses, as the history of loss in general may be traced through the figure of 'the melancholy whale', to employ Philip Hoare's phrase, an expression which gestures towards both Romanticism and anthropomorphism.[14] Further, the disappearance of these large pelagic sea dwellers brings a premonition of future loss. The landscapes in Jamie's essays are populated by spectral animals: the ibex, the auroch, the wolf, which are no longer present in Scotland, their disappearance a result of human activity. In brief images and passing remarks, Jamie once again captures the ambivalence of technological advances, as, for instance, when she writes that a train is 'a metal box on a Highland moor, but the last wolf was shot long ago' (2012, 23). The image is also an example of Jamie's style, which often relies on stark juxtaposition: the train speeding through the landscape reminds us of modern acceleration; the absent wolf points to the effect of hunting down a number of species.[15] Yet it transpires that animals form a powerful presence even after they are no longer alive, as the recorded instances of biodiversity loss reveals a paradox of the invisible animals in the landscape: in the presence is the idea of absence. What remains are the whalebones as a reminder of their past existence. Animals become nothing other than a series of traces readable by humans in their absence.

A nineteenth-century photograph seen in the Shetland Museum bears witness to 'the ghost presence of the whales' (2012, 222), bearing metaphysical echoes. The sighting of a live whale leaves a sense of 'yearning', their presence appearing unreal, almost oneiric (2012, 200),[16] as a whale appearance becomes an event (discussed below). Being in the presence of creatures which evolved millions of years ago offers a glimpse of human rhythms by reflection enclosed in multiple temporalities.[17] The partial view afforded by the act of watching a live animal from a distance foregrounds its elusiveness as one has to imagine the *whole* whale. The distance from which they are watched reminds the reader that proximity often meant death for whales. Human agency manifested through the prosthetic of a deadly technological touch proved lethal to the animals who received the 'full gamut of human attention—from the exploding harpoon and flensing iron, to the soft sponge and the toothpick' (2012, 118). The blubber flensed from the body reveals the vulnerability of flesh; now the bones are treated with utmost care as part of 'adjusting our relationship with these greatest of animals, and with the non-human world as a whole' (2012, 236). Returning in the essay, the phrase 'do not touch the animals' (2012, 97, 119) emphasises the ironic belatedness of the museum notice. What remains is the need for tactile experience, the urge to be in the presence of the real thing, to 'reach out for the natural, in wonder or shame or excitement or greed' (2012, 236).

Whales emerge as bones erected in the landscapes. The whale relics 'seem imbued with a particular presence' (2012, 228), even 'otherworldly presence' (2012, 118), where 'otherworldly' returns in reference to whales, acknowledging the gap between self and other always already at work, and placing them in the role of the other. The concept of otherness is questioned and refuted at the end of the essay where whales are described as being '*of* this world, as they had been for a very long time, long before we appeared' (2012, 119). The italicised particle together with the repeated adjective add emphasis to the statement, as the '*presence* of all those whales' bones' exerts a powerful effect (2012, 98) (original italics). Tracing the whalebones placed in the landscape, Jamie considers their stories, offering a parallax perspective, characteristic of her style, as the position of the observer points to an orientation towards other inhabitants of the world, decentring human subjectivity. Further, focusing on other bodies shifts the emphasis from subjectivity to natural being and suggests that a human body is a variant of flesh, not separate but entangled in the fabric of the world, thus challenging the established ways of looking at more-than-human beings. Even if, as Jamie insists, 'in the end it's just a whalebone, anatomical and mortal' (2012, 237), there is another side to the entanglement of animals and technology in modernity. Animals become projections, where technology functions as 'the afterlife of language' (Lippit 2000, 161). It is visible in the use of metaphors which connect the animal world with technology: gannets' wings flash like 'paparazzi cameras'; the synchronized whale sound is 'like a Victorian machine' or 'like a steam pump in a basement' (2012, 198); the weight of the vertebra found on an island in the Hebrides makes the bone akin to 'an engine part, with three smooth, propeller-like vanes' (2012, 219).

Tracing animal artefacts deposited in the landscapes, Jamie considers the possible reasons for their placement there, the effect that they exert and the manner in which they alter the landscape.[18] Offering a chance of human reckoning, the sense of melancholy emanates from the land as reliquary with the remnants of other animals placed in the landscape with a human hand, in a form of memento, possibly a celebration, a way to mark the place. As Jamie suggests, there is 'something else, something about the whale', which, due to its size, appears 'near mythic': 'part mammal, part architectural, inhabitants of an imagined otherworld' (2012, 230). Erected on hills, these passageways leading from the sea inland frequently take the form of an arch due to their monumental size and shape, reminding the viewer of memorial gates originating in ancient Rome. Yet, rather than a form of elevation signifying empowerment, these monuments – true to their function as something that reminds and brings recollection – are a memento: a commemorative object. Whalebones placed in the landscape are a form of *memento mori* and sign of our culture, a reminder that 'every whale relic represents a disaster for that individual animal, a death, a wreck, a stranding, a slaughter', and, as Jamie adds, 'something of that atmosphere cleaves to their bones' (2012, 230). The jawbone from the bowhead whale brought by William Scoresby from the Arctic takes the form of an arch, yet, as Jamie insists, it is not a triumphal arch or a trophy, but 'something, at least in this country, like atonement' (2012, 235). The whalebone 'frames . . . the grey and depleted North Sea' (2012, 224) in its physical shape as well as in a metaphorical dimension, marking the disappearance of the pelagic species. The bones placed in the landscape become 'festooned with meanings', a reflection that humans cannot help but map meanings onto objects and phenomena. 'Such has been our violence toward these animals', Jamie observes, 'that we sense in a jawbone arch a memorial not just to that particular whale, but almost to whalehood itself', an object become metonymy. Her understated reaction – an expression of helplessness ('Shame and shame' [2012, 119]) – sums up the grim history of industrial whaling.

It is possible to imagine that the whales 'heard a sea change' (2012, 234), that the advent of the twentieth-century energy industry offered '[t]he beginnings of deliverance' (2012, 234), replacing whale oil with that extracted from the seabed. The transition from whaling to extracting oil from the seabed augurs transformations in the landscape through the expansive development of petrol cultures, exploited energy shaping the world. The whales would 'have heard', as Jamie suggests, and 'felt, the drill bits biting into the seabeds, oil tankers sliding over the surface above, signalling a development in human technology' (2012, 234). Not mentioned explicitly, the stories of empire, colonialism, the exploitative capitalism of global industry, and commerce are ever present. The northern landscapes are filled with traces of the whaling industry such as the chimney and slipway on Harris, which was a Norwegian station dealing with hunting blue whales and fin whales off the coast of Scotland. Considering a whale presence, Jamie reverses the perspective: 'put the whale's way', she writes, 'these islands are a surprising, sometimes disastrous presence in the sea' (2012, 220), and even if the whales' own narratives are unrecorded, 'given that these bones date from Victorian times, the whale stories don't take much guessing' (2012, 221). In search of such stories, Jamie creates a catalogue of whalebones scattered around the British Isles. Whalebones are used to ornament private gardens. On the island of Stroma, uninhabited now, Jamie finds among some abandoned items a '[m]ottled and mossy whale's vertebra', looking like 'a piece of classical statuary, a winged male torso' (2012, 227).

At Sumburgh Head on Shetland the back of the skull of a sperm whale, resembling 'a fragment of a chariot', serves as a scratching post for sheep, as demonstrated by tufts of fleece. Another skull nearby used to belong to a rare minke whale. The arch in Whitby was brought as a gift from the people of Alaska, replacing a whalebone arch, 'weathered away', the latter a gift from the king of Norway; 'this gifting of whalebones between nations', which includes '[w]hale jaws and pandas', is simply 'strange' (2012, 226). Sometimes jawbones erected in the landscape were sourced from stranded or already dead whales, as one in Caithness. A whalebone which forms an archway at the entrance to the Meadows, in Edinburgh – the Jawbone Arch – is the remaining structure of the Shetland and Fair Isle Knitters' Stall set up during the International Exhibition of Science, Art and Industry of 1886, when the Meadows 'were filled with the confidence of Empire', boasting of new invention and technology. Being 'real, animal, anatomical, announcements of the natural' (2012, 221), the fin whalebone in the Edinburgh urbanscape constituted a normalised oddity. Similarly to other whalebones 'stranded' in urban environments and human-made green areas, which are 'out of sight of the sea' (2012, 221), the placement of these relics foregrounds the strangeness of the situation. Shifting the perspective, Jamie considers the animals which 'went up in the chimneys of the nineteenth century', when 'Science, Art and Industry [. . . were] smoothed and lit by whale oil' (2012, 222).

As the anthropocentric focus is reversed, the reader's attention turns to the whales represented as more than the sum of their components: 'There's the story (of course, there's always a story) of how these huge bones came to be stranded in a city park, out of sight of the sea—it concerns girls, and knitting, but such stories are not the whole story' (2012, 221). The reversed perspective creates a sense of defamiliarisation and reminds us that this is usually just 'the human side of the story' (2012, 221). A twenty-foot-high whalebone in Bragar on the Isle of Lewis, attached to a stone wall with metal rings (in itself a powerful image of entangled matter: metal on bone on stone) 'comes with a terrible story—a whale's story' (2012, 229), as Jamie puts it, that of a dead whale found about 1920 with wounds from an explosive, 'wretched' harpoon, which suggests a long whale death. This jawbone with shrapnel still lodged in the middle of it – 'the whole affair has a feel of the gallows' (2012, 230) – symbolises the dark irony of whale–human entanglement. Similarly to other bones located in a museum hall or in the landscape, this whale appears '[l]ess an animal, more a narrative . . . [that of perhaps] [t]he ancient mariner' (2012, 97). The reference to Coleridge's poem places whales within human culture not merely as objects or minor characters but as fellow beings who suffer. Thus, acknowledging the stories of other beings as stories subjectifies them and creates a sense of compassionate fellowship.

Whalebones placed in the landscape – 'raised around the country at large' – offer a hint of the sublime, as there is 'something venerable about' them, which may be compared to the effect that an ancient yew tree exerts (2012, 227). The sense of sublime in the presence of whale jaws is captured by such phrases as 'just monumental', 'the most majestic and unsettling' (2012, 228), their 'solemnity and slightly luminous quality' (2012, 228). Their placement in 'an apparently empty landscape' (2012, 229) additionally heightens the sensation. Resembling a shrine, the jawbone on Harris suggests a certain cult of whales, the remnants of which may transform the place into a site of worship. It may also represent the cult of capitalism reified in the form of the detritus produced in the rendering of animals. Thanks to their bowed shape and imposing size, whalebones make a good church door, as in Whitby, where a jawbone was placed in the decommissioned church turned into the Heritage Centre. A jawbone of a blue whale is 'like a wayside shrine' (2012, 229). Another monumental bone can be found in the grounds of Glastonbury Abbey, provoking a puzzling realisation that these whalebones came '[f]ar from the ocean', transported onto the 'hallowed ground, in the heart of Albion' (2012, 230). Jamie's ironic remark that this was 'a kind of whale-inspired religiosity which must have suited the Victorian mind—whalebone corsets and religiosity' (2012, 230) sums up the role of whales in taking part in forming the nineteenth-century material and spiritual culture of the British Isles. The above images depict the changing meaning of the whale throughout time. Before, a washed-up whale would have been 'a bonanza', its different parts consumed, used for lighting, to support roofs or make corsets. At present, to the dissatisfaction of local people, institutions claim washed-up whale carcasses. In one such case, the islanders hid a whale's jawbone, planning to use it for an arch, but it was claimed by the National Museum of Scotland. The described situation captures a conflict between institutions claiming authority and the local inhabitants whose claim to the land is dismissed. A wistful comment made by one islander – 'It seems everything disappears, and we have nothing to remember the whale' – is a sad conclusion that '[e]verything disappears into a vault in a museum' (2012, 234). The islander's complaint unveils 'another meaning to the whale arch, to whale relics', as Jamie suggests, 'something elegiac' (2012, 234). For the inhabitants of coastal regions, the monumental whalebones function as an homage, a memento, marking an event in local history.

The stunning sculptural aspect of the whalebones is emphasised in their placement; yet they tell another story, that of the landscape, itself changeable, whereby these transient, ephemeral objects, extended in time, become entangled with place and assume the role of a witness to change. Transformed by the weather and pollution the bones start to resemble tree trunks in their texture and colour, '[m]ouldered and corroded' (2012, 220), simultaneously standing out from and merging with the surroundings. Everything is a matter of time. In search of authenticity, Jamie traces the transformations of whalebones, which can be found on the Orkney Islands near the Brough of Birsay, where the vertebrae of a whale resemble 'some huge bird, perched on a pole, hunching its wings to lift away, or even a standing stone, but it is, again, the vertebra of a whale' (2012, 237), as if a bird became stone, became bone. Another image shows how matter in a state of constant change is propelled by the weather's equalising powers, which make a once-living being look like a tree: 'on a curved stalk which looks like wood but is a rib from the same long-dead, presumably washed-up animal' (2012, 237). Whale bones partake in the exchange of matter with another form of matter, as their cracks seep oil, and layers of dust settle, gathering for over a century. A close look reveals past trauma: a fractured rib, a memory of flesh. The recurring phrase 'in life' (2012, 104; three times on 108; 114; twice on 233) is a reminder that these were once living beings, even if it looks like 'a shred of tyre' (2012, 108). Baleen is hard, 'the same stuff as our fingernails', but 'in life', as Jamie repeats, it is 'soft, and frayed where the whale's huge tongue licks against it' (2012, 108). The oscillation between lifeless matter and an imagination of a living organism places us on a temporal plane: life transmogrifies into another life form, exemplified in the image of a whale bone in the process of being colonised by sea pansies. Brought home and kept in the attic, becoming 'a splendid thing, part anatomy, part sculpture' (2012, 219), a whalebone becomes 'a sign of the pelagic world' (2012, 220), a metonymy for the marinescape.

One whalebone described by Jamie differs from the others. Placed in North Berwick on a hill formed after an extinct volcano, it is 'quite a landmark, announcing to seafarers the entrance to the Firth', where, during the past three centuries, a whalebone after a whalebone was deposited, replaced a new one when the old bone weathered ('the weather did what weather does' [2012, 235]). Following a decision not to source another whale jaw, a fiberglass replica was erected in that place. While it demonstrates care for the animal world, replacing the real bone with a copy is nonetheless an ambivalent gesture. In Jamie's own words, 'in the presence of a whalebone you look at the sea differently and, because attitudes have changed, you look out, always in the secret hope that there might be living whales out there, which one day might appear' (2012, 236). The material with which the replica is made – reinforced plastic – while durable, appears uncanny through its timelessness. The act of replacing a whalebone with a whalebone-shaped piece of plastic is an example of historical irony. Made by human technology, it is another anthropogenic construction rather than a story of a deep-sea creature. Forever lifeless, the fiberglass replica fails to signal the work of the sea, which 'pulls animal body, land and sea together in one huge stitch', resisting the weather, it remains unchanged, unchangeable, in contrast with the real bone 'worn' by the wind and the sun, 'transforming what was once alive' (2012, 236). The sea wears at the bone and the process of usury continues to take place on land. A simulacrum, it is hollow, failing to signal a meaning, empty of a 'story that I know or wish to know, no knitting or harpoons or interpretation boards' (2012, 237). Finally, unlike the real whalebone, it does not undergo the weathering process which suggests a temporal dimension: the passage of time which may be traced in the transformation of things undergone together with the surrounding.

A Matter of Time

As discussed in the previous section, references to bones, whether bird ('The Storm Petrel' [2012, 211–17], 'On Rona' [2012, 179–209]), whale ('The Hvalsalen' [2012, 95–119], 'Voyager, Chief' [2012, 219–37]) or human ('The Woman in the Field' [2012, 43–71]) abound in Jamie's writing, concerned as they are with the negotiations between metaphysical and physical presence, between trace and matter. As Matt McGuire points out, Jamie engages with Norman MacCaig's work through 'this metaphysical combination of earthy and Eastern' (2009, 153).[19] From bone collections in cairns to whalebone arches erected in the landscape, in their organic physicality bones are a remainder of the past and a reminder of the time to come. Considered to be 'a beautiful material, a wonderful material' (2012, 105), they hold the function of relics, serving as registers of time, which emerges as a 'hint among bits of bone, a speculation among skulls' (2019, 130). The thought of what remains – and what will remain – haunts Jamie's essays. Temporal and material traces in the landscape include anthropogenic deposits suggesting past (or still-present) human occupation and other findings, which become a collection of venerated objects such as 'bits of birds, a cradle of seals' ribs, the exquisite skeleton of a starfish, no bigger than a thumbnail'. Both the 'archaeological' essays ('The Woman in the Field', 'In Quinhagak' [2019, 13–99], 'Links of Noltland I' [2019, 107–73]) and the 'island' ones ('On Rona' [2012, 179–209], 'Three Ways of Looking at St Kilda' [2012, 131–63]) attest that landscapes are explored by looking closely at what is on and in the ground, as a handful of earth, 'spanning centuries', reveals 'a glimpse of a life and a time' (2019, 177). Handling the earth at the Neolithic henge dating back four thousand years, which hid the Bronze Age burial site, the diggers had 'Neolithic dust under their fingernails' (2012, 68), which creates an intimate, tangible connection with deep time. Sifting through the grass or soil on hands and knees – 'a curious task, very intimate' (2012, 189) – resembles religious rituals of a penitent or a pilgrim, suggestive of a form of atonement and/or veneration. Similarly, to the images of the exploration of Rona and St Kilda discussed above, they allow for a different way of reading the landscape.

A selection of found objects taken home is a display of reverence for the world of remnants and vestiges on the part of collectors who are 'the arbiters of so many fates', as they decide which things are 'worth keeping' (2012, 112). In an essay examining material 'value' in 'Findings', Pippa Marland suggests that a plastic doll's head is 'a ghost of human consumerism, resistant to processes of decay, which is also able to evoke in us a sense of being scrutinised by the very materials we have created and junked' (2015, 121). Produced and jettisoned by our culture, the doll's head carries in it the ghost of another culture, another identity, another time, as the material is always haunted by the immaterial. Plastic objects exist outside human temporalities, enabling a realisation that 'the doll's head with her tufts of hair and rolling eyes may well persist after our own have cleaned back down to bone' (2005, 67). The notion of durability – an archaic value – recurs in a number of essays (cf. the above discussion on the fibreglass replica of a whalebone). In a time which produces avalanches of anthropogenic artefacts, the value of more erosive materialities becomes questioned as landscapes have been transformed into '21st-century midden of aerosols and plastic bottles' (2005, 66). Observing that 'we pick and choose' (2005, 67) among things 'valued enough to keep' (2005, 66), which sometimes are 'the useful' (2005, 66), but most frequently are not those that 'endured, but those that had been transformed by death or weather' (2005, 66), Jamie describes a process which also metaphorises the work of a writer, as the cited words of George Mackay Brown attest (2005, 6–7). The theme returns in *Surfacing*, where geological remnants of the past under the poet's feet contrast with 'the detritus of our own age' (2019, 113).[20]

Significantly, the awareness of the intertwining of organic matter with human-made objects resurfaces in an essay from *Sightlines* titled 'The Snow Petrel', which depicts a desiccated corpse brought home from Fianuis on North Rona with a metal ring, 'soldiering on while the bird's corpse withered' (2012, 215–16). There is 'something uncomfortable' (2012, 215) about the imperishable object juxtaposed with a biological organism, 'the only man-made object in all that place'. Yet it comes with a special purpose as it bears information traceable on a chart about the distance that the bird travelled in life: 'the scale of its journeyings made it seem even wilder than before' (2012, 216). The ambivalence of the instruction 'Inform British Museum' found on the ring makes 'the bird-ringing project sound imperious and Edwardian', writes Jamie, 'which it was—Edwardian, anyway, because bird ringing began in 1909' (2012, 212). The size of the storm petrel's leg – 'so twig-thin' (2012, 212) – makes the imperative request seem incongruous: 'there is no room for an "inform"' (2012, 212). The information coded in the ring obtained through the museum website reveals that in life the bird flew from Shetland to Rona, 'down to the pelagic hibernaculum off Namibia and South Africa' (2012, 216). As Jamie learns, ringed twenty-four years before on Yell, the snow petrel maps a connection between this Shetland island and Rona, forming a link between them 'by a flight-path, straight as an arrow' (2012, 215), despite obvious differences between them. Taken home, the corpse offers 'something of the sky and spaciousness of that island, at least for a while' (2012, 211). What is left of the bird – 'just a tuft of feathers in a polythene bag, a tiny skull, and . . . that silvery ring above its shrunken, black webbed foot' (2012, 216) – is kept by Jamie in her 'own hibernaculum', for different reasons: for its smell, 'fusty, musky, suggestive of a distant island in summer', 'for the intimacy' (2012, 216) and 'out of sheer respect because, in life, this ounce of a bird had made twenty-four return trips the length of the Atlantic', which is 'not bad at all, for a waif, wambling' (2012, 217). These words end the essay on the snow petrel, whose metal ring fused with its desiccated corpse tell a story of frailty and resilience. A valued

122 *Landscape Poetics*

finding, worth keeping, 'at least for a while', as Jamie repeats, the snow petrel provokes a dignifying gesture of care, a demonstration of a certain regard and admiration for the life of the other.

The Thickness of Time

The ornithological ring uncovers a vast history, partly reconstructed, partly imagined. As such, it is a single example of a much larger process. In their cultural, historical and social formation, whole landscapes constitute 'an information exchange' (2012, 68), whereby perceptual interchange between the world and the perceiver establishes the relation between subjectivity and nature mediated through time. Compared with the planetary temporalities, the awareness of the brevity of biological life foregrounds the manner in which biological lifespans are inscribed in enormous totalities. Geological changes extended in time occur beyond human perception. Human constructions, which extend thousands of years into the past but which have fallen into disuse, reveal 'the earthfast notion that time is deep, that memories are buried' (2012, 43). Reaching into the earth to uncover a henge, a Neolithic enclosure which 'lingered a long, long time in custom and memory' (2012, 61), a Bronze Age cist burial becomes uncovered. The monoliths in North Mains (Strathearn on the Strathallan Estate between Crieff and Auchterarder in Perthshire) provoke reflections of the same place at a different time:

> This here. This same topography. I walked out into the middle of the fallow field on its plateau. With the enclosing hills and twin, east flowing rivers, it is still the landscape the Neolithic people had understood so acutely, the same earth into which the Bronze Age woman had been lowered. Eastward, vanishing into haze, lay the river valley I'd driven that morning, where once the wild aurochs roamed. (2012, 70–1)

The paragraph preceding the excerpt cited above, presenting the fate of the place, ends with the words 'this place, this here'. The henge and the artefacts gone, there seemingly remains little to connect the temporal planes. The phrase 'this here' reappears in the following paragraph, a device which performs as a verbal hinge, joining the place which served a purpose several millennia before as it does now. Opening and closing, it connects linked objects: the image of a hinge is used earlier in the essay to refer to the 'henge', which becomes 'a hinge', 'a turning place' (2012, 48, 65) where other people walked the landscape. The words 'this' and 'here' ground the subject, establishing a spatial and temporal link. Through the repetition of the verb, the statement beginning the next and final paragraph of the essay – 'You are placed in landscape, you are placed in times' (2012, 71) – binds two key nouns: 'landscape' and 'time'. Suggestive of deep time, geological formations seem a constant, immovable presence only from the human perspective; they are nested in time scales of their own. The knowledge about the placement of prehistoric sites alters awareness as we see what we know when reading the landscape. Cairns were 'ritually closed'; the archaeological digs are a 'ritualised undoing' (2012, 67). In the presence of ancient artefacts that the land reveals, it is possible to imagine, as Jamie does, 'the pulse of ancient energy in the land, quietly persistent even in the slushy suburban sprawl' (2012, 46). Possibly following Giambattista Vico, Jamie suggests that time is a spiral (2019, 161), whereby temporal verticality follows a downward movement.

In passing remarks, Jamie captures the changing functions of place transformed with time, referring to 'new deeds' which certain elements of the landscape 'fulfilled' (2012, 171). Daniel Weston's remarks on *Findings*, suggesting that in her essays the preoccupation with the pastoral and agricultural function of the land underlines 'the settled nature of these places' (2016, 135), could equally be applied to Jamie's writing in *Sightlines* and *Surfacing*. The familiar shape of the land, with a terrace, the rivers and the Ochils, with the Highlands in the distance, which was 'relevant' (2012, 47) thousands of years before, now has a different function. The image emphasises overlapping layers of temporality, demonstrating the manner in which '[t]he past can spill out of the earth, become the present' (2019, 31). The excavation work revealed that in the past the Links proved to have been 'a very successful wee bit of Orkney landscape' (2019, 111). On Sceapull, the path leading 'through a gap in an earthen dyke the land began to rise and fall in ridges', which 'curved downhill toward the sea': 'Hundreds of years ago oats or barley would have been raised on them, but now, long overgrown, they had become sculptural, land art' (2012, 184). These visible signs of the passage of time augur future transformations, 'when unimaginable change has come to the life we know, a few acres far out in the Atlantic might be pressed into service again' (2012, 207). In opposition to the phrase 'unimaginable change', the second clause pictures the future of these places.

Elsewhere Jamie suggests that imagination may help 'abolish all layers of time', bringing the past – 'the various pasts' – to the present as 'the past, the various pasts, were all present' (2012, 58). This is exemplified in the blend of different periods, objects and groups of people – the Neolithic henge, Bronze artefacts, the seventeenth-century English radicals, the Hurricane aircraft, the 1960s communal spirit which arises among the diggers – which creates a sense of one large temporal plane. The image poses certain problems, as through such a mode of perception difference is erased: to read everything in a present and collapse everything is acutely ambivalent. Being in proximity with the Neolithic henge, underneath which there lay Bronze Age objects – exploring them with one's hands, on one's knees – creates an impression of being in blended time, making one 'feel unhooked from time', 'to be uncertain which era one was alive in', with the sound of the plane nearby. The remnants of ancient occupation such as 'standing stones, tumuli, ley lines and all that' (2012, 45) are called 'earth mysteries' (2012, 45; original quotation marks), the sense of mystery heightened during work on an archaeological dig which may create an impression of being temporally 'dislocated', feeling 'unhooked from time', even though some elements of the landscape – '[t]he range of hills, the plateau where we worked, the twin flowing rivers, the pines and cawing rooks' – have not changed since ancient times, remaining 'constant'. In an attempt to domesticate the sense of temporal dislocation, the National Museum 'shows how the land was then' (2012, 58), miniaturising the landscape, and thereby harnessing defamiliarisation, in the form of a diorama, a nineteenth-century invention stemming from a newly gained awareness of geological depth, which offers a visual, if static, depiction of the movement of time.

The present moment contains past and future, as '[i]n the experience of the present, there is always a small difference between the moment of now-ness and the past and the future' (Lawlor 2019, n.p.). Time at once condenses and stretches on 'a square of ancient earth' (2019, 130) where a small space contains deep time. The extent of time in its immediacy, felt as 'a shock' at a realisation of being 'alone in the vast moment of now' (2019, 130), offering a reflection on a 'now' moment which may only exist if it is contrasted with another moment which highlights that 'now' in 'the living-present', to use Husserl's term. This is why the fiberglass whale and the doll's head produce the sense of discomfort. In the presence of a subject to itself, that 'now' contains a trace of a previous experience (Derrida 1973, 68) with which arrives a realisation that the meaning of a particular object is never stable, but always in the process of change, whereby past, present and future are in the process of transformation, the present entangled with the past and future. Thus, the living present is 'thick' (to invoke Husserl again), as it contains the past and future. Such thick time reveals itself most intensely in Jamie's essays when she depicts archaeological works requiring high concentration; for instance, when she describes how it was possible to 'lose yourself in that minuscule landscape' as, suddenly, a field in Perthshire with its 'unchanging, stalwart ridge of hills' resembles 'a tiny Sahara seen from miles high', only to be reminded that it is in effect part of 'the wider landscape' (2012, 55). The proximity already mentioned experienced during an archaeological dig changes spatial and temporal perspectives, making the place contract and expand in a thickening 'nowness'.

Other than revealing the past uses of the land, the objects abandoned in the landscape speak of disuse and forgetting. In this form, the memory of the land powerfully invades the present moment (cf. 2019, 138–9) as the material effects of the workings of time become visible in 'dereliction' (2019, 131), the word suggestive of a previous form, which now manifests itself as the ghost of a still-habitable landscape. The cairns, which 'fell out of use and out of memory', remain in the landscape 'to become the haunt of the fairy folk' (2019, 139). Hauntings reappear in *Surfacing*, marked by the word 'ghostly' that recurs in a number of contexts, as, for instance, when describing past uses of the building, revealing layers of time through different forms of matter, juxtaposing twenty-first-century plastic objects with a Victorian building and Neolithic artefacts (2019, 146, 119, 144). These and other similar images establish past and present connections with different inhabitants of the land, conjured in the second-person pronoun and thus summoned through a verbal bridge over time, constituting an accumulation of 'the stories, the voices, the dead' (2019, 177).

The motif emerges in the two previous collections in which the people inhabiting the same landscape are figured through the work of imagination. For instance, as Jamie crosses the river by the bridge, she visualises people living in Neolithic times crossing the same river in a coracle in an act, as she perceives it, endowed with a 'ritual significance, an arrival at the centre of the world, a plateau site held in place by the surrounding hills' (2012, 69). The realisation arrives that a familiar field in Perthshire forms part of 'the wider landscape', where the placement of the henge 'possibly with reason' functions as proof that, without modern aerial technology such which would 'reveal the face of the earth to them', prehistoric people 'could certainly read a landscape' (2012, 55). The ability to read the landscape among archaeologists and surveyors enhances the exploration of place, suffusing it with a deeper reading.

When encountering artefacts, or 'features' buried in the earth, being able to tell 'a something from a nothing, human intentionality from nature or chance' (2012, 59) is a question of experience and expertise. Nancy's remark about 'the endless accumulation of archives and expectations' is complemented by Jamie's statement about the awareness of human self-obsession: 'We know we are a species obsessed with itself and its own past and origins' (2012, 69). The obsession emerges in the reason for the excavation in North Mains, performed due to a projected construction of an aircraft museum and a runway for a Lancaster. The trope of the plane returns in the essay, an aerial object contrasting with earthly ones, a symbol of modern advancement and technology juxtaposed with the debris of ancient culture, a familiar device in Jamie's work. The image connecting the dual motion of excavating a site in Scotland and burying people alive in Dresden foregrounds the never-ending, cyclical process of human history concerned with a constant process of enfolding and revealing. In an ironic twist, the Lancaster is never displayed on the field but instead is disassembled for spare parts; thus, it becomes a symbolic image of transitory power and destruction which proves short-lasting.

As mentioned above, the ambivalence of late modernity manifested in the landscapes is displayed through a number of images blending technology and natural phenomena. During the archaeological dig described in 'The Woman in the Field', a crane, contrasting with the landscape with its bright colour and mechanical construction, becomes 'a strange trump of modernity' (2012, 64), overpowering the scenery. The wind turbine, which makes a repeated appearance in the essay 'Links of Noltland', functions as a reminder of the potential of new technological processes. Through a chain of extended metaphors, the wind turbine reflecting light connects with Maes Howe (2019, 151–2, 156), which echoes yet another image. Depicted in 'Darkness and Light', the method of 'passing light over these same stones, still making measurements by light and time' (2005, 24) creates a link between the old ways and the modern ones, thus binding two images in which the shaft of sun plays a central part: the wind turbine reflecting light resembles the structures of Maes Howe, capturing the sun. The double metaphor foregrounds the interconnections between the ancient and the new. In a blend of colloquiality and seriousness, the statement of one of the surveyors – 'if it all goes to hell on a handcart, we have the data, we can build a replica' (2005, 25) – offers a potent reminder of the frailty of the interconnected system whereby technology advances a recovery of a culture buried underground and aids in constructing its copy. Yet, as with the fibreglass replica of a whalebone, it will never be the real thing but a mere simulacrum.

Light and dark perform various functions in Jamie's essays. For instance, in a fjord in East Greenland, at 71 degrees latitude, the changing pattern of the aurora watched as the minutes of life pass becomes the measure of time. The energy of the Northern Lights appears to be working like a sieve, separating '[s]tars, souls, particles' (2012, 13), and the scientific explanation, offering a simple interpretation of the event, which is 'just charged particles, trapped in the earth's magnetic field' (2012, 16), not only does not unravel the mystery but deepens it, bringing a realisation that we are melded with the sky through energy and light. Primordial dark in Maes Howe connects contemporary visitors to the pre-creational world in the glimpse into the infinite depth of time. The absence of vision brings the faculty of listening to the fore, causing the subject to imagine Neolithic 'nocturnal soundscapes', which 'would have included the calls of nocturnal animals, the crackle of campfires, and the resonance of human communication' (Nowell 2018, 40), a reminder that sound is related to the experience of time. Similarly, in a passage which depicts mooring on the shores of St Kilda, Jamie imagines that, after the boat engine is switched off, its roar replaced with 'preternatural' silence, the sound of waves and the calls of birds are the only sounds for the St Kildans (2012, 147). The image reminds us that the sound of birdsong is a primary example of the subjective experience of time, which includes more than is immediately present. Weather soundscapes such as a thunderclap hold a similar function, inviting us to imagine that these sounds were heard by the Neolithic inhabitants of the same land. In 'The Woman in the Field', the evocations of the weather are intertwined with the imagination of the past, which creates a sense of movement between the ephemerality of 'now' as manifested in the elemental forces and the static background of the extended temporality, which results in a pointillistic image. Phenomenological presence emerges through sensorial interchange and movement, as when Jamie depicts geese in flight, the undulation of grasses, and an elderly man at work, all together 'listening to the language of this landscape, as expressed with the hands and eye' (2019, 94).

While sound fills the time of being in the landscape, there occur rare moments of seeming suspension, for instance when watching the aurora or sitting quietly to enjoy 'spells of quietude' (2019, 66). Due to our corporeality, 'true silence' proves impossible because soon 'you come to hear the high whine of your own nerves', which is 'the very nervous system which allows you to hear at all', itself a testimony that our 'animal bodies' cannot be still, want us to move, to '[k]eep warm, keep hunting' (2012, 5). These are the demands of a living organism, distinguished from inanimate entities, reminding us that we are 'not ice, not rock' (2012, 5). Such a self-reflective glimpse, revealing the experience of temporal becoming, as Maurice Merleau-Ponty suggests, aligns the human subject with time, which reminds us that it is impossible to say 'I' absolutely (2002, 431–2). Phenomenology understood as 'here' and 'now', where 'every appearance or every experience is temporal' (Lawlor 2019, n.p.), is heightened even more when immediacy invades the present moment in a form of a singular event. The landscape may become a 'quiet meditation' (2019, 67) when perception sharpens, colours become clearer and details not seen before appear: singular stems of grass, threads of spiderweb, and '[w]hen a pale bee entered a fireweed flower, it was an event' (2016, 66). Combined with its silence, the stillness of the landscape where a sighting of a bird such as a raven becomes 'visible as an event in the landscape' (2019, 31), contrasting with its otherwise immobile aspect, offers a reminder that it is not flat and lifeless, and thereby smashing the fleeting illusion. The opening of the event establishes the connection between perception and the experience of time. As Ted Toadvine suggests, the non-equivalence of the present breaks 'the fermata that holds each moment indefinitely suspended along a continuum of geologically extended time' (2017, 227). What Toadvine calls 'the *non-equivalence*' – that is, 'the absolutely unique and non-substitutable events and moments, that compose our quotidian experience' (2017, 227) – is evoked in constantly renewed singularities. The power of the event relies on its brevity and its singularity. The phrase 'a wing's beat and it's gone' offers both a brief glimpse of another being and a metaphor for the disappearance of certain species.

In Jamie's essays, the singularity of the event often takes a form of a gift, a serendipitous encounter offered at the convergence of space and time. In this, her work resembles that of Thomas A Clark. It may be a sighting of a bee, a raven, a whale. The latter holds a special significance in the light of shrinking ecosystems. Within the singularity of the event, the uniqueness of the whale reinforces the sense of loss. The realisation of losing whole ecosystems resounds throughout the essays where every sighting of a whale becomes an event in the sea landscape, transforming the scenery. After experiencing the 'orca's greater presence' (2012, 84), Jamie records the effect of the event on the body, which resembles 'a private miracle', resulting in feeling 'different, looser of limb, thrilled because the world had thrown me a gift and said, "Catch!"' (2012, 86). The sighting of five killer whales hunting near the coast of Rona turns the observers into 'spectators at a grand prix' (2012, 199), the encounter bringing transformation to the whole landscape: '[a]ll this was happening in a tiny corner of the sea, but the sea suddenly seemed different. It appeared vaster, more alive and knowing and expressive than before' (2012, 85). Having 'a wild glamour about them', whales leave a strong mark on the perceived landscape, 'as though sprayed with an invisible graffiti tag: "*Killer whale was here*"' (2012, 208), the power of the event changing 'the rocks we stepped from', which 'were different now', as Jamie writes. The killer whales bring 'another kind of vision—the sudden unexpected' (2012, 89), causing delight and excitement, manifested in language relating the event (e.g. 'yelling about fins', 'hollered', 'thumped', the use of exclamation marks [2012, 83]). The thrill, pushing the observers to run for fear of losing the whales from sight, provokes an awareness of the phenomenal engagement of a human body with other species, as 'suddenly I was reminded mine was an animal body, all muscle and nerve—and so were they, the killer whales, surging animal bodies, in their black and whites, outclassing us utterly' (2012, 199). Seen in their element off the coast of Scotland, elusive and fleeting, they contrast with their form when reduced to the bone, finless and static, placed on hills and in parks or museum halls. The elusiveness of the event enhances the sense of mystery, the moment between presence and absence in the rhythm of the world, so well expressed in the recurring phrase 'a wing's beat and it's gone'.[21] As discussed above, the decline of the whale marks a dramatic point in modern history. Often, however, the disappearance of a species from the landscape is a non-event, happening unnoticed, as in the case of gannets, for instance, whose vanishing brings to mind the Icarus of Pieter Bruegel's painting, reimagined by W. H. Auden's 'Musée des Beaux Arts', where people go about their business, philosophers philosophise, theoreticians theorise while a tragedy takes place. By citing the poem, Jamie proposes a reversal of a familiar image from Greek mythology in which Icarus constructs wings made of feathers, instead imagining a gannet. At the same time, she expands the cultural context as she recalls Bruegel's painting *Landscape with the Fall of Icarus*: 'What, the painting asks, is the fate of one boy—or one bird—in the scheme of things?' (2012, 79). By personifying these pelagic creatures, Jamie decentres humans, and through such literary references places them within European culture spanning thousands of years.

The Land and the Sky

The elements of northern landscapes, lying 'under a huge Atlantic sky' (2012, 229), feature prominently in Jamie's work. Mingling with the atmosphere, humans are inseparable from the elements, attuned to the elemental effects of the weather. The Orkney Islands near the Brough of Birsay are 'an elemental place in any season—loud waves surge between long skerries; eider ducks ride the waves and, often, seals watch you as you walk' (2012, 237); similarly, the 'sensation' on Atlantic islands in the summer season, 'when the clouds pass quickly and light glints on the sea—a sense that the world is bringing itself into being moment by moment. Arising and passing away in the same breath' (2012, 186). It is a world in constant becoming, appearing to view in an organic rhythm.

The Rona people, described by Martin Martin in his travel journal of the Western Isles published in 1695 and cited by Jamie, as the 'ancient race' oblivious of the ways of the world outside, living 'by dint of wind and weather' (2012, 190), took 'their surname from the colour of the sky, rainbow and clouds' (2012, 191). They must have 'known to every blade of grass, every stone' and were attuned with the land and the seasons: 'They must have felt acutely the turning of the seasons, the need to lay down stores and supplies, because summer was brief' (2012, 192). Jamie records moments of such attunement during work on an archaeological dig (see, e.g., 2012, 62) or surveying the land. The following passage exemplifies the effect on the body of a prolonged time in open space:

> Daily, our sense of time slowed, days expanded like a wing. The days were long in the best, high-summer sense; at night we put up storm shutters on the bothy window to make it dark enough to sleep. Time was clouds passing, a sudden squall, a shift in the wind. Often we wondered what it would do to your mind if you were born here, and lived your whole life within this small compass. To be named for the sky or the rainbow, and live in constant sight and sound of the sea. (2012, 192)

The archipelagic landscapes fill an individual with a 'sense of light and spaciousness' (2012, 208), creating an impression of 'bones . . . turning to flutes' and contributing to feeling 'lighter inside' (2012, 192).

'Wind', the essay concluding *Sightlines*, depicts the effect of walking on Glen Mor, 'getting clouted properly' and 'knocked down'; these resemble Shepherd's descriptions in *The Weatherhouse*. Violent weather leaves one 'frayed and weather-worn' (2012, 240), bringing the sensation 'of being thumped by an invisible pillow', which does not bear any resemblance to 'being tumbled like a leaf' (2012, 240). The force knocks the person down on her knees, 'as if beholding a miracle' (2012, 240), not unlike a revelation of one's body in the face of a storm – 'getting clouted properly' (2012, 240) – buffeted, having to struggle and contest against it, different from that of a leaf or bird. The latter, a dead whooper swan, found on the beach, whose wing 'formed under the wind's tutelage, formed by and for the wind', is a reminder of the disparity, as we 'are not creatures of the wind' (2012, 240). Technology corrects the omission: air travel enables the rescue action for those stranded due to bad weather conditions as 'this is the modern world', states Jamie, cautiously adding, 'at least for now' (2012, 241), as if to signal that we should not accustom ourselves or rely on its comforts too much. As if to prove that such undue reliance might be naively optimistic, the hopes for the rescue are dashed as the wind prevails and the helicopter is cancelled. In an extended metaphor, Jamie connects birds, the helicopter and the wind, which share the element, a relatedness which is highlighted in a number of similes. For instance, 'Like a bird it could swap the state of being on land with that of being airborne by a mere alteration of attitude' (2012, 242). Windows in the helicopter floor allow for a bird's-eye view, helping to imagine the whooper swan's perspective, so that one sees 'the sea below as the swan would have seen it on its last flight, migrating in its family group' (2012, 242). The final paragraph of the collection highlights transience: 'There are myths and fragments which suggest that the sea that we were flying over was once land. Once upon a time, and not so long ago, it was a forest with trees, but the sea rose and covered it over. The wind and sea. Everything else is provisional. A wing's beat and it's gone' (2012, 242).

The dialogic nature of the landscape is expressed in the image of the ocean 'brightly shifting everywhere' as it is 'meeting the sky in every shade of grey' (2012, 188), in recurring references to the sky which emphasise its vastness and relatedness to the sea. In contrast with these two seemingly infinite elements, the land appears to be 'a green unheaving bosom', its steadiness and depth '[b]lessed' (2012, 180). After a sea passage, the groundedness of the 'deep core of steady rock, reaching down and down' bring comfort, together with the tactile experience of the land's surface, the texture of grass '[l]ush-long and harsh at once' (2012, 180). The haptic sensation is followed in quick succession by sound and smell: birdcall and the scent of wildflowers (most probably thrift, an evergreen perennial which tolerates saline conditions and grows in coastal areas). Finally, sight completes the sensuous experience, creating the entire sensorium of the landscape.

As in Nan Shepherd's writing, the landscape evokes moments of the sublime, revealed through adjectives such as 'ravishing' (used with reference to light in *Surfacing* [2019, 16; 21]), 'stunning' (describing a view [2019, 151]) and 'astonishing' (2019, 9; 30). Almost absent from *Findings*, these words appear with increasing frequency in later collections, marking a departure from a style characterised by restraint from aesthetic judgement towards a more open appreciation of natural beauty. True to its etymology, astonishment experienced by Jamie at the sight of the Alaskan landscapes causes her to freeze: 'The landscape was astonishing. There was nothing I wanted to do more than sit quietly and look at it, come to terms with its vastness' (2019, 30). Thunderstruck, she observes 'a silent, shining realm', extending far ahead and around. Two features of the landscape stand out, namely its vastness and silence, the former foregrounded by the land fusing with the sky: 'Almost to the horizon, and for miles north and south, lay silver mudflats, with the sky reflected in shallow pools. The sky held every sort of cloud, every season, and through gaps in the cloud a dreamy turquoise I'd never seen before' (2019, 30). The verb 'astonish' is associated with such a powerful effect of wonder that it would cause a deafening, yet the result here is a silent image. Stunned in place, Jamie would sit and observe the landscape, 'this unfixed place', as she puts it, which shows 'how readily ... the visible shifts' (2019, 31).

On seeing Quinhagak, Jamie comments that it was 'the most flat and uninhabited landscape I had ever beheld' (2019, 16). Such is the ratio of water to land that the view appears to be 'a waterscape into which some land had been released' (2019, 16). The following remark, that it is 'barely a landscape at all' (2019, 16), suggests a precognitive need in the perceiver to pin down what she sees. The dominant feature of the perceived image, its vagueness, is expressed in the conjunction 'or' which opens the next sentence: 'Or land, through which water has been introduced, enough to make the land appear to float.' Unable to determine what she sees, Jamie abandons the attempt to decide which of the above it is, concluding that '[i]t was both at once'; it is 'a visual pun', shimmering with ambiguity and possible meanings. The undecidability of the view defamiliarises the landscape as it resists a direct reading.

Jamie's phrase 'a visual pun' suggests her insistence on the textuality of the landscape, a feature which returns later in the same essay, when she says that she was 'learning to read the village better' (2019, 69). Jonathan Culler considers puns to be 'lively instances of lateral thinking, exploiting the fact that language has ideas of its own' (1988, 15). Depicting the play of the landscape as something which needs to be deciphered, Jamie foregrounds its textuality. Vision, landscape, and language create a collusion. In a striking metaphor, Jamie compares the 'thrilling, transgressive' act of opening the burial chamber during a storm with writing poetry: 'The weight and heft of a word, the play of sounds, the sense of carefully revealing something authentic, an artefact which didn't always display "meaning", but which was a true expression of—what?—a self, a consciousness' (2012, 65). Highlighting the archaeological nature of writing, words are like unearthed artefacts. Comparing a river to a highway, where the silence gives salience to 'the scale of the vast land around, its pressing strangeness', emphasising one's 'exposure' (2019, 76), Jamie touches on the overwhelming sense of nature's peculiarity recorded when experiencing the landscape, with 'strange' (2019, 97) and 'strangeness' (2019, 76) recurring words, forming expressions of both an unfamiliar landscape and the effect it exerts, especially as it is contrasted with the inhabitants' intimacy with the land. For instance, 'In the silence of the shore, the strange light, it discomfited me' (2019, 97). Estrangement is captured in the recurrent references to the unusual effects of light as an experience of being-in-the-world – 'the strange light', 'ravishing light' – which stress the defamilarising power of an unknown landscape.[22] Jamie wrestles with the sense of a vastness impossible to capture in words: 'It's some landscape . . .' (2019, 38), she observes, the ellipsis prefiguring the failure of language in the face of immensity. Struggling to express the otherwise inexpressible, post-Romantic sublime, grasping the landscape itself, Jamie notes the placement of people in relation to the land. She adds, 'to the people of Quinhagak, living close to the land, attuned to its rhythms, it is just their refrigerator' (2019, 38). The reference to the kitchen appliance makes the sublime banal; it renders the unimaginable quotidian, demonstrating bathos in the inexpressibility of the world being reduced to the function of food storage.

Similarly to Shepherd (see, e.g., 2011, 99), Jamie reflects on the deceptive nature of perspective, the visual tricks that the landscape may play: 'Transformation is possible. A bear can become a bird. A sea can vanish, rivers change course. The past can spill out of the earth, become the present' (2019, 31). The experience is governed by 'a production of imagination'. Following Schelling, John

Sallis suggests that it is through imagination that 'we are capable of thinking and holding together even what is contradictory' (2012, 4). The eye comprehends the view: 'The hill's not high, only a thousand feet or so, but the reaches of land around it are wide. We could see plantation forest and mountains to the west, farmland and lochs to the south and east. A visitor from Texas once told us our landscape was human-scale. The wind packed itself into our lungs and hair' (2005, 111). Underneath the visible landscape, there hides richness, the layers of the lived experience of the land: it is as if the seen side contained the reverse. Very occasionally, the landscape presented by Jamie becomes flat, two-dimensional, as it resembles a still image when all movement ceases in rare moments suspended in time, freezing the view. In the passage below, visual illusions as three-dimensional space appear to become a flat surface:

> Silent as a stage, lying back northwards for a short mile, was a perfect high glen, in browns and subtle greens. A hanging valley, held, as it were, in the arms of its surrounding hills. It had been a steep climb up, but now the land relaxed, levelled. Through the middle of this high valley the river knew no urgency. It moved in wide, slow meanders, like a rope played out. From my vantage point, on a slight rise somewhat higher than the valley floor, the whole scene looked like . . . a photograph. (2005, 118)

The phrase 'silent as a stage' introduces an element of the spectacular, gesturing towards the experience of the sublime. The above passage refers to the tradition of the picturesque, yet it challenges the category. At this point it would be useful to refer to David E. Cooper's work on the function of aestheticism in representing the environment. Pointing to the ambiguity of such concepts as 'anthropocenic' and 'intrinsic' values in nature, Cooper rejects the claim that descriptions of the landscape, focusing on its aesthetic features, which demonstrate the manner in which it affects humans, are not necessarily 'instrumental', as the concept of values is a 'human product', and, as he asserts, 'we "endow" things with value or "confer" it on them, and that the things themselves are "valueless"' (1998, 97). The beauty and frailty of the landscapes need a language which would stand in defiance of representation. The recurrent questions posed by Jamie – 'how to engage with the world in language' (2005, 165) and 'how to deal with this mortal life in language, how to sculpt something beautiful out of silence'

(2005, 182) – are sometimes answered by the natural world with scribbles unintelligible to humans.

The vanishing time marked by elements which dominate the landscape – stone, wind and sea – are evoked by noun phrases devoid of verbs. The device, which brings to mind Thomas A Clark's poems (as we shall see), captures the experience of place, encapsulating the emotion as well as the scenery, emotion expressed through scenery, object and element. For instance, we read of '[s]urf, and seal-song, and petrel glee' (2012, 185) or 'the vaulting sky, the islands set in a turquoise sea, the mink worrying among the rocks' (2005, 178). Usually associated with a depiction of static images, nouns suggest a complete, still view, one that is already made. In Jamie's writing, nouns suggest a state in which a verbal response to the landscape becomes impossible, when language fails, as she writes: the use of nouns as in the examples above thus constitutes an act of surrender to the sublime experience which is prelinguistic. The engagement with the world takes place beyond language. As Jamie explains, 'If we work always in words, sometimes we need to recuperate in a place where language doesn't join up, where we're thrown back on a few elementary nouns. Sea. Bird. Sky' (2005, 164).

Notes

1. John Parham places *Findings* and *Sightlines* on a timeline which shows the Anthropocene and 'relevant literary works' (2021, xiii–xix).
2. As Jamie herself says, 'Poets use language as a form of "seeing". More and more, however, I think the job is to listen, to pay attention' (cit. McGuire 2009, 150).
3. Cf. Alec Finlay's and the wildlife sound recordist Chris Watson's collaboration which involves recordings of the natural world, for instance 'Cairngorms Fauna Jukebox'.
4. This is complemented by an image of a wound, as the extracting process makes the mines look like a gash in the ground. Cf. 'Reliquary' in *The Tree House* (2004, 37).
5. As McGuire notices, Jamie's prose writing has been compared to that of Gilbert White by Andrew Marr (2009, 141), adding that it 'resonates with the work of . . . Henry David Thoreau' (McGuire 2009, 150).
6. See the chapter 'Landscapes of the Body: The Poetry of Kathleen Jamie' in Yeung (2015, 111–28).
7. As explored in *Frissure*, which Jamie co-authored with Brigid Collins.
8. Jamie's first published poem, 'View from the Cliffs', evokes a scene from Orkney.

9. Also the title of the 1937 film, which documents the final chapter of the depopulation of St Kilda.
10. Puff Inn on Hirta mentioned in Jamie's essay was closed after fifty years in 2019.
11. Some place names – Claigeann an Tigh Faire, the Skull of the Watching House; the Lovers' Rock; Cam Mar; Mullach Sgar – have been recorded, but many remained undocumented and are now forgotten.
    Jamie also notes the colonial aspect of name giving. For instance, in 'Voyager, Chief' she writes about the geographical names given by William Scoresby, who sailed to the Artic: 'the headlands and inlets of the Greenlandic coast read like a roll call of the post-Enlightenment; from Cape Barclay in the south to Cape Bright in the north, the ice-capped peninsulas and ice-choked fjords are a long list of male grandees: as he put it, ". . . respected friends, to whom I was wishful to pay a compliment that might possibly survive the lapse of ages". Every fjord and island is for a friend or admired superior, the largest fjord of all, named in honour of his father, is Scoresbysund' (2012, 223). However, some corrections have been made, for instance, the name of the settlement, formerly Scoresbysund, was changed into Ittoqqortoormiit in the East Greenlandic language (2012, 224). Traces of colonialism remain with such names as Liverpool Land, a peninsula bounded by Scoresby Sund, where Ittoqqortoormiit is located.
    Jamie also remarks on the curious reversals involving naming and the natural world. For instance, while on Rona, she notices a fulmar's nest and thinks of Leach's petrels hiding in the walls: 'Seabirds, named for St Peter, who walked on water, had colonised a cell built by a saint named for a seal' (2012, 194).
12. While whaling may well be a by-product in some cultures of colonialism, there are indigenous non-colonial cultures such as Japan and Norway that have relied and continue to rely on whaling as part of their cultural identity.
13. Thomas Nagel, 'What is It Like to be a Bat?' (1974, 435–50).
14. The epigraph of 'Voyager, Chief' comes from a Stanley Kunitz poem entitled 'Elegy for a Whale' from *The Wellfleet Whale*.
15. Theoretical debates on 'humanity's relationship with other species' (2012, 22) are met with Jamie's impatience as they reveal incongruities and contradictions. For example, in 'Pathologies', Jamie notes that discussions on consumerism as the replacement for wonder are led while eating venison. Being 'exhorted to reconnect with nature' raises questions about the concept (2012, 22–3), so often narrowed down to the 'natural world', a problem which Jamie considers during a walk (looking for 'nature' 'in the trees' colours, in the tidal flux of the river; in the fieldfares arriving to the fields' [2012, 22]), on the train home ('a metal box on a Highland moor, but the last wolf was shot long ago' [2012, 23]), or, finally, when marvelling at medical advancements: 'What are

vaccinations for, if not to make a formal disconnection from some of these wondrous other species?' (2012, 23). Challenging the concept of 'nature' forms part of Jamie's work. This has been noticed by a number of critics. For instance, Matt McGuire cites Jamie, who says, 'I don't recognise the idea of "the outdoors", or of "nature". We are "nature", in our anatomy and mortality. Regarding nature as the other, different, an "outdoors", an "environment" speaks volumes about our alienation from ourselves' (cit. McGuire 2009, 146). Jamie's simple question in *Findings*, "And what's natural?" (2005, 126), reminds the reader that the term 'Nature' is a human construct and therefore the time of Nature *is just* the time of the Anthropocene. McGuire remarks on Jamie's perception of the 'environmental crisis', suggesting that 'for her the problem lies in our own growing sense of estrangement from the natural world' (McGuire 2009, 146). Deborah Lilley argues that 'Consideration of what is encompassed by the term "nature" recurs throughout her [Jamie's] writing from different perspectives, and in the process, the category of "nature writing" is reconfigured to accommodate those perspectives. Her versions of the form are composed from ecological, social and historical viewpoints, challenging both the idealisation of nature and the perceived externality of nature that enables such idealisation' (2013, 16).

16. Gairn links this aspect of Jamie's work with Bachelard as she notices that 'In *The Tree House*, Jamie recognizes the need for reverie as a way of examining our relationship with nature, and while some poems can be read as reveries themselves, others comment on the difficulty of reconciling the demands of everyday life, our "interhuman relationships", with "our need for reverie"' (Gairn 2007, 242).
17. It should be noted that Thomas Hardy is one of the first writers to apprehend multiple temporalities. The idea informs Hardy's novel *A Pair of Blue Eyes* (1873) in which the amateur geologist Henry Knight hangs from a cliff, contemplating a vision of deep time, a scene which involves an eye-to-eye encounter with a trilobite.
18. Jamie's preoccupation with human–non-human entanglement is present in her poetry. For instance, the poem entitled 'Migratory III' (2015, 46) is accompanied with a note about the finding of Paleolithic flutes made from swans' bones, which date back 30,000 years (2015, 61).
19. Other references to MacCaig include the lines 'even the raven' in a poem of the same title ([Jamie 2012, 49]; Jamie changes MacCaig's line, which reads 'even the ravens') as well as the phrase 'antlers of water', employed in the title of the nature writing collection edited by Jamie. Both phrases come from a poem 'Looking down on Glen Canisp' (MacCaig 2005, 181).
20. Some objects retrieved from the landscape undergo a process of appropriation, becoming transformed into marketable commodities. One such example of a contemporary cultural change of a material artefact

into a brand is the Westray Wife, the Neolithic figurine, becoming a brand of cheese (2019, 160).
21. We are reminded that there is 'no such thing as "natural harmony"', but rather 'a dynamic', because '[p]opulations expand, then crash' (2012, 214). As the ornithologist cited by Jamie concludes, 'Mysterious things happen—catastrophic things sometimes, on the island, everywhere. Nothing stays the same' (2012, 214). For a very good discussion on the subject, see Ursula K. Heise, *Imagining Extinction: The Cultural Meanings of Endangered Species* (2016).
22. A similar sensation is depicted in 'The Wind Horse' (2019, 195–235). Jamie is wary of exoticisation, but perceives that, similarly to the notion of remoteness, it is not entirely possible to avoid. The word 'exotic' appears in 'A Tibetan Dog' and returns in various forms in 'The Wind Horse', both essays from *Surfacing*. When remembering a group of Chinese students, she wonders, 'Maybe they were exoticising the Tibetans, but weren't we all?' (2019, 218).

Chapter 4

'A patch pegged out for closer examination': Thomas A Clark's Poetic Practice

Not ostentatiously self-advertising, Thomas A Clark's poetry does not attract attention to itself with elaborate design or language. In this, it resembles a modest flower that thrives in the shade, not unlike the self-effacing *Adoxa moschatellina* – the moschatel. This delicate plant with slender stems and slightly lighter-green five-petalled, clocklike flowerheads prefers shaded places, growing under leafy deciduous trees in woods and on the shaded banks of rivers and streams where it forms a carpet undergrowth, disappearing in late spring after a brief period of flowering. The moschatel eluded botanists for a long time as they were unable to classify it. Its genus name is derived from the Greek word *adoxos*, meaning 'without glory' – a fitting name for a plant with such an unassuming appearance. Yet, it is also the only species of its genus and thus unique.[1]

Founded in 1973 by Thomas A Clark and Laurie Clark, Moschatel Press derives its name from *Adoxa moschatelina*. The significance of the name in Clark's practice is best revealed in a parenthetical line from the colophon of the Hawkhaven Press edition of *An Lochan Uaine* (2008): below the information about the text, endpaper, cover stock and cover wrapper on which the book is printed, there appear these words in parenthesis: 'and the soul of the moschatel'. The choice of this botanical name for the name of the press suggests a carefully tended marginality, but also a singularity. Clark's poetry frequently concerns itself with wildflowers found on verges. Explaining his literary interest in flowers that began early, Clark admits that such a clichéd motif as flowers in poetry presented itself as a challenge (Clark 1977, 12).[2] The passing reference to the flower sermon from which the Zen technique developed (Clark 1977, 14) provides a valuable hint concerning the influence of Zen which pervades Clark's practice, not only demonstrated in his use of minimalist style and form but also explaining the meaning behind the use of flower motifs and revealing a profound philosophical dimension.

What appears particularly significant here is the epistemological approach, or the idea of silent transmission in Zen. Clark's early poems may appear 'gnomic, abrupt' (Ward 1984, 58), summarised as a practice that Geoffrey Ward ingeniously calls '[t]he Zen rockery', extending the garden metaphor when he writes that it was 'supplanted by a more formal and extensive garden of verses' (1984, 58). The garden metaphor appears apt in the context of Clark's practice, which nonetheless moves away from the erstwhile representation of flowers in poetry wherein they serve merely allegorical or symbolic purposes. Clark eschews such gestures, instead focusing on plants and things as they become part of a sustained inquiry into the world. According to Clark's view on the language of flowers, poems are everywhere; in effect, this is the world 'made totally ... of language' (Clark 1977, 14, 16). The consequence of the belief in the verbal structure of the world is the approach to poetic creation which relies on the retrieval of poems from the surroundings, thus placing emphasis on the world and not the poet. Such grounding of language is bound with the grounding of the body, with perception formed in its perceptual environment where language is but one of the functions of the body. Coupled with restraint in introducing elements of adornment, Clark's found technique relies on an expressed astonishment with things and phenomena.

The motif of the garden encapsulates an inevitable reference to the Garden of Eden. Described as 'resolutely paradisal' (Ward 1984, 57), Ward argues that Clark 'promises' paradise 'with unwarranted cheerfulness', which, according to the critic, would situate him in the Romantic tradition, as one of the prevailing Romantic myths is the projection of a paradise (1984, 57).[3] This is an important point worth developing elsewhere. Without specifying what he has in mind, Ward remains dissatisfied with Clark's 'cheerfulness', insisting that Clark's poetry 'sidesteps' or even 'excludes' some matters, 'the sheer weight' of which is 'troublesome' (1984, 58) – as if expecting incorrectly or, what is worse, even demanding that poetry should address a number of mandatory issues.

Yet it is the phrase 'resolutely paradisal' that is of particular importance here. Clark himself mentions the function of the motif of paradise in his work, which constitutes a strong theme in his poetry.

In an interview with Glyn Pursglove, Clark cites Walter Benjamin's 'dialectics of happiness', which includes the hymnic and the elegiac – Paradise Lost and Paradise Regained or 'Glimpsed' – admitting that his poetry 'tends to oscillate between the two' (1977, 17).[4] This remark may be argued to constitute the key to Clark's practice for two reasons. The first, more direct explanation is that by referring to and employing various garden conventions, Clark attempts to construct 'a kind of Arcadia', as he puts it (Clark 1977, 16). The other explanation may be sought in the recurrent structure of delay and deferral which bodies forth the paradise-to-come in Clark's work. In further sections of this chapter, I shall demonstrate the extent to which these two features shape his practice. It is important for now, though, to highlight that the notion of paradise in Clark's poetry does not bear religious connotations but appears in secular form, bringing to mind Merleau-Ponty's concept of Wild Being, or the true, authentic being which is attainable only briefly. Clark evokes the world as a paradise that is elusive, merely glimpsed, and which constitutes a form of a personal Elysium. In the poet's own words, he believes in the concept of 'an earthly paradise', influenced by Ezra Pound's teleological approach to a life's work and attempt 'to write Paradise' (Notes for CXVII et seq./822, cit. Pryor 2011, 2), or to build one's work; this has exerted an influence on Clark's approach undoubtedly. Expanding this concept, Sean Pryor proposes a tantalising theory, defining poetry in terms of paradise. In Clark's practice, this aspect is significant, yet there strongly appears another one, which takes the form of a quest, embodied in the figure of St Brendan whose belief in finding paradise on Earth was formed during his indefatigable visitation of islands. In further sections of this chapter, I will address those direct references to St Brendan in Clark's poetry. Thus oscillating between 'making and finding' paradise,[5] Clark creates his practice.

In this chapter I argue that Clark's poetic practice relies on moving through the landscapes, in the process of which each element, each encounter and each glimpse are perceived as a gift. Resulting from the ambulatory immersion in the world, the poems emerge through openness and are marked by corporeal apprehension. Tracing some of the recurrent tropes in Clark's poetry such as the fold and the glade, I argue that what determines a large part of this practice is *aletheia*, or unconcealedness. I wish to extend and to some extent redirect the discussion[6] on the concepts of givenness in Clark's work, which represents truth-force through the process of opening the fold. The idea of openness is emphasised in certain aspects which performatively enact the unfolding. Considering the fold as a philosophical as well as structural concept, I examine the ways in which it reveals itself in the poems focused on minute objects as well as larger entities of the landscape. Part of the discussion is devoted to the significance of Gaelic place names found in the landscapes of the Highlands and Islands recurring in Clark's practice, which foreground the function of language in the polysemic experience of landscape, and which, in turn, enables an examination of the manner in which Clark's poetic practice becomes an expression of the resilience of Scottish landscapes.

A Poetic Methodology

Before discussing the ideas enumerated above, in order to place Clark's practice in a wider context it is important to address the inspirations, affinities and methodologies on which he draws and by which he is influenced. After his early fascination with the Beat Movement ('I used to write spontaneous prose in Kerouacian manner' [Clark 1993b, 97]), which functioned as an introduction to Zen, Clark became inspired by Ian Hamilton Finlay, in turn developing his own distinctive style. In arguing that the poem is not 'a spontaneous outpouring', Clark not only abandons the influence of the Beat writers but moves away from the Romantic idea of the extemporaneous arrival of poems. Instead, poetry appears as a result of 'very careful, small, meticulous making' (Clark 1993b, 97), a practice producing works created by elimination. Even more than the brevity, which 'feel[s] like confirmation of the innovations of concrete poetry', as Matthew Welton argues (2020, xiv), it is the focus on things as opposed to ideas or feelings that Clark's practice shares with concrete poets. Furthermore, the insistence on particularity confirms Clark's affinity with objectivism. Perceiving the poem as 'a thing made' (Clark 1993b, 97), he demonstrates affinities with objectivism and such poets as Louis Zukofsky, Charles Olson, Robert Creeley and Frank Samperi. In Zukosky's definition of objectivist poetics, a poem is an object relating to the world with clarity and sincerity, the features of which he describes in detail in the manifesto 'Program: "Objectivists"' and in 'Sincerity and Objectification: With Special Reference to the Work of Charles Reznikoff' (1931, 268–84), published in the 1931 issue of *Poetry*.[7] While the distinction between the two proposed features – clarity and sincerity – may not be entirely obvious, but are the essential requirements of objectification, writing as 'the detail, not mirage, of seeing' and 'thinking with the things as they exist' (1931, 273) constitute significant elements of this method. The poet remains attuned to the world, waiting for 'shapes' to 'suggest themselves', while 'the mind senses and receives awareness' (1931, 273). Things emerge from the surrounding world; they are not created by the poet whose mind perceives them in 'rested totality' (1931, 274), or objectification, in 'complete appreciation' (1931, 274) of things. 'Attention to detail revives the sense of scale' (Clark and Clark 2016), as we read in an untitled work composed of a card with bluebells. This approach brings to mind John Ruskin's celebrations of the natural world's beauty and, in particular, his claims that the close observation of the minutiae of the natural world could evoke the sublimities of vaster landscapes. Clark's practice demonstrates affinities with Ruskin, and not merely because of Clark's collection, *A Ruskin Sketchbook* (1979): attention to detail enables a close, authentic look at things, as '[t]hat preoccupation with the accuracy of detail in writing' (1931, 280) is what, according to Zukosky, constitutes sincerity.

This heightened awareness of things when consciousness reaches *towards* the world lies at the heart of Clark's practice. Cited in the title of this chapter, the poet's words reveal precisely that exploratory approach to poetry and the world: 'I tend to think of the poem as an heuristic device, a question you can ask of the world, or a patch pegged out for closer examination' (Clark and Tarbuck 2016, 36). Thus poetry functions as a practical method that enables the poet and the reader to find their way through the world by uncovering connections and discovering new things in the process of semiosis. Serving as an aid to discovery by experimental methods, it aims at the improvement of apprehension. Such an understanding of poetry emphasises its significance in the enquiry into the world, assuming experimentality as the main source of knowledge whereby, rather than declaring the truth, the poet poses questions. Such practice follows moments of heightened attention, which, according to Simone Weil, is a gift beginning with emptying one's mind and suspending thought in preparation for receiving it.[8] The reference to Weil is not accidental, since she is one of the thinkers who has exerted an influence on Clark's work.[9] Having read Weil in the early days of his practice, Clark has incorporated certain elements originating in her philosophy, including not only such concepts as the gift, generosity and grace but also, on a structural level, the practice itself, based on the sustained reiteration of particular terms.[10] These aspects of Clark's work will return in further discussion.

Among the aforementioned affinities between Clark and the objectivist poets, the strongest connection is probably with Lorine

Niedecker. Embodied in the combination of rootedness in the quotidian and formal experimentation, the influences of the minimalist ruralism of Niedecker's poetry may be found in Clark's practice with an overt tribute in *Wintergreen* (2004) which is dedicated to Niedecker.[11] As Gavin Goodwin notes, 'the fusion of folk and avant-garde traditions' (Goodwin 2019, n.p.) is shared by both poets. Following Rachel Blau DuPlessis's argument that Niedecker's choice of 'folk forms' demonstrates 'resistance' against 'class assumptions' (2004, 143), Goodwin suggests that Clark's move away from the page would 'enact a similar politically resonant fusion' (Goodwin 2019, n.p.). Arguably, this implicitly nullifies Ward's problematic assertion, above. Goodwin conjectures that, despite the placement of Clark's poetry in the context of the avant-garde, or, more particularly, the concrete poetry movement and the British poetry revival, it displays 'distinctly "commonplace"' features in terms of form and materials (Goodwin, 2019, n.p.). Yet, it should be emphasised that one does not exclude the other: innovative verse does not arise at the cost of ignoring the everyday, as has already been argued by a number of critics (see, e.g., Stafford 2010; Tarlo 2011; Willis 2008). In effect, the opposite may be observed: the tradition of the avant-garde engaging with the quotidian. Being 'always suspicious of the exceptional', Clark considers the commonplace 'an interesting concept' (Clark 1993b, 99). This statement may be combined with his voiced wariness of writers' exceptionalism. As he admits, 'I've always kept a distance from the idea that the writer is someone who knows or feels something special which is expressed in the writing' (Clark 1993b, 98). For Clark, the moment of real attention arrives from the outside, induced by being in the landscape, by things in the landscape.

The formalist aim of poetry to refresh language pervades Clark's practice, which favours de-habitualisation and defamiliarisation that in turn arrives through the attrition of routine. Among several quotations serving as mottos on the website of the Cairn Gallery (a space run by Thomas A Clark and Laurie Clark for minimalist and conceptual artists), there appear Viktor Shklovsky's words: 'making the stone stony'. It is worth placing the citation in context. Originating in 'Art as Device' (1917; also translated as 'Art as Technique') the phrase appears in the passage below:

> This is how life becomes nothing and disappears. Automatization eats things, clothes, furniture, your wife and the fear of war.
> 'If the whole complex life of many people is lived unconsciously, it is as if this life had never been.'

And so, what we call art exists in order to give back the sensation of life, in order to make us feel things, in order to make the stone stony. The goal of art is to create the sensation of seeing, and not merely recognizing, things; the device of art is the *ostranenie* of things and the complication of the form, which increases the duration and complexity of perception, as the process of perception is its own end in art and must be prolonged. Art is the means to live through the making of a thing; what has been made does not matter in art. (2017, 80)

The act of defamiliarisation enables and makes possible a refreshed perception of commonplace sites and things to which Clark returns in his practice. He achieves the 'ostranenie of things' through a number of devices such as minimalism and reiteration. I shall return to the latter in further parts of this chapter. The former device demonstrates itself in a direct, spare style which carries another aim. Behind 'the plain diction' of *Poor Poetry* (2016), 'a multiform work which is both a poem and a poetic methodology', there lies the refusal to draw attention to itself, or advertise its ornament and skilfulness:

a thin, inconspicuous poetry, persisting on the margins,
a neglected, threadbare, hedgerow school of poetry
light and resourceful, a common or poor poetry

a poetry without glory, using plain diction, withdrawn
from ambition, lacking in rhetorical skill, a spare poetry,
not given by the culture but passed from hand to hand.

Thus unadorned and modest, marginal, not flaunting decoration, poor poetry, marked by the absence of capital letters, democratises all words without prioritisation. Thus, in a direct manner, *Poor Poetry* enacts the declared methodology through its style and form. There is, however, another aspect of poetry making which is embraced by Clark. As he argues, 'by being . . . physically beautiful the poetry is quite self-effacing' (Clark 1993, 20). In the comment, which refers to Robert Louis Stevenson's *A Child's Garden of Verses*, a collection which has been an inspiration for his own work, Clark reveals the importance of beauty in his practice. I shall return to this point.

By aiming for compression, concision and exactitude, and focusing on verbal and formal condensation, Clark abandons the ornamental flourish characteristic of some ecopoems. Across his vast poetic practice there occurs variety as well as coherence, both thematic and structural, achieved through such devices as repetition and variation where the idea of recurrence forms a significant part. Recognising the importance of the sequence form in Clark's work, Harriet Tarlo suggests that landscape is explored in Clark's practice in two ways: through the manner in which space functions on the page and sounds beyond it (2011, 7–9). In the next section I will discuss the relation between poetic practice and landscape from which Clark's practice stems.

Clark returns to the same images – path, glade, sea – relying on sustained repetition with minimal changes. This includes different versions of the same work, as the incremental nature of Clark's poetry is emphasised by serial publications. The function of permutations, both within individual poems and the whole work, creates an incremental effect. Reiteration of the same words and images unravels meaning through repetition. What Clark calls 'this unfolding nature of language' (Clark 1977, 17) reverberates both in his self-enclosed, brief poems and the sequence poems linked with returning concepts and images, thereby constructing a coherent body of work. Many poems discussed in this chapter such as *By Kilbrannan Sound* (2012/2020c) and *An Lochan Uaine* (1993a/2008) are structured around permutations where the repetitive pattern rises incrementally through the addition of minimal changes in every line or stanza, a technique resulting in the engendering of a heightened awareness of things. As a result of the iteration of certain words, language gains an incantatory power, at times assuming a form of a secular litany or a rosary, the cumulative effect of which is haunting.

At this point it is necessary to highlight the importance of the formal aspects of Clark's practice, its total fusion of form and content. Clark's sustained interest in form results in the exploration of the potential of spaces beyond the conventionally perceived page, including poems on postcards, tote bags, bookmarks, stickers, kites and other 'poem objects'. Thanks to the placement of poetry in the public sphere, Clark enables it to enter 'the ordinary, everyday world, taking part in the occasion', as he writes about the 'standing poem' (Clark 2011, n.p.). Moved into the open, poetry 'sits quietly within the situation, making a difference, suggesting another possibility' (Clark 2011, n.p.). The verb 'sit' is a curious choice, returning in the above quotation. In the already cited 1977 interview, Clark employs the verb in reference to the poem-cards that 'sit there' just like flowers (Clark 1977, 15). It is noticeable that the poetry does not *do* anything but 'sits quietly'; it remains in place and this suffices to create a difference. The approach demonstrates defiance and protest against a self-advertising culture while raising awareness of ecological matters, with which his work has become increasingly concerned. Clark's practice explores the potential of concrete poetry, according to the classic definition proposed by Mary Ellen Solt, which determines that 'linguistic materials [are placed] in a new relationship to space'.[12] Frequently, a poem presents an image, engaging the space of the page or the spaces beyond and around it. Poems function as 'objects that have a life of their own in the world', as Clark puts it (Clark 1993b, 98). A single poem may become a portable object which, instead of forming part of a collection among other poems, enclosed between book covers and placed on a bookshelf, may be displayed on tables, dressers and windowsills. Thus it may serve as an ornamental object similar to those objects placed on nineteenth-century mantelpieces. The poem offers 'words for the mantlepiece',[13] making a presence that extends outside a book placed on a shelf. Clark thus effects a deconstruction of the usual binarisms associated with publications, such as text/context or text/*hors-texte*, inside/outside.

Described by Peter Riley as 'non-expository' (2010, 56), Clark's poetry presses the idea of modalities without representation, whereby the presentation of a landscape or a thing does not aim at re-presentation. By extending an invitation to a participatory presence – 'the literal presence of the viewer' as a result of 'a literal presence in the space' (Bishop 2005, 6) – Clark's poetry shares certain features with installation art as it escapes the flat surface of the printed page. What is more, it presupposes a form, or the manifestation of an embodiment and, with that, assumes the bodily participation of the reader who is not a disembodied viewing subject but a corporeally engaged self. The reader's involvement is invited through the recurrent device of the second person, appealing directly to active engagement, that second performing a summoning in an incantatory sense. The vocative case in Clark's poetry constitutes one of the persistent features. As Harriet Tarlo aptly notes, it 'leads or invites us into a very different response to the rapacity and ubiquity of humanity', offering a possibility to 'carve out a quiet space for an unobtrusive human presence in nature and [to] trace delicate shifts in experience' (2011, 17). This quality combines with the formal restraint of the poems discussed below.

Walking the Landscape

Landscape constitutes an overarching theme in Clark's practice. His performative writing – the terse, polished poems, interventions in the landscape and site-specific works that 'enact' or 'perform' the world rather than merely describing it – traces phenomenologically the line of the land, resulting in the intertwining of language and landscape, appropriately summed up in Gertrude Stein's phrase 'grammar and heather'.[14] Marking the importance of landscape in his work is *A Box of Landscapes* issued in 2010, 2016 and 2021 comprising a selection of Thomas A Clark and Laurie Clark's publications, the contents of the box changing in each edition, according to which works are published, each edition having ten copies. This is a poetry that demonstrates the fundamental need for 'local attachments', to use Fiona Stafford's term.[15] Apart from several poems,[16] most of Clark's practice encompasses the British Isles, more specifically Scotland, particularly the Scottish Highlands and Islands which he revisits. In such works as *One Hundred Scottish Places* (2021) as well as many others, Clark returns repeatedly to familiar landscapes, drawing inspiration from places in the Highlands and Islands, the poems arising from his walks. These are 'landscapes of great clarity and resilience', as he states, characterised by 'a surprising gentleness'. To cite the passage in its entirety:

> These are landscapes of great clarity and resilience; they often have a surprising gentleness – all qualities that I want to percolate into the poetry. But this is not where I live. I live on the east coast, above Edinburgh. So I'm always at some distance from the landscapes I write about. No doubt this distance sharpens desire. I always want to head out into the Highlands. Somehow I feel more relaxed there than anywhere else. I seem to be more responsive and resourceful than anywhere else. It's as if a whole set of cultural accretions has fallen away, or more likely, blown away. And this is one sense of *The Threadbare Coat*, the title of this new book from Carcanet Press. It's an image of poverty and exposure, as if there could be only the lightest membrane between you and the landscape. (Clark 2020a)

Clark's ambulatory practice expresses the tension between distance and desire as the recurrence of certain words throughout single poems and across the whole body of work, which creates an incantatory effect, iteration summoning the familiar places in an evocation of longing. The poems and essays, emerging from his 'daily practice of the short walk', allows Clark to place them within the tradition of 'the walking essays', including such peripatetic writers and thinkers as William Hazlitt, Robert Louis Stevenson and Henry David Thoreau (Finlay 2000, 11). Probably Clark's most frequently reprinted work,[17] *In Praise of Walking*, composed of a series of statements, assumes the form of a manifesto and 'has come to stand as something of a credo', as Finlay suggests (2000, 11). As Anne Mœglin-Delcroix writes, 'a personal practice . . . a deliberate way of being-in-the-world rather than before it. The walking body is the touchstone of this, because walking compels one to supersede the limits of a purely visual experience of nature to become the experience of the whole artist, with his body, in nature' (2015, 6).

Enmeshed in the meteorological phenomena, apprehending place through the senses, walking represents an intimate manner of responding to the world. More than merely hyperborean wanderlust, walking in Clark's work is a stylistic device.[18] In an early poem, *sea hand land foot* (n.d.), comprising a small booklet with the drawings by Nanette Godfrey, a line, a hand and a foot appear interchangeably on several narrow, horizontal pages. The undulating lines create visual metaphors foregrounding the connection between the lines of the landscape, the foot of a walker, and the hand of the poet and artist. When considering art in the landscape, Clark supports a minimalist intervention ethic, suggesting that 'the work should intrude as little as possible into its environment' (Clark 2014a, n.p.). As Clark comments, this rule is no longer observed by artists even though they claim to produce art 'which flaunts its "green" credentials'. Such art often does not respect the surrounding natural world, being interested instead with attracting attention to its own making. As Clark tells us, 'An art that persuades people to turn their backs on the landscape in order to admire the art cannot claim to be ecologically friendly' (Clark 2014a, n.p.). An 'occasional' placement of art in the landscape may only be accepted with the aim to reorient focus onto the location in which it is situated, Clark insists. In this manner, a poem may function as a signpost, or 'a patch pegged out for closer examination', functioning as 'an heuristic device', an inquiry into the world. Clark does not stop at art placed in the landscape, extending the comment to prose and poetry which, while pretending to be concerned with the surrounding world, focus instead on themselves, displaying 'the same self-centredness'. As he insists, art should not 'draw attention to itself', but rather 'redirect attention away from itself back onto its surroundings' (Clark 2014a, n.p.). Paying homage to the landscape cannot be a pretext for demonstrating the author's talent, skill or sensibility.

Poetry (and prose, especially one that deems itself 'nature writing' for that matter) that flaunts its own artifice and beauty does not celebrate the landscape but itself. Writing, says Clark, should serve as 'an exploratory device' (Clark 2014a, n.p.). As he concludes, '[j]ust as the use of natural materials is no guarantee that art will be environmentally sensitive, so references to the natural world are not enough to qualify prose or poetry as a form of "pastoral"' (Clark 2014a, n.p.). Following a truly ecological practice and 'an ethic of minimal intervention', rather than simply planting poems in the landscape, Clark *retrieves* them from the world in a process of placing emphasis on the environment.

One of the aspects of Clark's poetry highlighted by critics is, as I have suggested above, marginality (cf. Goodwin 2019). For Clark, maintaining a peripheral position and remaining at the wayside constitutes a political gesture of non-involvement. Considering Riley's suggestion that Clark's poetry is 'apparently unpolitical' (2010, 56), the word 'apparently' should be stressed. While he remains on the peripheries of any poetic or ecological mainstream, there should be no mistake that Clark engages in current debates, employing particular means, at times indirectly addressing the changing socio-ecological nexus. The early decision to focus on wildflowers is a form of political act, demonstrating appreciation for the inconspicuous, the marginal, the frequently ignored or overlooked. In recent years, following the rapidly unfolding environmental crisis, his politics have become bolder and he has become more outspoken on the problem, demonstrating an urgency to draw attention to such matters as species extinction. Clark's work has been discussed in the context of wellbeing, a concept which has gained some traction in recent times,[19] yet it is worth noting that his practice transcends matters of the condition of personal health or self-interest. By posing a question 'Can there be a poetry that is not yet another humanism?', Clark points to wider, non-anthropocentric concerns which ought to be considered. According to him, the major ecological concern of poetry, is 'not to write about birds or flowers, or the quality of air', but 'to care for words and their relations', considering the 'impact' of language on the environment (Clark 2020a). Confronted with disappearing landscapes, Clark engages in the ongoing debates regarding ecological concerns. In the past few years he has created a series of works which demonstrate involvement in the debate on the climate emergency.

Longing for the closeness of the natural world and an eschewal of distance, both of which characterise pastoralism, has occurred in a recreated form in Clark's work since the earliest publications, such as 'Pastoral' in *BO HEEM E UM* (1968). Writing about *Twenty Poems*, Geoffrey Ward points out that the tone indicates that 'pastoral charm may be gently mocking itself' (1984, 57). The poetic dialogue between Hamilton Finlay and Clark is sustained throughout the years; unsurprisingly, Clark's essay in *Wood Notes Wild: Essays on the Poetry and Art of Ian Hamilton Finlay* (1995) concerns the pastoral tradition. Finally, *Folding the Last Sheep* (2016) alludes to the work of an English nineteenth-century painter, Samuel Palmer, and also to Ian Hamilton Finlay's *Eclogue*, which Ross Hair perceives as 'pastoral continuum' (Hair 2017, 195; see also the discussion in Berridge 2004–5).[20] Pastoral and georgic elements present in Clark's practice increasingly concern the threat of loss, the fear that the harmony of the past can no longer return. The sense of melancholy at the loss of landscapes manifests itself through the awareness of its disappearing elements, most notably bird species which co-create erstwhile familiar aural landscapes. In August 2014, as part of the Edinburgh International Book Festival, a corncrake was heard in Charlotte Square in the evenings for the first time since the beginning of the nineteenth century when the city underwent a dramatic change. Where the New Town now stands there were fields and meadows. In *A corncrake in Charlotte Square*, Clark refers to Henry Cockburn's *Memorials of His Time* (1856), citing the following words: 'I have stood in Queen-street, or the opening at the northwest corner of Charlotte Square, and listened to the ceaseless rural corn-craiks, nestling happily in the dewy grass' (Cockburn 1856, 380) (2014b, n.p.).[21] The passage which precedes these words is worth citing here:

> It was then an open field of as green turf as Scotland could boast of, with a few respectable trees on the flat, and thickly wooded on the bank along the Water of Leith. Moray Place and Ainslie Place stand there now. It was the beginning of a sad change, as we then felt. That well-kept and almost evergreen field was the most beautiful piece of ground in immediate connection with the town, and led the eye agreeably over to our distant northern scenery. How glorious the prospect, on a summer evening, from Queenstreet! We had got into the habit of believing that the mere charm of the ground to us would keep it sacred, and were inclined to cling to our conviction even after we saw the foundations digging. We then thought with despair of our lost verdure, our banished peacefulness, our gorgeous sunsets. But it was unavoidable. (Cockburn 1856, 379)

The elegiac tone detected in the passage above – grieving beyond the human world – marks an example of solastalgia, a concept coined by Glenn Albrecht (see also his discussion in 'Solastalgia and the New Mourning' in *Mourning Nature: Hope at the Heart of Ecological Loss*, edited by Ashlee Cunsolo and Karen Landman), an elegiac expression and reaction to those landscapes damaged beyond repair. While for Cockburn the disruption was caused by rapid urban expansion during his lifetime, for the English poet John Clare it is the work and effect of successive Enclosure Acts. Mentioned by Kathleen Jamie in her essay 'Crex Crex', John Clare calls the corncrake, or 'the landrail' 'a sort of living doubt' (Clare 2007, 45). The corncrake has come to symbolise the rupture of continuity, as previously familiar landscapes disappear, transformed as a result of rapacious development. Shy and elusive, the corncrake has been driven to near extinction and now:

> if you were to listen
> from dawn to dusk
> you would not hear it.[22]

As an installation, A corncrake in Charlotte Square was a non-textual work placed in a public place, a sonic reminder of the loss of landscapes. A number of Clark's works which are printed on cards and car stickers thus becoming introduced into shared space and assume the form of slogans that draw attention to the disappearance of species. In this manner, through the appearance of bird names, lost rural sites infiltrate urbanscapes. Through the syntactic structure, the car sticker *before the traffic, the corncrake* (2021a) foregrounds the corncrake, highlighting the primacy of place that it should be granted. It brings to mind the argument posited by Jacques Derrida (2008, passim) that humans follow other animals: as non-human animals lead, we follow them in a reversal of anthropocentric self-importance.

As Clark reminds us, 'Whether we remember it or not, human life is dependent upon the non-human. I think it is imperative that we get to know this, physically, for ourselves' (Clark 1993b, 102). Apart from the corncrake, other birds recurring in Clark's practice include the plover, the curlew and the ptarmigan (see, e.g., *One Hundred Scottish Places* [2021b] and *wing of the ptarmigan: forty eight delays* [2018]). Preferring cold regions, the ptarmigan inhabits Arctic–alpine habitats and is exclusively found in the highest mountains of the Scottish Highlands. Historically widespread in the Southern Uplands and the English Lake District, it became extinct from these regions at the end of the eighteenth and the beginning of the nineteenth century. Now found only in the mountains of the Scottish Highlands where a sharp decline in its numbers may be observed in the past few decades, it is considered under threat of extinction. A shy bird, sensitive to disturbance, climate change, overgrazing and overharvesting, it is nevertheless still described as a gamebird ('The Ptarmigan'). One of the other threatened species, the curlew, appears in a folding poem published in 2020; printed on mud-coloured paper and featuring an illustration of a curlew, the poem contains the following lines:

> a shore is lonely
> with a curlew
>
> a shore is lonelier
> without a curlew

The lines point to the poet's connection with the local landscape of coastal Scotland, which he walks daily. Yet, as with most of Clark's poems, the voice behind the words does not attract attention to itself, but draws the reader into this scene of absence. With its characteristically high-pitched call, the curlew – a wading bird heard and seen on grasslands, moorlands, coasts, farmlands and heaths – winters around the coast on mudflats and marshes, landscapes which are becoming increasingly sparse. Encroaching on habitats and drying wetlands the disappearance of these birds accelerates, causing the continuity of landscapes to become ruptured as disrupted is the existence of these shorebirds, which have been part of the place for many centuries. The curlew is mentioned in one of the earliest extant works in the English language, the Old English elegy *The Seafarer*, the speaker of which confesses, 'I take my gladness in the . . . sound of the Curlew instead of the laughter of men.' The inextricability of Scottish landscapes with other avian species is underlined in the following brief poem by Clark:

> for what is the sea without an eagle
> for what is the wood without a warbler
> for what is the corn without a bunting
> for what is the house without a sparrow
> for what is the snow without a petrel

Drawing attention to the welfare of other species, Clark created a work titled *Curlew Lapwing Plover Whimbrel* (2021c). On a rectangular green card the following acronym printed in large black letters is the following text:

CLPW
RIGHTS

A comment below the poem published on the author's blog demonstrates the poet's unequivocal position on the matter: 'For thinking to be truly green, ethical concern must be extended beyond human interest' (Clark 2021e, n.p.). By employing a convention of human rights activism only to subvert it, Clark draws attention to the rights of animal species beyond the human. In a similar vein, three posters created by the poet for the UN Climate Summit (COP 26) which took place in Glasgow in November 2021 feature a related text: 'has anybody here / seen my old friend / curlew', 'has anybody here / seen my old friend / lapwing', 'has anybody here / seen my old friend / skylark'. The acknowledgements to Marvin Gaye indicate the rephrased source of the line, namely his civil rights song from 1969 about the assassination of civil rights leaders 'Abraham, Martin and John'.[23] The lines from the lyrics 'Can you tell me where he's gone' and 'I just looked around and he was gone' emphasise the absence. Similar posters with three different birds – eagle, plover and shrike – were installed at the Amtrak station in Hudson, New York State. The reference to the civil rights message emphasises the importance of artistic engagement, redirecting focus onto non-anthropocentric areas which have been, and still are, omitted and ignored, but which gained special urgency in the first decades of the twenty-first century. In this manner, Clark shifts focus from the anthropocentric debates around climate emergency, indicating that many other species have been affected by the crisis.

The consequences of the anthropogenic activity haunt a number of recent poems. Clark's increasing involvement in ecological matters is demonstrated, for instance, in his print *to redress the loss of the seagrass meadows* (2021d), published by Essence Press, a press run by Julie Johnstone, with part of the sales donated to the Seagrass Ocean Rescue project. The title 'Do You Know the Land' (2020, 156–9; originally published in 2019 as a separate book with Laurie Clark's drawing on the cover) alludes to a poem by Johann Wolfgang von Goethe, 'Kennst du das land?' (1795), which evokes a dream of the south with lemon trees, oranges, myrtle and laurel. Clark's poem reverses the geographical tropes and focuses on the north, 'a greyer, more sober beauty'.[24] In the poem composed of twelve tercets – the stanzas small and compact on the page – the first three stanzas lead towards the main motif of the poem through references to mist, wool and cloud, only to reveal it as bog cotton in line 9. The poem thus enacts the structure analogous to the plant. Another plant mentioned in the poem that opens onto the landscape is sundew, appearing in stanza 12. It is common in Scotland and can be found on peaty moors and bog pools, engulfing near insects by curling inwards. Yet, central to the poem is bog cotton, 'a conspicuous plant / of wet moorland / of bog and bog pools' (ll. 10–12), the lines evoking inflorescences which appear in the tufted growth: 'the cotton grass way / is to hover over / the information' (ll. 28–30). Two stanzas – stanzas 4 and 5 – are of a descriptive nature, offering exposition of the plant's physical characteristics. Appearing in the northern hemisphere, its distribution requires wetland habitats, places eradicated in certain parts of the British Isles in the process of land reclamation. Similar to the plover, bog cotton has been disappearing from the landscape due to the loss of wetland habitats. Intensive use of the land has largely depleted organic carbon stored in the soil. The poem may be read with the awareness gained in the past few decades of the usefulness of carbon sinks, which lower the concentration of carbon dioxide. A response to Goethe's lemon trees and laurel, bog cotton and sundew reveal the fragility of the northern landscapes. A sense of solastalgia returns in poems such as *Two Evergreen Horizons* (n.d.), evoking the depletion of the Scottish landscape. Composed of two pages with an illustration of rows of trees appear on each one, followed by the lines 'Neat Norwegian Horizon / Spruce' and 'Sad Scotch Horizon / Pine'. The alliteration underlines the choice of the adjectives, contrasting the tidiness of the Scandinavian horizon with the depleted Scottish landscape, which emphasises the melancholy of the latter.

Some Particulars

In 2020, following three previous collections by Thomas A Clark – *The Hundred Thousand Places* (2009), *Yellow & Blue* (2014c) and *Farm by the Shore* (2017a) – Carcanet published *The Threadbare Coat: New and Selected Poems*. While offering a good introduction to Clark's poetry, they are far from representative of the full array of his practice in which form is inextricably bound with content, text coupled with image. Published by Moschatel Press, the poems typically present themselves as small, handsewn objects, illustrated by Laurie Clark, the hues of paper on which they are printed, all of which carry meaning. The presentation enhances the overall message, entwining form with content. Continuing the form of the standing poem devised by Ian Hamilton Finlay whereby the text appears on the front of a folded card, Clark places emphasis on the spatiality of poetry, its placement among other things in the world enhancing the intimate envelopment in the world and the particularity of place. According to Matthew Welton, one of the characteristics of the use of nouns by Clark is their generic nature: 'The paths could be any paths, the meadows could be any meadows. If you tried to use this book as a map you couldn't be certain of where it would get you' (2020, xii). While it may be true for such poems as 'Of many waters', 'A walk in a water meadow' or 'At dusk and at dawn', in a number of poems the use of nouns includes species of birds such as the grey plover and plants specific to a particular region. Welton's claim that there is concreteness without specificity omits a considerable number of indicators in the poems which place them specifically in the northern hemisphere, in particular regions of the British Isles. Even though, as Welton claims, some nouns employed by Clark could be 'generic' (2020, 14), it should be stressed that Clark's practice is firmly embedded in the landscape, with Scottish place names and pointers to the regional flora and fauna recurring with regularity. These are names of plants and birds characteristic of the territory such as the ptarmigan, the curlew and the corncrake, discussed above. More general lexis also delineates the setting as, in many poems nouns serve both as topographical and linguistic indicators. For instance, 'lochan' (l. 2) and 'machair' (l. 11) in *Lullaby* (2018; 2020c, 164–5), or 'loch' in 'Nine paces' (2020c, 113–20), to mention just a few. What is more, even if there is no other indication, place names situate the poems firmly, locating them in the specifics of the land. Specificity appears in toponymic and topographical references, including a number of Gaelic titles which point directly to place names, to which I will return.

In Clark's practice the concept of particularity occupies an important place. Celebrating the *is-ness* of objects in their individuality and multiplicity, the predilection for particulars is associated with the poet's attempt to find form 'in the meadow of language' (Clark 1977, 13).[25] In an archaic sense, particular is a separate part of a whole – Latin *particula*, or a small part – an individual item contrasted with a universal quality. Focusing on individual features and distinguishing one thing from another, particularity belongs to Clark's repertoire of tropes which involve the emphasis on small things, the concreteness of language, a limited number of words circulating around and throughout various poems. William Blake comes to mind with an exhortation to 'labour well the minute particulars' and 'attend to the Little Ones'.[26] Blake perceives the small things with a reverence that manifests itself in the phrase 'Holiness of Minute Particulars'. As has been mentioned above, a slight and apparent religious bias reveals itself in some of Clark's poems, made manifest in the use of certain words such as 'affliction', discussed by such critics as John Freeman, as well as in the employment of some forms which share characteristics with such religious forms as the idea of litany. Focusing on the elusiveness of the real, Freeman unequivocally associates the manner in which Clark employs the notion of paradise with religion. For Freeman, even the phrase 'it is' in Clark's poetry 'is in a particular sense religious' (Freeman 1987, 8). While it may be true about the poem discussed by Freeman, it should be noted that Clark's work is not religious poetry in the strict sense.[27] Never explicit, however, these references appear as very distant echoes, as Clark retrieves these words and forms, endowing them with non-religious meanings. For instance, while for some the concept of grace may be inextricably bound with religion, in Clark's practice grace becomes secularised, carrying the meaning of giving thanks or praise, and the sense of beauty, which is combined with an expression of the search for a new kind of poetry resembling a quest for earthly paradise. Thus the phrase 'it is' discussed by Freeman may be argued to belong to a broader, ontological response to the world of things and beings. As Simon Critchley argues in his discussion of Wallace Stevens's poetry: 'things merely are.' In this manner, noticing the minute particulars constitutes the labour of perception of individual things. The poems arise from the close observation of the surrounding world whereby attention is a form of reverence to the singularity of things and their physical properties, the openness of the poet receiving things as they are, employing the energy and power of each word (Zukofsky 1931, 275). Through the demonstrated reverence, which does not originate in any religious system, instead of gesturing towards some transcendental realm the poems focus on things as they are. The expression of respect and praise emphasises the quality of secular grace that fills Clark's practice, the manner in which he articulates beauty in his practice being an expression of quotidian sacramentality. If anything, the poetry is pantheistic, evoking a world composed of irreducible distinct things in their infinite essence, where all is one substance, including the mind. Sharing attributes with the surrounding, the mind intertwines with the landscape suffused with noumenal particles.

Such 'minutely organized Particulars' appear in *Some Particulars* (Jargon Society 1971), an early poem the main section of which originated from found poems on flowers called 'anthology', a word which, as well as being a collection of poems, means 'a collection of flowers, a garland' (Clark 1977, 12), drawing inspiration from 'books on botany, Samuel Palmer, language primers, everything under the sun really' (Clark 1977, 12). From the exploration of theme Clark moves to form itself whereby 'poems that could *be* like flowers themselves' (Clark 1977, 12). In *An Affinity of Eye and Petal* (n.d.) the words appear underneath a drawing of an iris. The interplay of text and image highlights the polysemy of the unspoken yet divined word, which designates the flower and part of an eye. The riddle-like, minimal poem suggests or intimates the intertwining between the seer and the seen. Originating from *affinis*, composed of the particle *ad-*, meaning 'to', and a form of the noun *finis*, meaning 'a border' or 'a boundary', affinity suggests adjoining or adjacent elements. The affinity of the two irises – the eye and the flower – not only relies on their homonymous relationship but their closeness, or even touch, which David Macauley names 'caressing complicity' (2009, 234). The body constitutes a membrane, the formative organ between corporeal self and the world, part of the tactile landscape that it explores: to touch the world is to experience being touched by it, in an intimate reciprocity. Responsible for the amount of light that reaches the retina, the iris invites the form and colour of the flower, a reminder of the tactile properties of light. As light touches the iris at the front of the eye, the world becomes palpable. The act of brushing with its texture is described by Maurice Merleau-Ponty: 'Things attract my look, my gaze caresses . . . things, it exposes their contours and their reliefs, between it and them we catch sight of a complicity' (1968, 76). Thus Clark's 'quiet immediacy' (Finlay 2000, 11) arrives in moments of analogical apperception when the caressing gaze initiates affinity with things as consciousness – which exists towards something, not in isolation – extends to reach another object.

Focusing on particular flowers, the poet invites the reader to direct their gaze down at some inconspicuous plants growing on verges but also up, as he leads towards the horizon glimpsed from the garden. A measured 'overloading of floral imagery' (Clark 1977, 18), which the poetry of Clark shares with that of William Shenstone, fulfils the concept of 'the landscape garden' (Clark 1977, 17), an evocation of paradise whereby names serve as a place to explore the possibilities of language. Rather than using formal scientific nomenclature, Clark invariably chooses common names that demonstrate the close affinity between the land and the people who inhabit it through the centuries, coexisting with the environment. The intertwining of flora, fauna, land and language lies at the basis of many poems. Some of these old names are illustrative, based on analogies with the animal world, referring to some physical properties, as for instance in *Hart's Tongue* (n.d.):

Hart's Tongue

— a green speech
out of grey stone

An evergreen fern, Hart's tongue prefers shady places; it is hardy, and may grow on stone walls. Found clinging to cracks in rocks, sheltered locations, among boulders, between trees, it is 'named after the frond's similarity in shape to a deer's tongue'. The tongue-shaped leaves comprise an 'ancient-woodland-indicator plant[;] if found in woodland it suggests a rare habitat' ('Hart's tongue fern' n.d.). Its name stemming from folklore, Hart's tongue suggests intimate connections with the closely observed land. Similarly, the proverb form employed by Clark relates to folk literature originating from close observations of land and weather. A genre of folklore, proverbs originate in such intimate knowledge, suggestive of a life lived in close proximity to the land, in sync with seasonal rhythms. The short, usually rhymed and repetitive structure functions as a mnemotechnic device to dissipate wisdom passed down from generation to generation in the oral form, but also published in rural calendars characterised by metaphorical and/or formulaic language. Country proverbs embedded in the local place preserve archaic lexical items which remain after the referents have disappeared. Clark employs the form only to subvert it, as, for instance, in *Proverbs of the Meadow and the Mountain* (1986) and *Twelve Proverbs* (2001).[28] While formally similar – simple and pithy – they are marked by heightened literariness. Originating in the former work, the lines 'the hours are thistle-down / the days are swallows' (1986, n.p.) follow the construction based on parallel phrases common in proverbs, yet the similes elude the accessible style characteristic of most proverbs. Another proverb, 'vowels and consonants / clear water over pebbles' (1986, n.p.), comprises a declarative sentence based on an analogy, typical for the form, but semantically resembling a Zen kōan. Creating a similar effect as the running stream, the sonic particles of the language make the impression that the landscape is filled with speech.

The small-scale and particular combine with the landscape; they arise from it. Gazing down suggests respect and care in the act of giving attention to the smallest and seemingly insignificant particulars. In this, Clark shares the celebration of the small-scale with

Norman MacCaig. A jay feather found on a walk may bring relish, as *In small things, / delight is intense* (Clark and Clark 2010). Such tiny objects beckon to be noticed, offering themselves as 'gifts of meaning' (Clark 1977, 14), giving themselves to the perceiver, who becomes a witness to the presence of birds and plants. A bluebell offers itself and should be accepted unreservedly, as if to counter the observation that *Suspicion of beauty / is the new Puritanism* (Clark and Clark 2011). The givenness of the world relies on beauty which surpasses any teleological purpose for *a gift of wild flowers / is the gift of a gift* (Clark and Clark 2011).²⁹ The objects in the world are perceived as 'the miracle of expression' discovered by our gaze, 'prompted by the experience of our own body' (Merleau-Ponty 2002, 230). As Clark says about Robert Louis Stevenson's *A Child's Garden of Verses*, a collection which has been an inspiration for his own work, 'by being . . . physically beautiful the poetry is quite self-effacing' (Pursglove 1993, 20).

In some poems verbal minimalism yields to abstraction, as colour replaces text. Clark's botanical poems integrate the form of word and image, engaging in a dialogue between the two as one responds to the other. This intertwining is fulfilled formally through the design of folding cards which, almost invariably, offer text which relates, or responds to, an image on the front, as is the case with the poems above. At times, this practice is subverted; as, for instance, in *After Marvell* (1980), where the title appears on the cover, revealing cards in several shades of green. Even though Clark's poem operates through nonverbal means, the reference to Andrew Marvell in the title leads the reader to his poem titled 'The Garden' (1681), thus echoing the poet's evocation of the world within a world (for a discussion of the poem, see the essays by John Freeman, Robert Stacey and Ian Green in *Candid Fields*; see also Berridge 2004–5). In a later version of the poem with a slightly changed title, *After Andrew Marvell* (2015), the reader is presented with a foldable card containing a drawing of five rectangles in various shades of green. Rather than aiming at representation, these poems create associations, inviting the readers to make meanings for themselves. The removal of the verbal medium and its replacement with colour challenges the tendency to read the world through conventional language. Through the randomness of the loose cards, the poet relinquishes authorial control in favour of contingency and readerly choice. As opposed to literary texts that exert representational control, Clark's poems concern themselves with ways to eschew, or at least divert, representation. Demonstrating affinities with the concrete tradition, Clark's poems lack punctuation and capitalisation, a gesture which erases the difference between words, abandons arbitrariness and democratises relations. The lack of punctuation gives a freedom to the reader in terms of emphasis and liberates meaning, allowing them to walk through poetry lines, through a book, not rushing, letting them decide. The haphazardness of encounters on a walk and of things perceived while walking is evoked through permutational poems whereby the reader receives a random choice of cards which may be shuffled, their order changed. The chance element involves the limited number of possibilities.

Redolent of Mallarmé's poem 'Un coup de dés jamais n'abolira le hasard' (1897), the aleatory element constitutes a highly important aspect of Clark's practice as the composition left to chance and the reading experience thus resemble a walk which depends on chance encounters. The radically open form of the poems allows the reader to determine the order of pages, resembling the experiments of the French authors forming Oulipo such as Raymond Queneau and Jacques Roubaud, or the English author B. S. Johnson's novel-in-a-box, *The Unfortunates* (1969). This freedom appears in the abundance of blank space around the lines, which allows for moments of pause, and equally, by the eschewing of language that might exert representational control, leaves meaning to the determination of the reader. *A delphinium border* (1981) contains five sheets of card of various colours in a blue folder. At the bottom of each card one word is printed: 'purity', 'harmony', 'sentinel', 'fidelity', 'destiny', alluding to and challenging the tradition of floriography. Through the association of colours and virtues and the employment of the convention of the language of flowers, Clark indicates the arbitrariness of the convention which attributes meaning to plants, and which, in turn, anthropomorphises them and subjugates them to human purposes.

While the tactics of the avoidance of language by endowing things with symbolism offers an escape from the representative mode, doubtless representational or mimetic language cannot be eschewed completely. Instead of imposing symbols only to supersede them, Clark demonstrates that the names of flowers and plants themselves are sufficient as they pull us towards the things themselves. In this manner, the poems remain devoted to the evocation of their presence or particular – perceived, not imposed – features. Recurrent colours such as blue and yellow, a pair of complementary colours, when combined, make green. A poet of spare verse, Clark revels in the textures of vowels and consonants. In *yarrow & marram grass* (2021), where the visual aspect of language prevails with the double 'r', 'm' and 'w', the consonantal rhythms become highlighted by the visual presentation: the double 'r' is placed in the middle of the first two nouns, while the 'w' is mirrored in the 'm'. Then there is the sound orchestration in the echoing of 'r' in all three words, which ties them together even more strongly, and the labiovelar 'w' prolonged in the doubling of the labial 'm'. The choice of colour makes the distribution of the vowels appear in between the consonants. The visual aspect is the primary sense in the poem, the isolation of each noun creating a visual image in a semantic play. The presentation on the wall of visual patterns, as in a painting, constitute 'a poem playing with visual and vocal and semantic elements. That the vowels are distributed among the consonants, as two flowers or colours might mingle on a beach, is the metaphor.'[30] A flowering, perennial plant, yarrow grows in grasslands and open forests, attracts pollinating insects, is a source of food for them, and is used in traditional medicine for a wide range of ailments; it is widely distributed, from sea level to alpine areas, in a variety of habitats. Present in folklore, marram grass is found on coastal sand dunes. The poem combines the landscapes, extending from the coast inland. Thus the multiplicity of the smallest elements of the landscape, as the individual letters in a language, is brought to the fore. Various grasses appear in *Adjectives for Grasses* (1980) and in a more recent poem, *a promise of happiness* (Clark and Clark 2021a). The latter is composed of a list of sixteen types of grasses combined in four quatrains, their names accompanied with adjectives such as 'sweet', 'slender', 'perennial' or 'pendulous'. Together with the title, the poem structure evokes Eden, the symmetry suggestive of divine harmony. In these poems the speaking I is withdrawn in a gesture of self-effacement not dissimilar to Kathleen Jamie's, as both authors attempt to avoid placing a heavy filter on the landscape through the withdrawal of the authorial voice.

In another poem, *Bindweed Stitchwort Knotgrass* (2017b), the text is composed of a white card which bears the lines printed in green italics:

> *bindweed*
> *stitchwort*
> *knotgrass*

Centrally placed, the strong, two-syllable nouns and their trochaic rhythm impose a presence on the page and in the ear. The three words designate plants typical of uncultivated ground and to be found on border paths, widely distributed in the temperate and boreal regions, accompanying walks. Bindweed is widespread along paths, roadside verges and in uncultivated areas. While the Royal Horticultural Society deems bindweed 'troublesome for gardeners', the RHS also indicates its nutritional properties, providing pollen for bees and leaves for the larvae of convolvulus hawk moth ('Bindweed' n.d.). Lesser stitchwort grows on meadows, along hedgerows and grassy banks, and may be encountered in open woodland. 'Greater stitchwort is visited by bees, butterflies and hoverflies looking for spring nectar, and is the foodplant of the marsh pug, plain clary and yellow underwing moths' ('Greater Stitchwort' n.d.). A type of dock, knotgrass may be found along the seashore, on fields and waste ground. 'Common knotgrass can be used to make dyes of indigo, yellow and green' ('Common knotgrass' n.d.). As well as along roadside verges, all three growing in gardens where they are defined as 'The Problem' (cf. Mabey 2010) and subject to 'control', whether cultural (not involving weedkillers) or/and chemical. Their distribution is widespread, which contrasts with the scarcity of rare and endangered species, or charismatic plants, which grab attention and often become fetishised. By devoting a poem to these species of plants, Clark brings to our attention the elements of the natural world which have often been ignored, neglected, rejected or 'unloved', as Mabey puts it. Additionally, turning to the margins subverts the convention of garden poetry, challenging the cliché of employing flower references in poetry (cf. Clark 1977, 12).

Naming has an incantatory function, their repetition conjuring the invoked things. Clark recognises this magical function of language which call upon beings and things where repetition serves as a ritual familiarising humans with the world. This role of naming is explored in the poem titled, simply, *Names* (2006), complete with a photograph of a grove. The first stanza enumerates various kinds of trees growing in the temperate climate:

> Repeating their names, you gather
> the things around you: larch, pine,
> birch, beech.

The second stanza replicates the structure with minor changes: the verb is replaced and the names of trees yield to those of animals which may be encountered in the woods:

> Repeating their names, you bring
> the things to you: wildcat, deer,
> badger, vole.

Significantly, the replacement of the verb entails a change of preposition, as 'around' in the first stanza is replaced with 'to' in the second and third. The choice of the verb in stanza 1 foregrounds the multiplicity of things which surround the subject and also with which the subject surrounds him- or herself. In the second stanza the preposition indicates the movement towards the subject, its recurrence in the final stanza stressing the closing of the gap. The employed verb may suggest bringing these things closer to oneself but also carrying them home from a walk, taking them – the event of the encounter, the memory, their image – with oneself. In the third stanza the verb changes into 'keep' while the preposition 'to' is retained. Here the choice possibly means keeping some things close to one but also keeping them to oneself, as one would keep something secret. The names resemble intimate knowledge gained on forest walks. In the final stanza the selection of nouns becomes varied, extending beyond one group and including physical objects – mineral and vegetal – but also abstract nouns referring to spatial and emotional concepts: 'stone, flower, / distance, joy'. Specific names of trees and animals yield to a generic, unspecified 'flower'. Repetition possesses incantatory power, through which things are gathered and retained. The continuous form of the anaphoric 'repeating' underlines the infinite nature of naming which relies on iteration and recurrence.

Names conjure up things and phenomena, sparking imagination or recalling encounters. Yet, even if occurring repeatedly, every encounter and sighting is nonetheless singular. Composed of three lines, *every time you find* (2019) is worth citing here in its entirety:

> every time you find
> a primrose it is
> the first primrose

In this brief poem, enjambment organising the three lines constitutes the most significant structural device. As in the poem discussed above and in many other poems, Clark employs the second-person singular pronoun. The frequent use of 'you' in his poetry may have a threefold meaning: the second-person singular, 'you' as a form of referring to people in general, and finally, 'you' as the form of address to the poem. The indefinite article which describes a single item transforms 'a primrose' into 'the first primrose'. The transformation occurring between lines 2 and 3 marks a moment of realisation: every thing we perceive reveals itself in its singularity, as if it were appearing for the first time: the thisness of the thing, or the irreducible thingness of the thing; a quality that makes the thing what it is, its essence, 'the essential structure of the thing' (Merleau-Ponty 2004, 75).

Place Names

Clark's in-placeness reveals itself in his keen interest in topography, resulting in the poetic exploration of names which relate to particular areas. With every minimalist poem, the proper name in the title 'speaks' for itself, serving as a synecdoche, *pars pro toto*, for what cannot be apprehended. Repositories of memory, place names are bearers of the collective past, relating to the presence of people in the land. Referring to language that designates place, Clark foregrounds the textuality of landscape, as well as the manner in which it is perceived by humans: we constantly read and translate landscapes in an attempt to decipher the embedded meanings. Exemplary of a number of Clark's other works, *The Hidden Place*, realised as a site-specific wall painting at Ingleby Gallery (29 July–25 September 2010) and a three-colour screen print, offers an alternative map of Scotland, whereby place names have been translated and replaced with names of animals and plants in English. In this manner, the landscape appears as multidimensional rather than flat; they are multi-layered, palimpsestic. By using the format of a map on which he places alternative names, Clark challenges the arbitrariness of language and emphasises the personal nature of the landscape, the intimate knowledge of which reveals aspects invisible on official maps. Such practice is a recurrent technique in Alec Finlay's work. In in the next chapter, I discuss the exploration of the linguistic history and literary archaeology of places as it has been practised by Finlay, particularly notable in *Gathering* (2018).

The vicissitudes of the Scottish land are present in Clark's practice, most notably in the Gaelic place names serving as poem titles, for instance 'Creag Liath', *Coire Fhionn Lochan, At Loch Grinneabhat* or *By Kilbrannan Sound*. This device allows Clark to gesture towards topographical features such as bodies of water or mountain peaks, while also referring the reader to the cultural and historical aspects of the region, and offers a powerful reminder of the loss of names ensuing from, and commensurate with, the erasure of Gaelic culture. Similarly, the use of the proper name demonstrates respect, as the name connects the bearer with the sign of their identity, indicating certain social, spatial and temporal features. Denoting a summit in the Cairngorms, 'Creag liath' (2020c, 11–14) evokes a landscape, which exudes melancholy as it is marked by 'ruined dwellings on green moors' (l. 29) that are passed on a walk. There 'among the sedimentary deposits' (l. 33) a multiplicity of rock and stone enumerated in stanzas 8 and 9, including granite, 'crystals of amethyst, topaz, blue-beryl, smoky quartz' (ll. 35–6), expose deep time visible in the geological materialities among the anthropogenic ruins. In another poem entitled *Tràigh Bhalla* (2007), an envelope contains a card with four words: 'harebell celandine Caroline clover', subsequently presented in blue, yellow, pink and green print. Isolated from the page, centred and surrounded by white space, the name thus boasts its singularity. Referring to the name of a beach on the Isle of Tiree, the title appears only on the envelope, as if it were addressed to the landscape, and as if the correspondence with the female name among the names of flowers were a postcard with several telegraphic impressions, omitting inessential words. In other minimal poems such as *Dun na mairbhe* (2017c) or *Allt Garbh Beag* (2019), place names correspond with a nominal phrase. Completing *Dun na mairbhe* is the line 'the fort of stillness', evoking the memory of a construction on North Uist. Identified as a possibly Iron Age broch, the remains of the fort are situated on a small islet surrounded by water at high tide ('North Uist, Dun na Mairbhe'). Similar in structure, *Allt Garbh Beag* contains the phrase 'rough little stream', which refers to a stream falling into Loch Sligachan on Skye.

The Grove of Delight (2014) is an example of a poem form practised by Clark in which the line or lines inside or on the reverse respond to the title. Enclosed within green covers, a line printed on a bright yellow page announces: 'you are almost there'. Blending the sense of longing and deferral, the line contains the promise of paradise almost already there. On the back, an explanatory note reads:

> Doire shòlais
> the grove of delight
>
> See *place names* of
> Sleat, Skye (Clark 2014d)

The note uncovers the geographical reference in the title of the poem: Doire Shòlais, which translates as 'the grove of delight' and denotes a place in Sleat, a part of an Ostaig farm situated opposite Linne na Dunach ('Placenames' n.d.). Through this paratextual method,

Clark directs readers to explore the topographical and literary references in the process of uncovering the meaning. The grove of delight reappears in another of Clark's works: *Admit one* (2017d) is composed of a small green card, the size of a matchbox, with a yellow box in the middle, the text on the front:

> the grove of delight
> ADMIT ONE

Printed in capital letters, the second line stresses the message through the resemblance to public signs, which endows it with an imperative, emphatic tone. In contrast to the previous work, the topographical context is not revealed, remaining outside the poem.

Apart from such minimalistic works, a considerable number of longer poems also refer to place names in their titles. These are, for instance, 'Riasg Buidhe' (2000a, 95–104, cf. also 'Tobar Na Cailleach' [2000, 85–90]), originally published in *Tormentil & Bleached Bones* (1993). Differently from *The Grove of Delight*, the interpretation of which was aided by the additional note placing the poem, the Gaelic title in 'Riasg Buidhe' suffices to situate it. Printed under the title, the statement 'A visit to the island of Colonsay, Inner Hebrides, April 1987' elucidates the title and situates the poem. In this manner it becomes personalised by spatial as well as temporal detail. Meaning 'yellow moor grass', Riasg Buidhe denotes an abandoned village on the Isle of Colonsay with an early medieval chapel and burial ground ('Colonsay, Riasg Buidhe' n.d.), where ruinous terraced cottages mark the derelict landscape. While the poem notes the dereliction, it offers hope in the form of flourishing, 'a garden of daffodils' (2000a, 104), the landscape 'as resilient as heather' (2000a, 101). Composed of a series of statements, the poem in its final part refers to the accepted routines which 'can strangle us', contrasted with the chosen rituals which 'give renewed life' (2000a, 104). Similarly to Norman MacCaig, Clark writes about the elementality of 'a landscape of Torridonian sandstone and heather moor, green and gold lichens on the naked rock' (2000a, 101); the lithic in the form of recurrent references to rock, pebbles, stone, and cairn dominates. Yet the final statement in the poem offers an expression of release and renewal in the image of a singing lark.

An Cidhe Beag (2002) evokes a place situated on the west side of the harbour in the town of Scarinish on Tiree, the most westerly island of the Inner Hebrides (*An Cidhe Beag* n.d.). In its four quatrains, printed on every second page, the poem relies on variations of the same lines, thus resembling the boats which 'try out variations' (l. 15):

> every day the same boats
> appear in a different order
> red, white and blue
> within the curve of the harbour
>
> every day the same boats
> blue, white and red
> sit in their own reflections
> or turn slowly on the tide
>
> within the curve of the harbour
> red, blue and white
> every day the same boats
> dip on the spreading light
>
> in the same wide curve of the harbour
> the same boats every day
> try out variations
> on white, red and blue

An Cidhe Beag, or 'the small pier', forms a scene composed of a few objects and elements: variations of the same landscape transformed by light and movement constitute the reverberations of being. Through its structure, the poem enacts modalities of repetition and difference, investigating the manner in which the modality of each phenomenon and thing affects the perceiver's experience, who sees 'the same boats every day' (l. 14), even though their perception becomes slightly transformed through a series of minimal changes. Employing a similar method, *To Scalasaig* (2000b) equally relies on line variations. *To Scalasaig* was published as a small white booklet, the title printed in blue italics, each stanza, slightly off-centre, occupies a separate page. The blue of the title conjures the blue of the distance as the light dispersed in air enfolds the faraway landscape in the patina of blue. As the colours become interchangeable – blue-grey, blue-green, green-grey – the separation between the island, the sea and the sky dissolves. Composed of eight stanzas, each based on a repetition of three adjectives – grey, blue and green – and three nouns – sky, island and sea. The permutations appear with regularity – three, six, twenty-four – emphasising interchangeability. Preceded by the preposition, the place name in the title – Scalasaig – is a small port village on the Isle of Colonsay – evokes a direction, a longing to be transferred to a place with an uncluttered horizon where the recurrence of a limited number of phenomena creates a sense of calm. Journeying to or advancing towards this horizon becomes an expression of a dream to be relocated in a placid place of the minimal landscape pared down to the elemental things: sea, land, sky.

First published by Moschatel Press in 1993, *An Lochan Uaine*, takes its title from the Green Loch in Glenmore in the Aviemore area in the Cairngorms with its ancient Caledonian pines. The poem was exhibited at the Star Gallery, Fushimi Underground Mall, in Nagoya, Japan (9–30 August 2013), with a model lochan realised by Eiji Watanabe. As in many other works by Clark, the structure of the poem relies on repetition with minimal alterations:

> coming in the morning
> to the green lochan
> and sitting for a while
> by the water
>
> coming in the evening
> to the green lochan
> and sitting for a while
> by the water

At times places in the title combine with a line of poetry that evokes a moment grasped by the poet's consciousness, by association creating a series of textual correspondences, highlighting Clark's literary affinities. In *Lochan a Bearta* (2000c)[31] the title points to a particular place, the blue line of the poem printed in italics on a narrow card – 'the ceaseless weaving of the uneven water of the little loch of the loom' – sonically evoking the trickling of water in the long vowel [i:] in the first part ('the ceaseless weaving of the uneven') and the return of the liquid consonant in the second ('the little loch of the loom'). The third movement of the poem contained in the note – 'after Charles Reznikoff' – connects the poem with 'Aphrodite Vrania'.[32] Through the employment of these three skeins – locality, sound pattern and literary reference – the poem creates a fabric of meaning.

Apophatic discourse reveals poetic truth, uncovering, disclosing beyond language, all things numinous. Language has the power to summon the world. Iteration constitutes the ordering principle in a number of poems, such as, for instance, *Coire Fhionn Lochan* (2007a; 2020c, 15). Constructed around the repetition of a noun phrase, it resembles a litany. In a string of twenty lines divided into five quartets, the words 'the little waves' return at the end of each, preceded by a participle form of a varying verb. The liquid consonant 'l' found in more than a half of the verbs – 'lapping' (l. 1), 'idling' (l. 4), 'rippling' (l. 5), 'settling' (l. 6), 'swelling' (l. 8), 'trembling' (l. 9), 'slanting' (l. 12), 'scribbling' (l. 14), 'lilting' (l. 15), 'sparkling' (l. 16), 'leaping' (l. 17) and 'splashing' (l. 20) – doubly returns in the adjective 'little', binding the words together and enhancing the flowing quality of the verse. The emphasis on verbs creates the impression of movement thanks to which the landscape is represented as a living thing rather than a static image. Reiteration marks the graphic arrangement of the lines visually foregrounding their rippling quality. Through the minute changes from one line to another, from one page onto another, Clark's sequential work creates an incremental effect comprising linguistic and perceptual changes.

An early work entitled *A Short Tour of the Highlands* (1979) takes the form of a small, white booklet with a drawing of a landscape on the cover: a slope, a ridge with some stones, a brook; inside are three images with the following titles: 'The dark waters of Loch Awe', 'The peeled antlers of Glen Tilt', 'The bare crags of Ben Hope'. Referring to the tradition of the picturesque, *A Short Tour of the Highlands* playfully subverts it by reversing the scale and introducing invented names. The miniature format of the poem challenges the concept of the tours invented in the eighteenth century and responsible for the commodification of the landscape in the Scottish Highlands.[33] Thus we are presented with a polemical view on the Highland Tour, challenging nostalgic manifestations of Scottish culture.

With poems such as those discussed in this section, which, of course, represent only a small selection of his practice, Clark evokes the past of the landscape which has left a mark, in a manner similar to MacCaig exploring his Gaelic ancestry in Assynt or Alec Finlay's mapping of various onomastic attributes of the Cairngorms. All the poets evoke absence, powerfully sensed in the landscapes, as places are named and conjured, whereby the invoked toponyms remind the reader of the Gaelic legacy in Scotland. Many of the poems discussed above – including *To Scalasaig*, 'Riasg Buidhe', *By Kilbrannan Sound, Dun na mairbhe, Allt Garbh Beag, Tràigh Bhalla, The Grove of Delight* – refer to island place names, emphasising Clark's archipelagic preoccupation. The next section focuses on another function of the island trope in Clark's practice.

Islands

Similarly to Kathleen Jamie, the island is a recurrent trope in Clark's work, which, together with the Scottish Highlands, belongs to one of the most frequently imagined landscapes in his poems. Unlike Jamie, however, Clark evokes the longing to find oneself on an island far more than expressing an actual experience of being there. For instance, in 'The far-glimpsed island', the title announces the distance which remains in place through the six lines of the poem. The hyphenated adjectives, which dominate the poem, gesture towards a longing for connectivity. In a revealing comment, Clark deplores the insistence in British poetry on experience. In his own words, 'My quarrel with contemporary poetry, at least as it exists on these shores, is that it speaks of the people's experience (at best) whereas I want to speak of their desires, their longings' (Stacey 1987, 36). Through the devices of delay, interval and pause, Clark evokes a sense of longing, particularly evocative in his island poems many of which are structured around deferment.

Islands reappear in Clark's poetry as sites of longing, locations where the idea of the earthly paradise could be fulfilled. Even if the place is never reached (or never reached again), if the state of bliss remains unachieved – unachievable, even – the thought itself extends towards a possibility. For instance, one might consider the poem *and then an island floated past us like a promise of happiness and we rocked in its wake* (2016) with its single line printed in the shape of an island on the horizon, complete with an image of a boat on the shore. Another poem entitled *island* (2005) depicts 'a place we might go', its potentiality expressed in a form of 'a name on an old chart', but it is equally a site of condensed emotions, 'a moment out of the flow / a wild region of the heart'. In *I say island* (2003), the very idea arises in the mind once the word is uttered:

> I say island and out of the forgetfulness where my voice
> banishes any contour, inasmuch as it is something other
> than known harbours, musically arises, an idea itself and
> lonely, the one absent from all maps.

The note 'after Mallarmé' added to the title of the poem indicates the provenance of the poem and ties it with the oft-quoted statement, 'Je dis: une fleur!' from *L'Avant-dire au Traité du verbe de René Ghil* (1886), repeated in *Variations sur un sujet* (1895) and finally published in *Divagations* (1897) in the essay 'Crise de vers' ('Crisis in Poetry').

It is worth citing Mallarmé's passage again here: 'I say: a flower! And, out of the oblivion where my voice casts every contour, insofar as it is something other than the known bloom, there arises, musically, the very idea in its mellowness; in other words, what is absent from every bouquet' (2007, 210). Clark refers to the Mallarméan mode of abstraction whereby the pure idea of an object – 'idée même', the very idea, or 'an idea itself' in Clark's version – is conjured by the mystic power of the word. The idea is described by Mallarmé as 'suave', or delicate, the word replaced by Clark with 'lonely'; thus a conventional description of a flower replaces an equally clichéd adjective describing an island. The music of the name summons the island in one's imagination; yet in its light-grey print, the word – and the idea – emerges, standing out from the rest of the text but at the same time, paradoxically, appearing faint, distant.

At times, the poetry of absence relents in favour of material presence, when the name of a flower in effect bodies forth the world, as in, for instance, *The Lord of the Isles* (originally published 2018; 2020c, 143–6), the title of which refers not only to Norse and Gaelic rulers in the Western Isles of Scotland who owed their allegiance to the kings of Norway before the Treaty of Perth in 1266, but also the yellow iris on the cover, gesturing towards the non-human world, its continuous presence contrasted with the disrupted human history. The verbal texture of the poem highlights the flower's uninterrupted governance of the islands. In stanza 4, the nouns 'depredations' (l. 14), 'drift' (l. 15), 'decline' (l. 16) enact the pattern of repetition and return in the dental consonant, followed by a short vowel in the first word, rolling through the liquid consonant, then returning to the vowel again, reverberating in the assonance and rhyme of the last line: 'decline in elm and lime' (l. 16). Everything is 'perpetually perishing' (l. 8) in the dialectics of presence and absence demonstrative of the resilience and vulnerability of the natural world. The rhythm and rhyme in the poem unfold in the combination of the words, teasing out the 'melody' of things (Zukosky 1931, 273): as in music, delay creates an echo-like effect, with densely overlaid textures of notes. The islands are there, but they are 'to be held at a distance/in perpetuity' (ll. 55–6), never really reached, as if an ungraspable ideal.

The sense of the unattainable expressed in the form of the unfulfilled desire reappears in a number of Clark's poems. The trope of islands representing Eden is explored in *The Earthly Paradise* (originally published in 2013 and included in *The Threadbare Coat: Selected Poems* [2020c, 46]). In the original version, the poem is printed in a small-sized booklet with one line on every page, where the text is accompanied by images of rowing boats. Thus on six consecutive pages one line appears with a slight variation, arranged as alternating minimal pairs: 'not on that island' and 'not on this island'. The adjectives 'this' and 'that' modifying the noun refer to a particular place within reach, one closer and the other farther away, interchanging between the two in a rocking movement. In its insistence of the negation, the use of anaphora enhances the repeated deferral. The spatial indicators – not here, not there – are also temporal – not yet, not now. The principle of delay with the lacunae, gaps and pauses in between governs many of Clark's poems, which evoke deferment and respite. Absent from the Carcanet edition, the note '*after* The Voyage of St Brendan' at the end of the original edition illuminates the poem, providing literary and historical context, referring to the account of St Brendan's journeys recorded in the ninth-century *Navigatio Sancti Brendani Abbatis*. St Brendan the Navigator travelled around the Hebrides, along the western coast of Scotland, Wales and Brittany. According to accounts, during a journey to 'The Promised Land of the Saints' he saw a phantom island in the North Atlantic, which was probably a mirage but which was included in maps for several centuries afterwards. Without the note, the poem acquires universalising qualities, evoking a desire which pushes some to travel to ever new, remote regions in search of fulfilment, reflected in St Brendan's attempts to discover an actual paradise by sailing around the islands, in quest of paradise.

The poem entitled *Garvellachs* (2021b) challenges the view of islands as places to be reached, which may be extended to any landscape transformed into a tourist commodity. The title refers to a group of islands in the Southern Hebrides, the Garvellachs – An Garbh Eileaicha, the 'rough islands' – the most southerly of which is Eileach an Naoimh ('Isle of the Saints') with the remains of an ancient Celtic monastery, and is believed to have been founded by St Brendan in 542 CE. The poem opens with a repeated appeal:

> let them be
> the isles of the sea
> leave them alone
> leave them to their own
> let them be

Relying on repetition as an organising principle, the poem becomes a resonant chant, with the alternating phrases 'leave them alone' and 'let them be' returning in stanzas 2 and 3 consecutively, the latter line expanded by the adverb 'there'. The line is repeated in this form in the last stanza:

> let them be there
> let them be far
> keep their distance near
> the isles of the sea
> let them be

Small places such as 'the bee hive cells' (l. 11) and 'the hay scented buckler fern' (l. 14) should remain 'unvisited' (l. 12, l. 15). However, once reached, the islands suggest an effusion and inspire serenity and silence, as in *The Quiet Island* (2015; 2020c, 42–3) or *Doire Fhearna* (2007b). The latter was published as a folding card with a triptych structure composed of three tercets on each page, the title evoking a place on Islay in the Inner Hebrides. The name 'Doire Fhearna', signifying 'the alder wood' ('OS1/2/70/41' n.d.) can be found in old original object name books. The poem is preoccupied with the state of assumed distance as the site becomes transformed into a place of quiet stillness.

Such 'small pockets of quiet', as Clark writes in 'Riasg Buidhe' (2000a, 100), remain undisturbed except for the iterating sound of waves. Indirectly associated with the island landscape, a brief poem entitled 'Thainig Na Naoi Sonais', published in *Carmichael's Book* and edited by Alec Finlay (1997), alludes to a poem from the *Carmina gadelica*, a book of hymns and incantations collected and translated into English by Alexander Carmichael (1900), and considered by scholars 'this mysterious text' (Kapalo, Pócs and Ryan 2013, 53). The narrative preceding the poem relates to Carmichael's encounter with John Beaton, an illustrious botanist on the Isle of Uist. Devoted to the figwort, a rare plant found in Uist said to possess magical properties, which 'grows in sight of the sea', the reciter cited by Carmichael says that it is 'full of the milk of grace and goodness and of the gift of peace and power and fills with the filling and ebbs with the ebbing tide' (Carmichael 1900, 78), which resounds 'with the dew of bliss, while the tide is flowing' (Kapalo, Pócs and Ryan 2013, 55). Clark borrows two lines from one of the incantations, 'Eolas an Torranain' ('The Charm of the Figwort') – 'thainig na naoi sonais le na naoi marannan' – which serve as the title of the poem. Employing the lines, 'came the nine joys / with the nine waves' (Clark 1997, 39, ll. 1–2; Carmichael 1900, 91, ll. 5–6) and 'of thousand blessings, of thousand virtues' (Carmichael 1900, l. 9), Clark refers directly to

Carmichael's text, which he recreates, thereby enacting brief waves through the repetitive structure of the poem.

The Fold: Aletheia, or a Bright Glade

Doubtless, the fold, another Mallarméan figure, constitutes one of the recurrent themes and motifs of Clark's practice, as well as proving a sustained organising principle, employed through form and meaning in multiple ways. Appearing in the title of a considerable number of works,[34] the fold is also present in their design: their formal potential explored in the folding-poem, appearing on a structural level in concertinas and folding cards frequently employed by Clark. The significance of the concept transpires in the early references to the fold as the Japanese way of making garments which does not involve cutting, stitching and sewing but is 'to get a fold of cloth and fold it' (Clark 1977, 14), an act forming 'something discreet', as it occurs 'with a kind of grace one couldn't make oneself' (Clark 1977, 14). The device belongs to the conceptual aspect of his practice, and with it a view of poetry encompassing and welding form and content. In the poet's words, as we read in the description of *A Box of Landscapes*:

> Poetry is an art of condensation, *folding* whole landscapes and discourses into a verse or a line, to be unfolded later by the reader. Designed for a jacket pocket, or for a table or mantelpiece, rather than the bookshelf, often holding only a phrase or an image, you can open the box and *unfold* a range of landscapes, trees, hills, orchards, rivers. (Clark and Clark n.d., emphases added)

The reader's active participation in the exploration of individual poems reflects the poet's role in retrieving the elements of the landscape in the process of creation. In both acts, a function of folding matter is revealed in various ways as consciousness is folded infinitely in intricately complex ways. The flesh is Being as the relation founded on the intertwining of silent vision and verbal expression. To unfold means to grow or develop, and brings to mind the concept of the fold put forward by Gilles Deleuze (1988), when he discusses the theory of monads developed by Leibniz as the idea of the world as a body of infinite folds of matter.[35] The combination of Leibniz's metaphysics and Deleuze's materialism appears apt in reference to the concept of the fold in Clark's practice, whereby matter that is variously folded produces interiority which may be uncoiled.

In his self-referential poems, Clark indicates the enfolded nature of the artworld. Such poems as *pli selon pli* (2013) explore the intertextual potential, as it refers to Pierre Boulez's piece *pli selon pli* (fold by fold) (1960), the subtitle of which is *Portrait de Mallarmé* (*Portrait of Mallarmé*), thus indicating palimpsestic musicological and poetic associations. Most frequently, however, the fold in Clark's practice refers to the landscape with its multiple variations whereby the motif itself represents an infinite number of encompassed possibilities. For instance, a fold may enclose an image or an event in the landscape which appears to be composed of infinite pleats, or folds of space and time, revealed through movement. The concept of the fold is introduced without evoking a sense of mystery or noumenalising nature as an entity hidden from the subject, as is the case in some Romantic poems. For instance, *In a fold of hills* (1999) one reads as follows:

> In a fold of hills there is a patch of
> blue (is it a flax field or is it the sea)
> that is a surprise each time you come
> to it, and that will retain its value
> whenever you return to it in thought.

Perceived or remembered, 'a patch of blue' enfolded in between hills is 'a surprise', with its ambiguity, and lack of definition expressed by the phrase. Returning in lines 2, 4 and 5, the pronoun 'it', replacing the object for lack of a precise name, eschews identification. During a walk, when consciousness follows the gaze, I am at the end of my vision as Merleau-Ponty suggests in *Phenomenology of Perception*. In the perceptual field of landscape, 'the inner horizon' becomes enfolded in the outer horizons of an object (2002, 77–9). In blue remembered hills (n.d.), a harmonica card with words printed on each side in four different colours reveals the poem, line by line:

> blue remembered hills
> grey imagined hills
> green observed hills
> purple awaited hills

As one row of hills hides another, to be uncovered through the unfolding, the act of walking the landscape is evoked. The nouns suggest the colours in the landscape as they appear to the eye, while the verbs evoke various modalities of experience. The repetition enhances a sense of plurality of things in their infinite number, hidden in the folds of the landscape.

The above poem belongs to a series that evoke the fold by enacting it, form welded with theme, structured around conceits that aim at astonishing and delighting the reader. Another, entitled *Bookmarks* (2001) performs the opening of a book, finding a bookmark, a place where we left off, analogous to an experience of walking into the landscape:

> *as if to lose yourself*
> *between the covers of a book*
> *was to find yourself*
> *in a fold of the hills*

The text printed on the bookmark which may be found among the pages transports the reader outside in a motion reminiscent of the transcendence of the subject in relation to the world. It offers a reminder of the immersive experience of walking into the landscape and being enfolded by it. In a dual motion, the poem evokes a sense of the textuality of the landscape whereby each hill resembles a page turned, unfolding.

The fold also occurs in minute particulars, as in *On a Grey Day* (1999), whereby the repetitive rhythm of language enacts the visual rhythm of the folded forsythia petals which hide those unfolding interchangeably with those folded. The act of opening suggests a revelation achieved through 'this unfolding nature of language'. Composed of twelve couplets, *a forest grove* (2001) suggests the enfolding qualities of the material and immaterial elements of the wooded area. With two couplets on every page structured around repetition and minimal variation, the poem revolves around dialectics of presence and absence, gathering and intertwining the birch and alder, the goldcrest and siskin, shadow and sunlight, song and silence. Structurally, the couplets are built around the anaphora carrying the preposition 'in' in every second line, thus enfolding the object *in* the previous one: 'the branches of alder / in the branches of birch' (ll. 1–2), 'the song of the goldcrest / in the branches of alder' (ll. 5–6), 'the shadows of birch / in the branches of alder' (ll. 9–10). Towards the end of the poem the intertwining intensifies and complicates, binding the aural and visual with the material: 'the songs and shadows / in the branches of birch' (ll. 17–18).

In the final two couplets transfiguration may be observed as matter becomes light:

> the branches of sunbeams
> in the branches of alder
>
> the branches of sunbeams
> in the branches of birch (ll. 21–4)

Through the intertwining of birdsong and tree branches, braided with light and shadow, they are enfolded together. Repeated twelvefold, the preposition 'in' gestures towards the cyclical enfolding of things and phenomena which twist and weave through the body of the world where all the objects are 'apprehended as co-existent' (Merleau-Ponty 2002, 79).

As has been mentioned, the reiterating words and phrases, reappearing and functioning as a refrain, serve as an integrating principle of Clark's practice. Among the most persistently recurrent motifs is the word 'glade', which, similarly to 'fold', appears frequently as or in the title of various works. It is among the most regularly recurrent terms in Clark's practice, the concept recurring with a great intensity and frequency. More than a dozen works contain the word in the title: from the early *The Dappled Glade* (1979) and *The Pocket Glade Dictionary* (1980) to *The thought of a glade* (2019).[36] The proliferation of poems and other works bearing the same title or its modified version suggests the plurality of forms of in the landscape, where this multiplicity does not erase their singularity. In a rhythmic pattern of difference and repetition, each time we encounter a new glade, the landscape retains its singularity, its particularity. The glade names an open space surrounded by woods, originally meaning a sun-filled place, and possibly drawing from the word meaning 'shining', 'sunny', related in turn to the Old English word *geolu*, 'yellow'. Clark explores these associations. The line printed on one side of a yellow card reads 'In its green envelope', and if the card is reversed, one word appears in block capitals: 'GLADE'. The poem alludes to, continues and recreates the tradition of riddles, popular in Old English literature. In another poem entitled *Glade* (1994), in the form of a wall drawing from the collection of Greville Worthington, the text reads as follows: 'In the darkness of the forest, there may be an open space, an interval or gladness, that once discovered can be visited again and again.' The gap revealing a glade heralds the arrival of the earthly paradise embodied in that space of brightness.

The noun 'gladness', originating from Old English *glæd*, meaning 'bright', 'shining' or 'gleaming', highlights brightness and suggests a state of elation, which appears in other works. A similar work is the screenprint on paper entitled *Glade* (1996), from the portfolio Travaux Publics, Public Works, at the Scottish National Gallery of Modern Art (Modern Two), containing the following lines:

> This space may be considered as a glade
> or clearing, an area open to a brightness
> which may be found again in other spaces

The exhibition of books, cards and prints of Thomas A Clark and Laurie Clark entitled *A Bright Glade* organised at the Scottish Poetry Library from 1 April to 4 June 2006 was accompanied by an exhibition prospectus. When opened it reveals a sentence printed in bright yellow: 'In the darkness of the forest there may be an open space, an interval or gladness, that once discovered can be visited again and again.' When unfolded, the following words, printed in light blue capital letters appear:

> stepping out
> into the open
> you open to
> space and light

As already mentioned, the use of the second-person singular pronoun, recurring in Clark's practice, in this poem is as powerful as anywhere; it functions to shorten of the distance, as if the speaker were approaching a friend with an invitation for a walk. This mode becomes reinforced in the employment of the vocative case, as in the poem 'The High Path' (2020c, 17–20), which opens with the line: 'let's take the high path'. With poems in which a single line is placed in the middle of a page, as for instance in *One Hundred Scottish Places* (2021), Clark invites the readers to decelerate by making them focus on a limited number of words and pause before turning of pages. A similar effect is achieved with compact couplets, tercets and quatrains preferred by Clark, as in *The Hundred Thousand Places* (2009) where the space of the page is filled only with one or two stanzas, at times as brief as three or four lines. Surrounded by white space, the sparse text unites the eye and hand in movement. Blank pages which separate the stanzas create a longer pause as one might stop on a walk. The placement of brief lines or stanzas amid the open space of a page allows for contemplation, thus creating space for slow, uncrowded concentration as Clark refrains from dictating the speed of reading, offering readers the freedom to choose their own pace. Inscribed in the strategies of deferral and delay, the poems open up as a glade would.

The trope of the glade brings to mind the Heideggerian concept of a clearing – *Lichtung*, or 'a clearing, a lighting'[37] – bearing a similar philosophical function to a site of thought where truth may be glimpsed, where illumination occurs. In Heidegger's writing, a clearing becomes associated with the uncovering, or understanding, which reveals itself to the subject and discloses the world. Interestingly, in English the word is associated with a human-made gap in the woods, while 'glade', favoured by Clark, refers to an opening created without human involvement.[38] The distinction between the glade and the clearing is explored in a poem the title of which is also its text: '*Go to a clearing, / come to a glade*' (2011), which possibly suggests a kind of understanding that eludes active involvement and which may become revelation arriving without a conscious effort. In this respect, the glade in Clark's practice represents a glimpse into Merleau-Pontian Wild Being, whereby the embodied subject arrives at a realisation of the co-extensiveness of all objects and beings. In an undated poem titled *glade*, published in the form of a small booklet in the landscape mode, the verge of the cover is decorated with oak leaves, the following lines printed consecutively on separate pages in green font:

> sunbeams and oak boughs
> oak boughs and antlers
> antlers and sunbeams

Appearing alternately, the three nouns evoke distinctive realms: light intertwines with the plant and animal world, in their plurality, all corresponding in form, even if made of diverse matter. A recurrent word, 'sunbeam', is light visible, a meteorological phenomenon, the shaping of light in shafts. By joining these three nouns with the conjunction 'and', which functions as a hinge, Clark reinforces a sense of the stillness of the image, in the absence of movement entailed by the absence of any verbal form. As in a forest grove discussed above, the enfolding of things and phenomena reflects the landscape formed around coexistence.

Endowed with a vocation, the world beckons to us. As indeed all the authors discussed in this volume do, Thomas A Clark does not engage in 'world spectatorship', where spectatorship would suggest watching an event without taking part in it, letting the accent fall on the gaze with its imperial power. Instead, Clark, like the others, takes a participatory, experiential approach, which allows for the elimination of the problematic relation between the spectator and the spectacle. In his practice, Clark encourages participatory response as he recognises the limitations inherent in relying entirely on vision. In the opening sentence of an essay entitled *The World Brought Near*, he highlights the distinction between vision and other senses: 'While touch, smell, taste and hearing bring the world close, sight pushes it away again, creating a space of separation' (1998, 3). Conventionally understood, sight tends to create a distance. However, as Merleau-Ponty demonstrates, it is nonetheless possible to apprehend vision as an active process: 'To see is to enter a universe of beings which display themselves, and they would not do this if they could not be hidden behind each other or behind me.' Significantly, the perceiving subject 'enters' an object; what is more, as he writes, 'to look at an object is to inhabit it, and from this habitation to grasp all things in terms of the aspect which they present to it.' When seen, things 'remain abodes open to my gaze' as the subject is 'potentially lodged' in them (Merleau-Ponty 2002, 79). While sight performs an important function in Clark's practice, most often it functions in an active manner, the gaze enveloped in the perceived object. Further, Clark's statement cited above is a necessary reminder that all the senses are harnessed in the exploration of the landscape. For instance, the five-line poem *The Bright Glade* (n.d.) indicates the sensual play when encountering various trees:

> see elm
> touch oak
> smell pine
> taste lime
> hear poplar

The imperative form of the verbs invites the all-encompassing corporeal experience of the world of individual objects in the landscape whereby the natural world appears as 'the schema of intersensory relations' (Merleau-Ponty 2002, 381). The recurrent employment of the verbal form underlines active engagement with the landscape, while the elimination of pronouns and articles intensifies the points of contact between the self and the arboreal subject. The verbs referring to perceptual experience pull the reader into the present.

182 *Landscape Poetics*

A movement towards the world is enacted in such poems as *Of Woods & Water: Forty Eight Delays* (2008, reprinted in *Selected Poems* [2020c, 56–67])[39] which is composed of quatrains, originally one on every page surrounded by ample space, their compact form enacting an unhurried pace during a walk, with brief glimpses and sensations during the many moments for pause. At times, Clark resorts to photographs in order to convey the otherwise incommunicable experience, as in *One Moment Walk* (2007), which consists of three photographs on postcards: thick greenery – a fern with a moth: wildflowers; a cascade of water in a verdant place. Originating in the openness to random encounters, these works explore the motif of *aletheia* as the open space is emphasised by formal means. In the folding poems, some of which have been discussed in this chapter, the Heideggerian disclosure, or unconcealedness (*Erschlossenheit*), becomes enacted through their structure. These poems are constructed around such moments of disclosure not dissimilar to that space of brightness, a glade in the wood. Frequently positioned in the centre of the page, sparse lines surrounded by blank space further reinforce a sense of openness. As in *Rothiemurchus* (2021), the poem which evokes a landscape of generosity, where in its dazzling abundance light returns with every stanza in an incremental mode. As in *A Bright Glade*, the revelation brought by open space and light inspires a sense of gladness bearing paradisial qualities. The statement 'here they are', followed by 'here you are', first grounds the observed things and then the poet/reader in place and time. The appearance of the red deer at the end of the poem, which simply 'occur' in the illuminating, all-enveloping, flooding light, becomes symbolic.

Conclusion

As opposed to writing *about* landscape, whereby the preposition creates a situation in which objectification occurs by removing the object and creating distance, Clark's work relies on writing the landscape. In a series of ambulatory observations which avoid language that captures and fossilises as he seeks to eschew representational control, the poet meaningfully engages with the world. Through the sustained investigations of the natural world, in his emplaced practice, Clark evokes the landscapes in their rigour and beauty, but also suggests a sense of emanating melancholy resulting from the awareness of their complicated human history and the disappearing species of animals and plants. The memory of the past is honoured in the incorporation of Gaelic place names which remain, denoting the landscape. The unhurried pace of the poems as well as various typographical devices, the use of pause, lowercase and empty space emphasise the sense that the landscapes are not to be explored in a modern, consumerist manner; rather, they beckon to us to linger and dally. Continuing and expanding the tradition of objectivist poetry, Clark's poem-objects highlight language in its materiality. In the dedication to compression and brevity, the reduction of superfluity constitutes the dominant aesthetic of the work. Resulting from self-effacement is the erasure of authorial control, which in turn shifts focus onto the poem itself and, further, through the poem onto the surrounding environment. Thus inclined towards minimalism, his poetry forms 'the lightest membrane' which connects the poet, the reader and the landscape. Introducing a form of mobile poetry, the book-length poems are composed of stanza-length glimpses separated from one another with blank space around sparse lines that provide space for pause, for breath. Liberated from the ordering principles of punctuation, the poems offer themselves to the reader, as the unique space formed between reader and poem creates release from authorial control in which the reader unfolds landscapes and reveals their true form in the alethic process. Through attention to tiny particulars, Clark tends to the peripheries, refreshing clichés, which in turn allows for the retrieval of the poetic from the commonplace, thereby exploring meaning in the margins. The longing for paradise is expressed variously through iteration, delay and deferral, and invoked formally in the concept of the fold. The Arcadian convention explored by Clark offers possibilities of framing the landscape as a form of an ideal/idyll. Between finding and making the earthly paradise, Clark's practice is akin to a rhizome: delicate in appearance but perennial, and possibly endlessly expanding. The rhizomic is also a quality of the work of Alec Finlay, as the final chapter will explore.

Notes

1. For the discussion of the name, see also Alan Tucker's Preface to the catalogue of the 1979–80 Moschatel Press exhibition (1979, n.p.) and Ross Hair, *Folding the Last Sheep* (2016).
2. *Wu-men-kuan*, 'one of the most famous kōans in the Zen tradition', relates the story of Mahakasyapa, the Buddha's disciple, who reacts with a smile when the Buddha shows a flower to the assembly. 'Mahakasyapa receives the transmission when the Buddha acknowledges his intuitive understanding' (Heine and Wright 2000, 8).

3. See Ward's discussion of *Twenty Poems* (Ward 1984, 57).
4. The concept of pleasure in Clark's practice has been explored by Gavin Goodwin, who describes it as 'hedonistic' (Goodwin 2019, n.p.).
5. Correspondence with the author, 20 Dec. 2021
6. See Gavin Goodwin's discussion of Clark's *Generosity* (2010).
7. The essay was reprinted in 1967 in *Prepositions* without the references to Charles Reznikoff.
8. See Simone Weil, *Gravity and Grace* (2002).
9. See Simone Kotva's insightful discussion of the affinities between Weil and Clark.
10. Conversation with the author, 7 September 2021, Pittenweem.
11. Writing about the influence of Lorine Niedecker on British poets, Peter Middleton suggests that 'A more lasting but indirect influence was: the confirmation that poetry could continue in the absence of support from the academy, the reviews, and literary marketplaces' (2008, 268). Middleton mentions Thomas A Clark among poets who 'drew sustenance from examples like Niedecker's of the possibility of flourishing despite neglect' (2008, 268).
12. It is worth mentioning other contemporary artists who explore textuality through various media in a similar fashion such as Lawrence Weiner and Julie Johnstone, who also runs Essence Press.
13. *Words for the Mantlepiece. Moschatel Press and the Printed Editions of Thomas A Clark and Laurie Clark*, The Gabrielle Keiller Library/ The Dean Gallery, 24 Feb.–29 Apr. 2001.
14. The words appeared as one of the mottoes on the Cairn Gallery website.
15. Fiona Stafford, *Local Attachments: The Province of Poetry* (2010)
16. *From Sea to Sea* (Italy), one work in Andalucía (*Through White Villages*. 'Andalucia, Winter 1988') and one or two? works in Portugal in the 1980s (*Forest, Mountain, City*. 'Portugal, Winter 1990') and *The Castles of the Good* ('In the land of the Cathars, Languedoc, France, Winter 1991'). All published in *Tormentil and Bleached Bones*. There are also several poems inspired by other places such as, for instance, *Ruin Wood* (1981) accompanied by a drawing of a map of a place in Gloucestershire, Hobbs Hole Wood, Stroud.
17. First published in 1988 by the Cairn Gallery. Some reprints include: 'In Praise of Walking', in *Distance & Proximity* (2000); *In Praise of Walking* (2004), *In Praise of Walking & On Looking at the Sea* (2007). See also Christian McEwen's review in 'Thomas A. Clark: *In Praise of Walking*'. *The Dark Horse*, no. 23 (Summer 2009): 42–7.
18. In her insightful discussion of walking as 'the art of passing through', Camille Manfredi places Clark's work together with that of Andrew Greig and Hamish Fulton (Manfredi 2019, 47–73). See also Garry MacKenzie in *Walking, Landscape and Environment* (2020, 22–5) where he discusses Clark in the context of Tim Ingold's theories and Heidegger's concept of *Holzwege*.

19. Alice Tarbuck draws a link between wellbeing and poetry based on Clark's 2009 commission to contribute to the design of New Stobhill Hospital in Glasgow, in which Tarbuck uses Edward Soja's concept of 'third space'. Goodwin employs the term after Winnicott. Goodwin argues that Clark's New Stobhill Hospital text ('A Brightness in A Stillness / A glade') 'encourages an imaginative act of self-care, helping to soothe – both biophilicly and through imaginative agency – a mind having to cope with painful and anxious experiences' (Goodwin 2019, n.p.). Commenting on the commission for New Stobhill Hospital in Springburn, Glasgow, which opened in 2003, Clark said: 'While breaking up the density of the building, bringing in light and space, the larch courtyards also introduce a contemplative element. Patients spending time in waiting areas here have access to a different scale of time, that of the seasons or the growth of trees, or to the timelessness of looking' (Clark 2009, 79). In an earlier interview, Clark talked about the necessity for open spaces: 'There are some situations in which one needs to escape. If one lives in a crowded culture it might be useful to have images of empty landscapes, broader spaces. [. . .] It is a wish for certain things that are absent, or not sufficiently present, which are deliberately conjured up in order to further or to heal. To me that is how the poems work' (Clark 1993b, 101).
20. The pastoral tradition in Scottish poetry extends to the eighteenth century, with Allan Ramsay's *The Gentle Shepherd: A Pastoral Comedy* (1725) set in the countryside of the Scottish Lowlands, the probable setting being Penicuik, not far from Dunsyre where Ian Hamilton Finlay and Sue Finlay created Little Sparta. Robert Burns, in his 'Poem on Pastoral Poetry', pays tribute to Allan Ramsay, drawing a link between him and Theocritus.
21. I would like to thank Thomas A Clark for drawing my attention to this project.
22. Thomas A Clark and Laurie Clark, from *The teachings of Huang Po* (2014). Cf. also Clark, *The teachings of Huang Po* (1991).
23. Written in 1968 by Dick Holler, the version recorded a year later by Marvin Gaye became a hit in Great Britain. It was released by Tamla Motown in 1970.
24. Correspondence with the author, 20 Dec. 2021. I would like to thank Thomas A Clark for drawing my attention to this analogy.
25. Cf. Welton 2020; Tarbuck 2017.
26. Blake's *Jerusalem*.
27. One of the recurrent words, grace echoes Christian theology as the favour of God, often understood as unmerited or undeserved. See Simone Kotva's *Effort and Grace: On the Spiritual Exercise of Philosophy* (2020). Weil was Clark's early influence. See also Kotva (2019, n.p.)
28. See Clark 1993b, 99.

29. See Clark in conversation with Alice Tarbuck, who mentions 'the idea of givenness in the Husserlian sense' (2016, 40).
30. Correspondence with the Author, 10 Sept. 2021.
31. W. J. Watson gives a fascinating account of Lochan na Bearta, or 'Lochlet of the Deed', in *Place-Names of Ross and Cromarty*: 'Near it are said to be uamhagan (little caves, holes), that would hold twenty persons. This seems like a description of earth-houses. Unfortunately the place is remote, and those who knew the uamhagan in their youth are too aged to guide one to the spot.' *Place-Names of Ross and Cromarty*. Inverness: The Northern Counties Printing & Publishing Company, 1904, p. 242.
32. In his essay 'Objectivists', Zukofsky considers Reznikoff's poem in terms of sincerity. For the problematic distinction between sincerity and objectivism, see Eliot Weinberger's comment in 'Niedecker/Reznikoff' (Jacket 30, July 2006).
33. For a discussion of the Highlands, see Nigel Leask's substantive study *Stepping Westward: Writing the Highland Tour, c. 1720–1830* (2020).
34. For instance, *a fold* (2010), *folded* (2010), *Folding the Last Sheep* (2016), *The fourfold* (2017), *a recumbent fold* (2011), *unfolding brightness* (2011), *water fold fall* (2012), *In a fold of hills* (1999).
35. Gilles Deleuze, *The Fold: Leibniz and the Baroque*. Deleuze includes discussions of Heidegger and Mallarmé, as well as Pierre Boulez.
36. *The Dappled Glade* (1979), *The Pocket Glade Dictionary* (1980), *glade* (c. 1980), *The Bright Glade* (n.d.), *A Bright Glade* (2006), *go to a clearing, come to a glade* (2011), *glade* (2017), *The thought of a glade* (2019).
37. See §28 of *Being and Time*.
38. Conversation with the author 7 Sept. 2021. I would like to thank Thomas A Clark for pointing this out. See also Clark (1993b, 102).
39. Cf. *wing of the ptarmigan: forty eight delays* (2018).

Chapter 5

'Acts of communal memory': Landscape, Memory and Place Names in Alec Finlay's Work

Alec Finlay is a poet and artist whose work traverses conventional boundaries, bringing together poetry, place names, visual arts, linguistics, vocal processing and social practices. Finlay works across various media, intertwining text with visual and audial aspects, which include, but are not limited to, photo-poems and audio walks. He explores landscapes, feeling his way through place in detailed itineraries, with the use of various media such as QR codes and *tanzaku* in the form of Tanabata wish cards. The fluid crossings between different literary and artistic forms characterises Finlay's work. The use of diverse media includes blogs as live pages where he publishes the progress of his projects, accompanied with print publications, or 'catalogues', in which poems and comments are often followed by a bibliography. As Alan Riach points out, Finlay 'followed his father's [Ian Hamilton Finlay's] example not only in his own aesthetic precision and sharp but generous humour, but also in his publishing of others in a freshly imagined series of anthologies' which enables 'collecting work by writers whose ethnic and cultural history complicates any simple, single sense of what being "Scottish" might be' (Riach 2009, 15). Rather than national identity, however, the dominant feature of Finlay's work is ecological awareness: his engaged art is environmental in that it seeks solutions to resolve ecological problems. Finlay's ecological sensitivity manifests itself in such projects as *ebban an'flowan* (2015), *th' fleety wud* (2017),[1] described as 'a mapping of the Upper Teviot watershed and proposal for flood remediation' (2017, n.p.), and *Gathering* (2018), to mention just a few titles. Finlay's work is placed outdoors, because, as he says, 'some of the biggest possibilities exist in the landscape, especially the wild landscape' (Monaghan 2021, n.p.). Human intrusion into the landscape causes the erosion of the territory, whereby territory is understood as 'a measure of energy (animal), or arena of power (human)' (Finlay 2020, 259) according to Finlay's definition in 'From *A Place-Aware Dictionary*'. Among the themes in his ecologically focused projects are renewable energy, biodiversity, loss of habitats, rewilding, deer stalking, grouse shooting. Placed in the landscape, most of his works do not leave a permanent mark, avoiding a profound intervention as they refrain from interacting irreversibly or altering the environment for the viewer; instead, they are ephemeral, responding to individual characteristics of place.

In 2010 Alec Finlay and Ken Cockburn set out on a journey on foot through Scotland, guided by Matsuo Bashō's *Oku no Hosomichi* (*The Narrow Road to the Deep North*). Their responses to the encountered landscapes are gathered in a volume titled *The Road North* (2014), which may be Finlay's most discussed work.[2] The choice of a non-Western text to serve as a guide on the journey through Scotland demonstrates an attempt to introduce a non-Eurocentric perspective. Stepping over temporal and geographical limits, Finlay and Cockburn enter into a dialogue with the seventeenth-century text, offering a phenomenological mapping of place focused on corporeal experience and a blending in elements of cultural and historical survey of the land.

In his work, Finlay frequently maps the terrain with his feet, feeling his way through place in detailed itineraries. Exploring the relationship between language and landscape, Finlay does not strive for fixed meanings, but concerns himself with the rhizomic dissemination of sense, which is illustrated by his use of *tanzaku*, or 'place name translation'. His place writing and sited projects become moveable maps focused on 'place-awareness'. '*MAP*: a memory of landscape or an illustrated poem' (2020, 254), as Finlay proposes. As he jettisons systematic representation, Finlay challenges the view that perception of place is stable, demonstrating that any 'monolithic map' is too large to apprehend and that sense making is a dynamic process which occurs constantly on location. The lines which serve as the first part of the title for this essay – 'a monolithic map / of we know not what' (Finlay 2014, 51) – foreground that which the map is not for the artist: a monolith, which suggests an entity too large and too regular, something unchangeable, devoid of differentiation in its whole. An embodiment of modernity, maps foreground the primacy of reason, they represent an obsession with quantification, and privilege sight over other senses; yet Finlay's maps reverse that, offering a different approach. His work underlines the primacy of physicality which involves other senses than mere vision, and so illustrate a point made by Maurice Merleau-Ponty, who observes that '[s]ensory experience is unstable, and alien to natural perception, which we achieve with our whole body all at once, and which opens on a world of interacting senses' (1962, 262). For the readers of Alec Finlay's work, maps created in the open field enable complex interpretative practices. The ecopoetic maps made by Finlay do not form flat surfaces, yet they offer a survey of the territory aimed neither at representation nor the superimposition of divisions. Working with and against factual maps, often during a series of field trips (performed in person or by proxy), Finlay explores local topographies in their actual form as he does, for instance, in *th' fleety wud*, tracing the Upper Teviot watershed from the source (Teviot Stone) to the Rule Water. 'Fleety Wud', the name found on the OS map, means 'The Flooding Wood', as Finlay speculates, whereby the name of the wood denominates its main feature: flooding. The textuality of the landscape is foregrounded by Finlay who marks topographical features by typographical elements such as font, colour and fading.

An attempt to read the landscape, Finlay's texts propose a response to and active engagement with place. Reading the ecopoetic maps, Alex Hodby observes 'the breadth of Finlay's approach to landscape and nature and his treatment of such themes as play, wounded nature, philosophical topography and genetic modification' (2005, 6). Thus, Finlay's ecopoetic maps combine the concreteness of experience and the abstraction of language, evoking locations through various means and allowing the reader to imagine the walk. Embedded in the landscape, Finlay's art foregrounds body knowledge, experiencing the world corporeally rather than in an abstract fashion. Thus, his maps do not privilege vision but combine all senses, the artist immersed bodily in the landscape, while immersing the viewer in a number of sensual ways.

This chapter aims to explore ways in which Finlay's work combines mapping and ecopoetics. It will discuss how his various projects, concerned with chorography, which focuses on small regions and specific locations, entwine language and topography. It aims to explore the special function of the proper name as it occupies a prominent place in Finlay's oeuvre. Finally, following J. Hillis Miller's statement from *Topographies* that 'Landscape "as such" is never given, [it is] only one or another of the ways to map it', I will argue that in his numerous collaborative projects, Finlay proposes open texts onto which are mapped various consciousnesses. His words may be taken to summarise his work, whereby '[p]eople are invited to interact with a world book and to take part in a wandering journey, which no individual will ever be able to complete in its entirety' (Finlay 2005c, 47). As has been mentioned above, a considerable number of Finlay's projects involve a textual aspect, often in the form of mapping a region. Through works such as *Some Colour Trends* or *Gathering*, Finlay explores the manner in which the self engages with the landscape bodily and textually. Mapping the landscape takes different forms in his poetic and artistic practice: these may be conventional, cartographic, linguistic or aural, as is the case of sound maps. In this last example, in an attempt to transcend a two-dimensional image – the flatness of a map – Finlay employs both verbal and non-verbal art forms in order to explore the manner in which landscapes shape human experience of timespace, whereby place is considered as dynamic, heterogenous and multiple. Frequently, explorations of place assume a collaborative form, one which is favoured by Finlay, as for instance in *Shared Writing: Renga Days* (2005). By definition a collaborative form, a *renga*, or a chain-poem, is 'a study of shared consciousness' (2005, 121), its interlinked nature combining creativity and contemplation through a shared process, the dynamic of which is based on linking, each verse connecting with and departing from the previous one. *Renga* is '*a situation*, an *experiment* with the nature of poetry and language' (Clark 1992, 32; original italics), a form of communal art.[3] While employing a traditional Japanese form, Finlay's project recreates it creatively in an attempt to avoid 'japanoiserie' (2005, 10), as he puts it. Placed on a platform, which 'toured around' the British Isles 'from sea to sea' (2005, 33) along Hadrian Wall, including places such as galleries, parks and orchards, *renga* proposed a spatial poetry practice in which the poets responded directly to the surroundings, being in the landscape and responding to it.

The Alignment of Place, Body and Time

Finlay's work focuses on the self's relation with the landscape, on being-in-the-world experienced corporeally through site-specific installations and walking, a down-to-earth activity which enables direct contact with the physical world. It creates a deeper sense of place, an awareness of the local and regional as it incorporates small-scale elements of the landscape which, when combined, form a large, interconnected, rhizomatic whole. Embodiment is an inextricable element of Finlay's emplaced creations. To cite Merleau-Ponty, 'Our body and our perception always summon us to take as the centre of the world that environment with which they present us' (1962, 333). Being in the landscape, walking through and responding to it in a poetic manner, foregrounds the alignment of place, body and time. Imagining the context in which the reader receives his work affects the formal aspect of his work. As Finlay says, 'A lot of the formal resolution comes from thinking how people will *physically* be when they experience it' (Finlay 2014b, n.p., my emphasis). Thus, his work is a consideration of the corporeal experience of the landscape, the phenomenology of being. Composed of moveable maps, it captures the phenomenology of place and its changeable, fleeting nature.

Embedded in place, making poetic cartographies, Finlay's poems 'focus on the temporal in terms of the momentary-sensations, thoughts and feelings that emerge briefly and pass away' (Tarbuck 2017, 18). As already suggested, Alec Finlay's poems transcend the boundaries of the page and assume the form of material objects: the sound poetry, visual poetry and found poetry practised by Finlay traverse textual borders from and into the real landscapes, exploring the relations between the space of the page and place. By planting poems in the landscape in various media – in the form of *tanzaku*, nest boxes, bee boles – Finlay foregrounds the interconnectedness of text with place. Grounded in the landscape, Finlay's writing represents open-field poetics (see Tarlo 2013 and Bloomfield 2013), a term which refers both to the importance of locality and to the Black Mountain poets,[4] whose poetry celebrates an 'open field', whereby the form of the poem responds to its content, being less constrained by conventional poetic forms, linked by the significance of breath and free verse. Essential to his poetic consciousness, the inclusiveness of form and its multidimensionality demonstrate 'joint recognition of modes as well as joint occupation of spaces' (Tarbuck 2017, 20), to use Tarbuck's words. As mentioned above, Finlay creates in various forms and media, which include poetry, collage, sculpture and audio-visual; the hybrid and interdisciplinary nature of his work, which includes poems, narrative text, maps and drawings, foregrounds the multimedia approach to representation. Employing different media in the service of poetry enables Finlay to explore language, as, '[o]nce you know how to play with it you own all its meanings' (Finlay 2005a, n.p.). His is a work imbued with playfulness, but the playful aspect of his art does not avoid ethical questions concerning our being-in-the-world but foregrounds them. Finlay's ecologically aware work draws attention to ontological and epistemological aspects of being-in-the-world. Finlay believes in art that is 'a mixture of play and complexity – questions and answers squashed into one' (Finlay 2005a, n.p.). I follow George Hart's argument here that in works which focus on 'textuality, verbal surface, and wordplay', ecologically aware authors focus on the treatment of 'nature' in literature as 'a referent and a subject' (2000, 315). Finlay's engagement with landscape is 'much more than simply formal playfulness; this aesthetic strategy constitutes a formally embodied investigation of environmental aesthetics and ethics,' as Mandy Bloomfield puts it (2013, 122).

Finlay underlines the communal nature of his work, emphasising the importance of 'shared consciousness', as he calls it (Finlay 2014b, n.p.), which refers not only to its reception but also its collaborative conception. I shall mention briefly just a few of Finlay's collaborative projects in this part of the essay in order to demonstrate a sample of the breadth of his artistic imagination. In 2008 Finlay's collaboration with Jo Salter created *Specimen Colony* (2008), an open-air installation of nest boxes painted in the colours of birds from foreign postage stamps, exhibited at Bluecoat, Liverpool, which refers to the city's connection with the rest of the world by trade and migration. Working in another medium, sound, together with Chris Watson, Finlay realised *Siren* (2006), a field recording. Many works involve the audience, as for instance *Avant-Garde English Landscape* and *Some Versions of Landscape. A survey of artist projects in the landscape (1998–2006)* and there are also numerous projects involving *renga*, crosswords and participative walks to which I shall return further in this chapter.

The multimedial, collaborative nature of Finlay's work draws our attention to the relationality of space by 'detotalizing' it: as '[s]pace becomes detotalized by virtue of its relational construction and because, being differentially understood and produced by different individuals, collectivities and societies, it can have no universal essence' (Tilley 1994, 11). Interventions in the landscape demonstrate direct interaction and interconnection with place that goes beyond linguistic means as 'spatial modes of organising materials . . . [offer] alternatives to "description"' (Finlay 2012, 29). Abolishing straight lines, concrete poetry as practised by Finlay represents 'a new relation to syntax' (Finlay 2012, 29), one that allows for introducing a more open, rhizomic, less linear mode of reading. Poetic form matters for Finlay as it extends into the reception of a work of art, 'a formal quality that we might be able to recognize together' (Finlay 2014b, n.p.). He gives as an example a circle poem, which becomes 'a space that we could both occupy, in looking at. We would have a relationship to it, and that might be a bit more confidently shared than a solipsistic, confessional poem, say' (Finlay 2014b, n.p.). Finlay's sparse, minimalistic style relies on pared-down language, often presented in a non-standard layout on the page or in the landscape. As Tony Williams notices, Finlay writes 'fragile poems, using lineation to draw attention to the felicities and poky bits of language, leaving things unadorned, cutting away everything but the nub' (2012, n.p.). Employing concrete or pattern poetry, which is 'both visual and literary artvisual poetry' (Higgins 1987, 3), Finlay foregrounds an organic relation between linguistic and non-linguistic objects, creating poems which are to be perceived phenomenally, like the landscape, experienced through immersion in place. A recurrent practice, topological label/text placement, refreshes language and makes the reader perceive it anew. However, it is not language that is at the forefront in Finlay's work but the experience of being-in-the-world. Through an interactive mapping of landscape, Finlay focuses on place-awareness, which reveals dynamic relationships between various elements in space, highlighting connectivity, an interleaving between topography and self. In his book on the phenomenology of landscape, Tilley argues:

> A centred and meaningful space involves specific sets of linkages between the physical space of the non-humanly created world, somatic states of the body, the mental space of cognition and representation and the space of movement, encounter and interaction between persons and between persons and the human and non-human environment. Socially produced space combines the cognitive, the physical and the emotional into something that may be reproduced but is always open to transformation and change. A social space, rather than being uniform and forever the same, is constituted by differential densities of human experience, attachment and involvement. (Tilley 1994, 10–11)

By walking *through* and placing textual elements *in* the landscape, Finlay explores the interweaving of consciousness with the world, while emphasising the intertextuality of any perception of that world as he examines examining layers of social and cultural significance of spaces. Interactions between human and non-human environments, explored on the move, form the centre of many walking projects created by Finlay for whom walking is to 'become habituated to the landscape, learning place-names, reading the tell-tale signs that decode the texture of the land and its weather' (Finlay 2018, 150). In response to such work, critics have, of course, stressed the significance of walks in Finlay's art practice. For instance, Andrew Sneddon suggests that pilgrimage is an important mode of response in Finlay's interaction with other authors as it enables him 'to see what they saw' (2008, 6). Similarly, Alice Tarbuck and Simone Kotva argue that Finlay's work is an example of non-secular pilgrimage as a form present in environmental writing. Yet such emplacement through walking does not only foreground vision but also touch as, whereby sight possesses tactile qualities, as Merleau-Ponty notices: 'My eye for me is a certain power of making contact with things' (2002, 325). The palpability of sight highlights the corporeal intertwining of the self with the surroundings, binding them together. What is more, those who walk become subject to compounded rhythms as they 'repeatedly couple and uncouple their paths with other people's paths, institutions, technologies and physical surroundings' (Hägerstrand cit. Mels 2004, 16).

Finlay's walks map the Scottish landscape, leaving paper and digital trails and thus they expand the concept of travel literature, offering chorographic explorations of landscape and language. I wish to look briefly at some of these here. All were completed in collaboration with other people, and all exist in various forms, which is a signature of Finlay's work. In *White Peak, Dark Peak* which concerns the Peak District National Park (commissioned by *re*: place, Derbyshire Arts Development Group, 2009), Finlay proposes 'an audio-visual word-map' (Finlay 2010, n.p.), or a 'combination of walking, letterboxing, Japanese *renga* and field-recordings' (Finlay 2010, n.p.), which contains specific directions and employs geolocation and QR code technology. This emplaced nature of the artwork (and most of Finlay's art) is summarised in one of his short poems, 'Kinder North', the final line of which – 'words have no place outside what lasts' – foregrounds the inextricability of language and landscape. This embeddedness of words in place brings to mind what Finlay says in reference to his father's, Ian Hamilton Finlay's, work and which may be applied his own: 'The poem belongs here because this is where the poet first heard the wind' (Finlay 2012, 1). The form of the poems responds to place: in Finlay's pattern poetry the shape of the words depict the subject, creating a typographical effect, imitating the shape of mountains. Such arrangement of letters on the page is an attempt to capture the view.

Còmhlan Bheanntan / A Company of Mountains (2013) is yet another journey project, in which Finlay combines poems, essays, photographs, and what he calls 'word-mntn' drawings. The title is drawn from the first line of Sorley MacLean's poem 'Ceann Loch Aeoineart'. Inspired by MacLean's *An Cuillithionn* ('The Cuillin'), Finlay chose fourteen locations on the Isle of Skye, exploring cultural and historical aspects of place. The volume is preceded by a map of the island with numbered places, or vistas, which Finlay uses interchangeably with the word 'conspectuses'. Originating from Latin and signifying 'a sight', conspectus suggests an overall view of something, which justifies the book's subtitle: *14 views of the Isle of Skye*. In a long list of contributors, Finlay includes the poets Meg Bateman, Thomas A Clark and Roderick Watson, as well as Sorley MacLean and Iain Crichton Smith.

A 'collaborative audio & visual word-map' (Finlay 2014c, n.p.), *The Road North* published in 2014, and preceded by a blog, was completed during a journey undertaken by Finlay and Ken Cockburn. The paper-based version contains prose and poetic text, while the online version includes photographs and audio material, accompanied by an interactive map on which the reader may retrace the poets' path: a contour of Scotland with clickable squares placed around it. The itinerary projected onto a map enables the reader to follow the numbers or explore the fifty-three places at random. Departing on 16 May 2010, precisely 321 years after Bashō and Sora, Finlay and Cockburn pair places from a different geographical locations and historical periods. In the places which they visit they leave *hokku*-labels, referring directly to Japanese literary tradition in which *hokku* were written as opening verses of *haikai no renga*, since Bashō also wrote a separate poem. The *hokku* contains a seasonal word or phrase, to reflect the poet's current environment. Re-enacting Bashō's journey and transposing it onto another time and place, Finlay and Cockburn find a relation to the original walk, the act of walking and paying attention to the landscape binding them across time and space, *hokku*-labels materially linking them to place. In the book version of the walk, Finlay and Cockburn employ a series of questions and answers, which precede each section and each part of the journey, opening space and challenging the certainty of maps.

'Walking as art', to use Rebecca Solnit's words, is a new function of walking which has emerged since the 1960s (Solnit 2001, 267). A performance practice, walking can become a brief, ephemeral artwork, an invisible sculpture, a practice initiated by Richard Long, who in *Line Made by Walking* (1967) created something that was 'both more ambitious and more modest than conventional art: ambitious in scale, in making his mark upon the world itself, modest in that the gesture was such an ordinary one, and the resultant work was literally down to earth, underfoot' (Solnit 2001, 267). In some way, Finlay's practices are a continuation – but also an expansion – of Long's practices, and so the question Solnit asks about Long's artwork is pertinent also in relation to Finlay: '[was] the line ... a residual trace, or a sculpture – the line – of which the photograph was documentation, or was the photograph the work of art, or all of these?' (2001, 270). In Finlay's work, the traces left in the landscape enter in dialogue on multiple platforms, the centre – *the locus* – always being the place.

Finlay's Chorography

In its focus on the local, walking leads us to the concept of chorography. In its etymology, the word 'chorography' comes from two Greek words: *khōros*, meaning 'place', and *graphein*, 'to write'. A term which comes from antiquity, returning in the early modern period, chorography signifies topographical literatures, place writing. Rather than understanding the concept as 'writing about a country or region', Darrell J. Rohl argues that chorography translates *graphia* 'representation', and defines chorography as 'the representation of space or place' (2011, 1). After a period when chorographic writing flourished – the seventeenth century – the term chorography was rarely used even though it was still practised (Rohl 2011, 3), but nowadays landscape phenomenologists such as Christopher Tilley continue chorographic practice (Rohl 2011, 4). It is also pursued by artists such as Finlay, who is concerned with mapping place not only with reference to its geography but taking into consideration its history and culture.

While spatio-temporal, preoccupied with both place and time, chorographic writing decidedly puts place first, yet temporality is a significant feature in its historical dimension, which enables chorography to reveal 'the bidirectional connection of past and present through the medium of space, land, region or country' (Rohl 2011, 6). One more feature of chorography makes it a suitable concept for the examination of Alec Finlay's work, that is 'an inherently multimedia approach, including written description, multiple modes of visualization, and performance', which makes chorography 'generative, or creative' (Rohl 2011, 6).[5] I use the concept of chorography in reference to Finlay's projects to denote local geographies, place writing focused on a small part of the world rather than attempting to cover all of it, projects which work by 'calling places into being, not just by naming topographic features, but by dramatizing in the process of revealing the landscape how they matter' (Bossing 1999, 153 cit. Rohl 2011, 6). What is more, emplaced literature focused on place awareness as practised by Alec Finlay partly realises the concept of a 'deep-map', described by William Least Heat-Moon in *PrairyErth: (a Deep Map)* (1991), reflecting on eighteenth-century antiquarian approaches to place, which included 'history, folklore, natural history and hearsay', aiming to capture 'the grain and patina of place through juxtapositions and interpenetrations of the historical and the contemporary, the political and the poetic, the factual and the fictional, the discursive and the sensual, the conflation of oral testimony, anthology, memoir, biography, natural history' (cit. Rohl 2011, 5) and anything else pertaining to place.

Etymologically, chorography contains an element which has proved philosophically fertile, germinating meanings: *chora*, or *khōra*, which designates place, site, locality. Originating from Plato's *Timaeus*, *chora* has been employed by Julia Kristeva, who, in *Revolution in Poetic Language*, underscores the difficulty in defining the concept, which remains forever ungraspable, as it 'lends itself to phenomenological, spatial intuition, and gives rise to a geometry' (Kristeva 2011, 25–6); and which is used 'to denote an essentially mobile and extremely provisional articulation constituted by movements and their ephemeral stases' (Kristeva 1984, 25). As Kristeva argues: 'Although the *chora* can be designated and regulated, it can never be definitively posited: as a result, one can situate the *chora* and, if necessary, lend it a topology, but one can never give it axiomatic form' (Kristeva 1984, 26). Its elusive nature is also grasped by Derrida, who writes:

> this 'thing' that is nothing of that to which this 'thing' nonetheless seems to 'give place'—without, however, this 'thing' ever *giving* anything: neither the ideal paradigms of things nor the copies that an insistent demiurge, the fixed idea before his eyes, inscribes in it. Insensible, impassible but without cruelty, inaccessible to rhetoric. *Khōra* discourages, it 'is' precisely what disarms efforts at persuasion ... Neither sensible nor intelligible, neither metaphor nor literal designation, *neither* this *nor* that, *both* this *and* that, participating and not participating in the two terms of a couple, *khōra*—also called 'matrix' or 'nurse'. (*Prière d'insérer* cited in Translator's Note, xv–xvi)

Chora is 'analogous only to vocal or kinetic rhythm' (Kristeva 2011, 26). Finlay's chorographic works present or stage a space filled with voice and movement, and are an attempt to capture spaces in between, spaces 'inaccessible to rhetoric', to show that landscape *is*.

Ephemeral and provisional, *chora* is a clearing which reveals itself, opening to the truth of being, explored by Alec Finlay, whose work is 'at the same time too dense and too fleeting: too connected with its place and procedures' (Hodby 2005, 6). In order to survey the landscape, Finlay employs a 'microtonal' method, which involves 'images of landscape, events, notes and conversations', or 'a succession of small notes heard across a wide field—a way of working that can animate the entire space without dominating one particular aspect of it' (Hodby 2005, 6). These comments regard Finlay's projects titled *Avant-Garde English Landscape* and *Some Versions of Landscape. A survey of artist projects in the landscape (1998–2006)*,[6] but equally could be used to describe a number of his other works. In these two projects, Finlay explores the space of the Yorkshire Sculpture Park, using the existing sculptures as 'navigational way-points on a walk through the park' (Finlay 2005c, 24). The focus on 'the kinetic rhythm', on moving through the landscape, is reflected in such works as 'A-GEL03 circlesthroughthepath', which proposes a walk which connects seven letterboxes containing circle poems that map a route around park, foregrounding the relation of landscape to thought through an imaginative use of language. As Finlay explains:

> Patterned poems—compound, modified or animated forms—
> permutations that imitate nature and horticulture—
> mesostic poems which grow like plants—
> circle poems which turn an arc in time and have silence in their
>   heart—
> grid poems made into sliding puzzles—wordrawings.
>
> The wounds we make in nature return to mark us.
> Our healing is turning toward living.
> (Finlay 2005c, 28)

In an artwork numbered SVOL06 and titled 'Mesostic herbarium' – *naMes makE Stems chOsen wordS Their growIng branChes* (Finlay 2015, 46), Finlay foregrounds the organic nature of text which can sprout letters in unexpected places. Names are intertwined with the vegetal world. As Finlay explains, 'Mesostic herbarium is an archive and book of poems written on the names of flowers and trees. Some poems have been animated as WORDWOOD, and others made into botanical name labels' (2015, 46). Scattered around the world, wooden boxes, each containing a circle poem rubber stamp and ink pad, are accompanied by guides published online, which highlights the openness of artwork and its interactive nature, forming an incomplete map.

The intertwining of language and landscape is present in various works, particularly more recent ones such as minn*mouth* (2016), which 'seeks a potential vocabulary that exceeds conventional orthography', offering the 'sequence of detached sentences', which 'proposes a fluxus, from poetic devices, sketching a history, part-lost, part-imagined, whose roots are bedded in the experimental analysis of wind' (Finlay 2016, 5). What Finlay calls 'tidal poetry', welds together language, sea waves and sand in an attempt to 'counter petrolio, and forge a post-carbon culture—or, at least, devise a poetics for a drowned world' (Finlay 2016, 5). Such elemental works are complemented with projects which focus on the vegetal world, including the 'mesostic' projects, emphasising the interchange between text and organic matter. In one such site-specific artwork, titled *I Hear Her Cry: anagrammatic poem-clues for The Oaks, Wellesley*, realised in 2012–15, Finlay offers place-aware work in a double sense: it focuses on types of trees as well as the literary heritage. Several poems are dedicated to American poets and thinkers such as Sylvia Plath, Emily Dickinson, Henry David Thoreau and Ralph Waldo Emerson, all of whom observed the vegetal world closely. In the epigraph coming from James Schuyler's poem titled 'October', the falling of leaves encapsulated in the American name for a season of 'mists and mellow fruitfulness': 'Fall has / come: unpatterned, in / the shedding leaves.' The moment of leaves suddenly detaching itself from a branch and falling is captured in the enjambments severing the auxiliary verb from the main one and the preposition from the rest of the prepositional phrase. The beginning of Schuyler's poem, three lines before the lines cited above, creates an image in which books are compared to leaves: 'Books litter the bed, / leaves the lawn. It / lightly rains.' The final two lines of the poem reinforces this image: 'The books / of fall litter the bed', which further emphasises the intertwining of organic and textual matter, combining the irregularity of 'unpatterned' leaves with the order of language.

Proper Names

I Hear Her Cry includes poem-clues, a device commonly employed by Alec Finlay, which may be seen as a return to the beginnings of English poetry with Anglo-Saxon riddles. For Finlay, clues open up language and enable us to 'know all the ways that a word can fit into the jigsaw of language' (Finlay 2005a, n.p.). Some of Finlay's projects rely on puzzles, taking the form of 'map-word crosswords' as in *Three Rivers Crossword* (2005), in which he follows the rivers Tyne, Tees and Wear to create a map of the north-eastern region of England. In an epigraph, Finlay cites William Empson's words, who remarked in the 1930s that the fashion for 'obscure poetry' coincided with the fashion for crossword puzzles, claiming wittily that 'this revival of interest in poetry, an old and natural thing, has got a bad name merely by failing to know itself and refusing to publish the answers' (Finlay 2005a, n.p.). By placing clues in the landscape and inviting readers to navigate them online in search for answers, Finlay creates a crossword map which includes words referring to place names in Latin, Old English and Norman language, flora and fauna found there and human-made structures, proposing a linguistic mapping of landscapes and landmarks. The intertwining of cultural history of Scotland with the elements of the landscape is already demonstrated in such works as *Some Colour Trends* (2014) in which Finlay focuses on place names in various regions including Deeside, Donside, Speyside, Strathbogie and Strath Deveron. By investigating their etymology, Finlay foregrounds the influence of several languages: Norse, Gaelic, Pictish and Scots, as well as English. This linguistic layering reflects various processes of coexistence and recreation in the course of name-giving whereby imagination and vision perform a significant part, whereby place names in response to the landscape. Finally, the employment of colour reflects contemporary coding used in marking routes.

Proper names, their function and meaning remain an important, recurrent theme in Finlay's work. Considering various linguistic possibilities through the exploration of place words, Finlay draws our attention to the manner in which they are made to signify in the landscape, designating its elements. A question of convention, proper names are of cultural relevance, pointing to social geography and history: they have a spatial and temporal function. Thus, proper names are cultural constructs; they do not exist outside of a specific context. What is more, they mark propriety, conveying power. 'The bruises of designation that scatter maps', place names are 'invisible when confronted with the geological fact', as 'the act of corroborating the empirical with its appellation is fraught with difficulties' (Morrison 2013, n.p.), as Gavin Morrison writes in an essay '14 Views of the Isle of Skye', written for *Còmhlan Bheanntan / A Company of Mountains*. These difficulties concern various aspects of naming the landscape, particularly in Scotland, where the linguistic past and present are complex, palimpsestic, where the Clearances erased previous names: 'even the burns and rivulets lost their denominations, lacking a populace to refer to them' (Morrison 2013, n.p.). Morrison's observations and questions reverberate through Finlay's work of mapping: 'Is there an ethical imperative to reclaim these peaks' and other topographical features' earlier names? How far back does one need to go to find the "true" or "original" name?' (2013, n.p.). This is our, human concern, while '[t]he mountains remain stoically obstinate to this flurry of labelling; the names on the map are a moment in an historic continuum' (Morrison 2013, n.p.). Indeed, the non-human world does not need names; proper names are our human invention, a gesture of appropriation we cannot seem to avoid.

The inevitability of naming has been a subject of philosophical reflection, preoccupying such thinkers as John Stuart Mill, Bertrand Russell and Jacques Derrida. In *Naming and Necessity*, Saul Kripke asks what the relation there is between names and descriptions, citing the example given by Mill in *A System of Logic*, who writes about Dartmouth, which supposedly stands for the mouth of the river Dart, based on which he claims that names have 'denotation but not connotation' (1972, 26). However, Kripke disagrees with Mill, insisting that names do have a connotation for some people even if it is 'not part of the *meaning* of the name "Dartmouth" that the town so named lies at the mouth of the Dart' (1972, 26). Kripke, like Frege and Russell before him, assume a different position from Mill on this matter, arguing that 'a proper name, properly used, simply was a definite description abbreviated or disguised' (1972, 27). Derrida, who wrote extensively on the proper name,[7] takes a different stance, focusing on the random nature of proper names: 'The proper name, in its aleatoriness, should have no meaning and should spend itself in immediate reference. But the chance or the misery of its arbitrary character (always other in each case), is that its inscription in language always affects it with a potential for meaning' (Derrida 1984, 118). For Derrida, the proper name is aleatory, random, depending on chance, arbitrariness being its most striking feature, yet, as he argues, '[i]t becomes meaningful once again, of limited range, once it is reinvested with semantic content' (Derrida 1984, 120). The proper name begins to signify once it is filled with meaningful content, thus resembling *khōra*, as Derrida points out in *Prière d'insérer* (Dutoit 1995, xv–xvi).

As a word serving to identify a referent in the world, the proper name is often believed to be unique but, as Julian Wolfreys notes, '[t]here is a degree of play in the proper name between singularity and generality' (1998, 18). As 'there is a name behind the name – / there is a mountain beyond the mountain' (ll. 6–7) (*A Far-off Land*). The problem with the proper name (or better: one of the problems with the proper name) is the hegemony of its written form as the proper name is 'typical of the effect of writing-power, of its ability to veil and unveil' (Wolfreys 1998, 17). Once transcribed, placed on a map, the proper name announces itself, wielding the power which it is granted. The ambivalence of the proper name is explored by Finlay, having assumed an increasing significance in his recent work and resulting in a series of art projects and publications devoted to the consideration of place names[8] as well as the relation between sign and referent, which has been shifted due to cultural and historical changes. Yet human history and culture do not always matter as 'some place-names record where the sun falls, some point to where/ the rain puddles, and some where deer sleep' (ll. 10–11). The lines come from the opening poem from *A Far-off Land* (2017), 'Up the Noran Water and in by Inglismaddie . . .', the title of which refers to a traditional Scottish song based on Helen Cruikshank's poem 'Shy Geordie' from her first collection, *Up the Noran Water* (1934). On one the first pages of *A Far-off Land*, Finlay considers various facets of place names and their frequently paradoxical aspects. Thus the line 'a place-name can be a shelter' (l. 21) is immediately followed by 'a place-name can be a wall or gate preventing entry' (l. 22). Incorporated by us and made intimate, some place names do not necessarily belong on any maps as 'there are names that have a place within us' (l. 36). When they are lifted off the map, proper names may become endowed with 'semantic content', a meaning unique for everyone. Conversely, as Finlay points out, 'when we can no longer walk place-names offer a path that leads / into inaccessible landscapes' (ll. 37–8): a path opened up by a map.

Finlay foregrounds the interweaving of human activity and non-human aspects of place as '[n]ames take root whenever people dwell, revealing flora and fauna according to the knowing eye of the farmer, stalker and forager' (Finlay 2018a, 150). The passage comes from *Gathering* (2018), the title of which refers to Heidegger's concept of the fourfold. Heidegger writes about the gathering of 'earth, sky, mortals and gods' (2013, 148), which are brought together in a 'simple oneness of the four' (Heidegger 2013, 148), suggesting an interconnectedness of things. Finlay's book was inspired by Adam Watson, *The Place Names of Upper Deeside* (1984), which revises Gaelic names on the Ordnance Survey maps of the Cairngorms in

Scotland.⁹ *Gathering* is chorographic work – which includes prose and poems, photographs, and references to many sources on place – and a detailed depiction of the region, 'a place-aware guide' (Finlay 2018a, 9), an 'eco-poetical guide' (Finlay 2018b, n.p.) to Upper Deeside and the Cairngorms, concerned with the topographical features, with flora and fauna as well as remnants of culture in the form of shielings and decrepit dwellings. The book is divided into sections, each devoted to different topographical features of landscapes such as paths, rivers, 'lithophones and lookout stones', mountains and hills, among others that demonstrate the proliferation of elements of landscape. It opens with an epigraph taken from Walter Benjamin's essay 'In the Sun': 'Isn't every region governed by a unique confluence of plants and animals, and isn't every local name a cipher behind which flora and fauna meet for the first and last time?' (2005, 664) This announces one of the main preoccupations of Finlay's study: names given to a place are frequently a response to the vegetal and animal world found there. Throughout the many chapters Finlay reflects on proper names, their past role and present significance, and their transfer between languages, as '[t]he once known, the native, the Gaelic mountain, will all have had names before their "proper" ones' (Finlay 2018a, 71), remembering that '[t]he experience of space is always shot through with temporalities, as spaces are always created, reproduced and transformed in relation to previously constructed spaces provided and established from the past' (Tilley 1994, 11). The work of reproduction and transformation is expressed through circular poems containing place names (2018a, 55–7, 111, 198), which revolve and turn towards being, to use Finlay's expression.

The Communal Component

One of the characteristics of Finlay's work is its predominantly collaborative nature, that which Camille Manfredi calls '[t]he communal component' of his projects (2019, 132). Practised by Ian Hamilton Finlay and, to some extent, also Thomas A Clark, and, more recently, Kathleen Jamie,¹⁰ collaboration is a mode of artistic work which underlines the importance of a communitarian spirit, confirmed, for instance, in *Mesostic Herbarium* (2004), *Shared Writing: Renga Days* (2005), *Wild City* (2018) and Alec Finlay's most recent work, *I Remember: Scotland's Covid Memorial* (2021), which are composed through various contributions not only from poets and artists working together with Finlay but also common citizens.

Alec Finlay's *Gathering* (2018) is a collaboration with Hannah Devereux, Mhairi Law and Gill Russell, and includes contributions from James Dyas Davidson and Guy Moreton. The subtitle 'a place-aware guide to the Cairngorms' suggests the genre: the readers may expect a publication containing information about a place. Thus suggesting the function of the publication in the subtitle, Finlay directs the readers' attention to the nature of the region in terms of its geography and history, and so the readers become travellers or tourists who are guided through the region of Scotland. Place names and keywords are printed in bold type, which, together with landscape photographs, gesture towards the aesthetic expectations of the guidebook convention. Yet these features merely allude to rather than confirm the adhesion to the generic category. The size and weight of the publication means that in effect it cannot be a portable guidebook, certainly not a guidebook one would pack when going on a hike in a mountainous area. What is more, in spite of its informative value, it quickly becomes clear that the text does not resemble a conventional place description. Rather, it is a chorographical study, 'an innovative mapping of the Highland landscape in poems, essays, photographs and maps' (Finlay 2018b, n.p.), Finlay engages in literary and philosophical deliberations, interspersing the passages with brief poems. The book contains suggestions for routes yet in the poet's own words, it is not 'another guide to mountain culture' (2018, 9), nor does it contain 'the pageant of The Black Colonel's Bed, Jacobite hot spots', or 'Balmorality', as Finlay assures us (2018, 9). The note under the title explains that *Gathering* was 'inspired by the place-name collection of Adam Watson'. Adam Watson was an ecologist, conservationist, biologist, mountaineer and leading authority on the Cairngorms who died shortly after the publication of Finlay's book. In a study co-written with Elizabeth Allan, *The Place Names of Upper Deeside* (published in 1984), Watson assembled over 7,000 local place names over thirteen years of work, covering the topography of the region, and in this way preserving a vital element of Scottish folk culture. Among the 260 local inhabitants of the upper part of western Aberdeenshire, Watson talked to the last speaker of Deeside Gaelic, Jean Bain, who died in 1984. Considering the rich oral tradition of Gaelic, 'The loss of live conversation renders patterns of meaning more difficult to discern' (2018, 11), to cite Finlay.

In *Gathering* Alec Finlay continues his interest in the exploration of Scottish place names. As he explains, 'Some place-names reach into the bedrock of linguistic archaeology and Proto-Indo-European culture. Names may be inflected by three or more languages – primarily

Pictish, Gaelic and Scots – as, for long periods, the Highlands were multilingual and multicultural' (2018, 11). To say that place-name nomenclature in Scotland is a contentious matter would be an understatement. As W. F. H. Nicolaisen – who, as Finlay admits, was an important influence on *Gathering* (2018, 11) – demonstrates in 'Celtic Toponymics in Scotland' (1977), this is a space of multiple errors, erasure and neglect. Nicolaisen refers to William J. Watson's *The Celtic Place-Names of Scotland*, published in 1926, which constituted a significant achievement in Gaelic toponymics, taking into account the native pronunciation as well as the old written forms. In order to verify that, Watson consulted local inhabitants in situ. Finlay explicitly expresses an approach to place which favours local *folk* lore over the prevailing knowledge, arguing that 'Cultural and ecological knowledge is defined by the variety of names represented, or suppressed, in a region and the extent to which their meanings are understood' (2018, 11). He points to the flatness of maps as a result of the imposition of 'dominant languages and standardised orthography' (2018, 11), putting forward an argument that some of the documented Gaelic place names should be 'recognised by the OS, as a living memorial' (2018, 11). However, as he insists, *Gathering* does not aim to become 'heritage' (2018, 11). The concept of heritage may be understood here as a product of the aestheticisation of place, an easy, often sentimental interpretation of the past, which is fossilised or otherwise fixed in collective memory. 'A living memorial' in turn suggests a breathing organism which undergoes change within its system. The mode of observation differs: 'a living memorial' presents focused, participatory attention as opposed to that proprietary stance assumed by the notion of heritage. Thus concerned with the dissemination of sense (in contrast to a fixed meaning), Finlay offers an approach whereby names designate the natural world in its material form.

In most of Scotland, following the process of erasure and imprinting, Gaelic, a language which has been used in the region for over 1,500 years, was replaced with English, the process brought about by the Highland Clearances, which resulted in the destruction of the traditional society and loss of culture. During the eighteenth and nineteenth centuries thousands of families were evicted, their cottages burned and destroyed, and replaced with large sheep farms. The evicted tenants were resettled in small coastal crofts, where they were forced to depend on fishing and the collection and burning of kelp, resulting in economic hardship. Cleared for farming, the land became depopulated, which resulted in the destruction of the clan system and the weakening of the social fabric as the dispossession led to the disruption of a traditional way of life and a dispersal of Gaelic communities, making the transmission of language increasingly difficult. Now, with a small number of Gaelic speakers, at times place names constitute the sole remaining trace of a vanishing culture. Connected with these events is the history behind the creation of the Ordnance Survey maps. Their ambivalence is revealed if one considers the etymology of the name: their initial military purpose related to surveying, the primary aim was to map Scotland after the Jacobite rising of 1745 (Bliadhna Theàrlaich), which staunched opposition to the English government in the Highlands. In the early eighteenth century, in order to pacify the clans, the English rulers constructed forts and placed soldiers in the Highlands ready to intervene. As the English troops could not proceed for lack of roads and maps of the Highlands, a network of roads was built, in combination with a survey of place. As Finlay puts it, 'Of this well-calculated and truly Roman procedure the names of Fort William, Fort Augustus, Fort George, and Kind's House – English names in the very heart of the country – remain speaking witnesses' (2018, 83). In this way, Ordnance Survey maps of the region were created. As the documents issued by the national mapping agency, they may be said to mark the hegemony of the map. Considering the historical facts, OS maps are far from neutral: official documents, they stand for the violence of imposition of an authoritative text from the colonial language and culture, 'the topographical nomenclature of a country being always . . . a fossilised record of the most notable tides of social change that have swept over it in the past' (Finlay 2018, 83).

Finlay's work foregrounds the embeddedness of place names in the landscape, local toponyms collected from the community. I wish to propose a reading of *Gathering* as an example of counter-mapping (also known as 'community-mapping'). As Sarah De Nardi suggests, the term is 'increasingly employed by indigenous peoples, often with the assistance of anthropologists, to defend and protest their homelands, artefacts, and knowledges or to set boundaries and stake claims to customary lands' (2014, n.p.). It is 'often remarkably detailed and including a great many named places and other spatial associations that go unrecorded in conventional topographical maps, the everyday mapping and map making of local communities can mount challenges to state hegemony, act as a medium of empowerment and resistance' (De Nardi 2014). In over seventy sections, Finlay offers a highly detailed and varied evocation of the Cairngorms, which becomes a kind of mnemonic-mapping in a form of ecopoetic archaeology that uncovers layers of the palimpsestic landscape. Often, there are many versions of the place name translated from Gaelic into English. In a section titled 'Toponym' (2018, 174–5), Finlay introduces a sequence of one-word poems, employing toponymic terms such as 'beinn', or mountain, 'cairn/càrn', or rock pile (also a burial mound), 'corrie/coire', a hollow on a side of a mountain, a glacial landform, 'slochd/sloc', a pit or a gap. The notes which follow the list of the one-word poems explain the etymology of the toponyms and provide topographical examples as well as a bibliography:

> THE HIGHER HIGH : BEINN
> A ROUND HEAD : CÀRN
> THE GLACIERS PARABOLA : COIRE
> MIND THE GAP : SCLOCHD
> (2018, 174)
>
> STONE-AGED XYLOPHONE : RINGING STANE
> (2018, 50)

In a blend of the poetic and linguistic, Finlay traces the language of the landscape with its non-living forms that 'help the rock speak' (2018, 51). For instance, the chapter on 'Lithophones and Lookout Stones' (2018, 50–2), devoted to the Neolithic carved stone balls and the Ringing Stane, or a resonating rock, depicts a set of struck sonorous stones, *rock harmonicon* set in the land. As Finlay writes, 'Rhythm in musicking and placemarks in language were some of the ways our forebears anchored meaning' (2018, 51). Thus the orality of place names becomes entwined with sound effects, or the aurality of the land. *Gathering* combines memory of place and time, intertwining topography, toponyms and temporality and celebrating place names which constitute 'acts of communal memory' (2018, 9). It aims to save them from loss, representing the landscape not as burial ground but 'a living memorial' (Finlay 2018, 9).

The theme of landscape as repository of memory reappears in Finlay's practice. At times it assumes a form of remembrance combined with the healing properties of the land, as exemplified by such works as *Mesostic Remedy* (2008) and *Taigh: a wilding garden* (2018). *Mesostic Remedy*, or 'a compendium of mesostic poems on the names of the 38 Bach flower remedies' (2008, n.p.) with contributions by Linda France and illustrations by Laurie Clark, offers reflections upon 'nature cure', following Dr Edward Bach's philosophy of homeopathy, which focuses on the connections between physical health and emotional as well as mental states. The typographically experimental poems take the form of brief statements concerning various aspects of wellbeing. In reference to the word 'mesostic', employed by the artist in several projects, some of which have been mentioned in this chapter, Finlay writes: 'The mesostic poem is an interleaved form, whose structure is suggestive of organic growth' (2008, n.p.). *Taigh: a wilding garden*, or 'National Memorial for Organ and Tissue Donors', was placed at the Royal Botanic Garden in Edinburgh. The title refers to healing stones at Taigh na Caillich,[11] exploring the relationship between stone and a dwelling place that humans make in the landscape. The placement of the memorial in the botanic garden underlines the importance of green spaces in the urban setting. In his practice, Finlay offers an original approach to the themes of illness and health, as well as the relation between wellbeing and nature, which have been explored extensively in the recent years in British art and writing on nature.[12] By focusing on collectivity, Finlay practises 'empathetic radicalism' and 'shared healing', perceived as revolution since political and cultural change requires 'radical gentleness', as Finlay argues (Riach 2020, n.p.). The collective experience of the global pandemic at the beginning of the third decade of the twenty-first century reminded humans of our vulnerability and the need for care and empathy. Created in the aftermath of the pandemic, *I Remember* is Scotland's Covid Memorial in Pollok Country Park, Glasgow, and offers a reflection on mourning and loss. Adapted from Joe Brainard's 1975 concept, *I Remember*, commissioned by *The Herald*, which launched a campaign for a memorial in the early days of the pandemic (spring 2020), not only functions as commemoration but also raises awareness about the importance of access to green spaces, a problem which became prominent during the lockdowns. Created in a communitarian spirit, the memorial is composed of a number of wooden supports with the words 'I remember' etched onto them in languages spoken in Scotland, including Scots, Gaelic, English, Italian, Polish and Japanese, among others. (The multilingual nature of this artwork confirms Finlay's dedication to the spirit of inclusiveness, as does the placement of text in sign language on his blog.) As with many other projects by Finlay, *I Remember* appears in a number of media, such as sculpture, a publication, audiobook and website. The memorial in its first phase was officially opened on 27 May 2022. The installation in Pollok Country Park 'will include 40 wooden supports bearing the words "I remember", along with QR-code linking to the audiobook, and memorial plantings of wildflowers' (2022, 90). Preceded by a dedication 'for the dead and those still finding their way to healing', the book is composed of lines, each beginning with the words 'I remember' by contributors whose names are listed at the end of the publication. Through such co-creative practices, the collective experience of the pandemic becomes particularly pronounced. Preoccupied with participatory, socially engaged practice and believing in the healing properties of the natural world, Finlay recognises the need for a more inclusive approach to the experience of landscape. Ethical responsibility and solidarity with those suffering from an illness lie at the heart of such projects as *Paths for All*. For its purpose, Finlay devised a 'Day of Access', which proposes a series of events enabling those with constrained walking to *be* in the landscape. 'Not walking won't stop me imagining walks or collaborating with people who walk for me,' declared Finlay (2020, n.p.), proposing the concept of a 'proxy walk', or 'a walk done on behalf of a person who is bed/house-bound with illness, describing the present reality of a landscape they recall; an act of imaginative solidarity and exchange of energy' (2020, 256). For those who cannot walk in the landscape, Finlay proposes a form of mediation of being in nature and landscape as a response to the ableism which dominates nature writing. Moreover, Finlay points out that the question of healing is dual: healing may come from the land, but it ought to be noticed that the land requires the process of healing as well. As he admits, working on the disability access project offered 'a way to come at rewilding from a fresh perspective – what does it mean to heal the land, to come at it from the thrill-based desire of hunting, or even climbing, and consider instead a culture of recuperation' (Monaghan 2021, n.p.), adding that a large part of Scotland's landscapes is 'dominated by the desire to hunt', which stands in opposition with '*new desires to heal*' (Monaghan 2021, n.p.). The search for alternative ways towards democratised, more just approaches to land, based on redistributive policies and cooperative ownership models, including the urban dimensions of land justice and their implications for locally autonomous food systems. The urban croft becomes an extension of the allotment as a communitarian space in the search for more politically and socially just solutions that foster localism. Inscribed within projects fostering sustainable forms of urbanism, *Manifesto for Urban Crofts* (2021), created by Finlay and composed of twenty colour risograph posters in a wooden seed tray, is aimed at raising awareness of bio-conscious approaches to the land. Ecological urbanism, which focuses on a culture of recuperation, involves rewilding in a city context. This is the theme undertaken by Finlay in another collaborative work – a recording of participative walks, public readings and workshops created in collaboration with Dee Heddon and Misha Myers from the Walking Library, poets Gerry Loose and Ken Cockburn, artist Kate McAllan and photographer Mhairi Law – *Wild City / Fiadh-Bhaile / Orasul Salbatic* (2018), which offers an exploration of encounters with the natural world in the built environment. The preoccupation with living and non-living elements of the landscape, as well as human interactions with the natural world, remains central to Finlay's work. This sustained interest is present in a number of projects revolving around bees: from installing beehives, bee boles, or 'bee-themed public sculptures' to planting fruit trees in collaborative creative responses to the natural world. In works such as *The Bee Libraries* (2012–14) composed of bee-themed books, converted into nests for solitary bees, Finlay not only highlights the continuity of the human relationship with honeybees which extends back to the neolithic era, foregrounding the significance of bees in history, but also points to the culture of beekeeping as well as bee symbolism in myth and philosophy. Part of Finlay's project is to build a global bee library with such locations as Sydney, Australia (2012); the Yorkshire Sculpture Park (2012); Brogdale, Kent (2013); Malham, North Yorkshire (2013); the University of Stirling (2014); Chelsea Physic Garden, London (2014); and Shandy Hall, North Yorkshire (2014). For instance, *Nether Hive* (2013), composed of three beehives placed on the University of Stirling campus, was created with Dunblane and Bridge-of-Allan Beekeepers in collaboration with Kathleen Jamie. *Swarm (ASX)*, with honey-bee recordings by Chris Watson, commissioned by the 18th Biennale in Sydney, is described by Finlay as 'an apicultural model of the global speculative financial system' ('Living Things' n.p.). Other 'poem beehives' include *The Beehives* (2015) on the Corbenic Poetry Path, located in Perth and Kinross, and *Succession*, comprising four painted beehives, with text, for the National Fruit Collection in Brogdale in Kent. *A Variety of Cultures* made of plum and apple trees in Jupiter Artland responds to and complements the nearby *Beehives* (2009) by Ian Hamilton Finlay. Yet while Hamilton Finlay's beehives were created in response to the pastoral landscape at Little Sparta, Alec Finlay's orchard at Jupiter Artland as well as his beehive works appear to be created with heightened ecological awareness, present in many of his other poems and artworks, underlining the significance of all the elements in the ecosystem. Formed by the elements and inhabited by innumerable living beings, the landscape is a communal site, filled not only with human language, memory and text, but also with plant and animal energy in the process of constant interchange.

Finlay's work shows that landscape is not a given; it is not a stable, monolithic whole; rather, there are various forms of mapping places that are always already multi-layered. As a result of such constant malleability, Finlay's writing responds to the ways in which landscape is protean, mutable, depending on the subject's perception. His phenomenological maps, created both on the page and in situ, on the move, challenge the idea of a cartographic representation. Joining together various elements of the non-human world – the ground, the vegetal and animal world, the Earth's atmosphere – Finlay creates 'poésie en plein air' (Finlay 2005b, 47). Finlay's chorographic, site-specific artworks, mapped directly onto the landscape, engage with place and uncover meanings arising from immediate perception entwined with cultural memory contained in place names. A succinct description of *renga*, then, one of the collaborative forms used by Finlay, may serve to encapsulate his approach to being-in-the-world in this conclusion, which in response to Finlay's work must admit its own provisionality: that is 'an art of listening and interpolation; a path that leads on and never ends' (Finlay 2005b, 11; 2005c, 44). So too, all the writers considered in this volume direct us, as readers, to paths of which they have had a part in making, and which lead on, never ending.

Notes

1. Similarly to Ian Hamilton Finlay and Thomas A Clark, Alec Finlay continues the concrete convention in the use of titles without capital letters: this avoidance of majuscules abolishes hierarchy, introducing equality.
2. See, e.g., Manfredi 2019 and Sanderson 2015.
3. Japanese poetic forms are practised in Scotland by a number of poets, including Alan Spence, Kenneth White and Kevin MacNeil. Alec Finlay is the author of *Football Haiku* (2002), as well as editor of *Atoms of Delight: An Anthology of Scottish Haiku and Short Poems* (2000).
4. This resemblance is no coincidence since it was Robert Creeley's collection which brought Alec Finlay to poetry (2001, 100).
5. Rohl describes the legacy of late seventeenth- and early eighteenth-century Scottish scholars such as Sir Robert Sibbald and Alexander Gordon and their chorographic practice (Rohl 2011, 7–17).
6. As Finlay explains, the title, *Some Versions of Landscape. A survey of artist projects in the landscape (1998–2006)*, comes from William Empson's critical study *Some Versions of Pastoral* (1935) and exhibitions devoted to English avant-garde filmmakers: *British Avant-Garde Landscape Films* (1975) and *Perspectives on English Avant-Garde Film* (1978) (2005, 80).

7. See, e.g., *On the Name* (1995), 'The Battle of Proper Names' in *Of Grammatology* (1997) and *Signéponge/Signsponge* (1984).
8. For instance, *th' fleety wud* (2017) is described as 'a place-aware mapping of the Upper Teviot watershed from the source at Teviot Stone to the Rule Water in the Scottish Borders. With a phylogenetic diagram and watershed map, place-name translations' (Finlay 2017, n.p.). Place names have a special significance in Scotland, as exemplified by the Scottish Place-Name Society and the journal devoted to the subject, *The Journal of Scottish Name Studies*.
9. As we may read on *Ainmean-Àite na h-Alba / Gaelic Place-Names of Scotland* website, the problem with naming was officially acknowledged in 2000, when 'the Ordnance Survey (OS) recognised that some Gaelic place-names on their maps were incorrect, and in some instances, inconsistent across their scales of mapping. This arose because most names of natural features were collected in the 19th century, with revision in line with the Gaelic spelling system of the late nineteen sixties and early seventies' (2019, n.p.).
10. Kathleen Jamie began employing the method after her appointment to the post of Scots Makar, with her first poem entitled 'The Life Breath Song'. A 'people's nature poem', it was made by the people of Scotland who were requested to submit a line of verse which was then shaped into the poem by Jamie. The poem was accompanied by three film poems created by the Scottish artist Alistair Cook premiered on 5 November 2021.
11. See Tarbuck (2017).
12. Critical books include *The Bloomsbury Handbook to the Medical-Environmental Humanities* (2022).

References

Abberley, Will, Christina Alt, David Higgins, Graham Huggan and Pippa Marland. *Modern British Nature Writing, 1789–2020*. Cambridge: Cambridge University Press, 2022.
Adorno, Theodor W. *Aesthetic Theory*, translated by Robert Hullet-Kentor. London: Continuum, 1997.
'Adoxa moschatellina'. *Online Atlas of the British and Irish Flora*. https://www.brc.ac.uk/plantatlas/plant/adoxa-moschatellina. Accessed 20 Aug. 2021.
Agamben, Giorgio. *Homo Sacer: Sovereign Power and Bare Life*, translated by Daniel Heller-Roazen. Redwood City: Stanford University Press, 1995.
Alaimo, Stacy. 'Elemental Love in the Anthropocene'. In *Elemental Ecocriticism: Thinking with Earth, Air, Water, and Fire*, edited by Jeffrey Jerome Cohen and Lowell Duckert, 298–309. Minneapolis and London: University of Minnesota Press, 2015.
Albrecht, Glenn. 'Solastalgia and the New Mourning'. In *Mourning Nature: Hope at the Heart of Ecological Loss*, edited by Ashlee Cunsolo and Karen Landman, 292–315. Montreal and Kingston: McGill-Queen's University Press, 2017.
Allen, Valerie. 'Matter'. In *Inhuman Nature*, edited by Jeffrey Jerome Cohen, 61–77. Washington, DC: Oliphaunt Books, 2014.
'An Cidhe Beag'. *Tiree Place Names*. http://www.tireeplacenames.org/scarinish/an_ceidhe_beag-2/. Accessed 7 Nov. 2021.
Andrews, Kerri. *Wanderers: A History of Women Walking*. London: Reaktion Books, 2020.
Andrews, Malcolm. *Landscape and Western Art*. Oxford: Oxford University Press, 1999.
Anon. *The Print Collector's Newsletter* 23, no. 3 (1992): 108–9. www.jstor.org/stable/24554413. Accessed July 13, 2020.
Anon. *The Voyage of Saint Brendan: Journey to the Promised Land*, translated by John J. O'Meara. Dublin: Dolmen Press, 1978.
'Archive Documents: The Conservation & Management Plan'. *Little Sparta*. https://www.littlesparta.org.uk/the-conservation-management-plan/. Accessed 6 April 2022.

Armitage, Simon, and Tim Dee, eds. *The Poetry of Birds*. London: Penguin, 2011.
Assman, Jan. *Cultural Memory and Early Civilization: Writing, Remembrance, and Political Imagination*, translated by David Henry Wilson. Cambridge: Cambridge University Press, 2012.
Ascherson, Neal. 'Seven Poets'. *Seven Poets: Hugh MacDiarmid, Norman MacCaig, Iain Crichton Smith, George Mackay Brown, Robert Garioch, Sorley MacLean, Edwin Morgan*, edited by Christopher Carrell, 17–31. Glasgow: Third Eye Centre, 1981.
Barbaras, Renaud. *The Being of the Phenomenon: Merleau-Ponty's Ontology*, translated by Ted Toadvine and Leonard Lawlor. Bloomington and Indianapolis: Indiana University Press, 2004.
Bateman, Meg. 'The Landscape of the Gaelic Imagination'. *International Journal of Heritage Studies* (2009): 142–52. https://doi.org/10.1080/13527250902890613 9
Bateman, Meg. Review of *Literature of the Gaelic Landscape: Song Poem and Tale / Litreachas na Tìre: Òran Bàedachd is Sgeulachd* by John Murray. *Scottish Place Name News* 44 (Spring 2018): 13–14. https://spns.org.uk/wp content/uploads/2020/02/SPNNews-44-Spring-2018.pdf.
Bateman, Meg, and John Purser. *Window to the West: Culture and Environment in the Scottish Gàidhealtachd*. Sleat, Isle of Skye: Clò Ostaig, 2020.
Bell, Eleanor, and Linda Gunn, eds. *The Scottish Sixties: Reading, Rebellion, Revolution?* Scottish Cultural Review of Language and Literature Series, vol. 8. Amsterdam and New York: Rodopi, 2017.
Bender, Barbara. *Landscape: Politics and Perspectives*. Providence: Berg, 1993.
Benjamin, Walter. *Selected Writings, Volume 2, Part 2: 1931–1934*, edited by Michael W. Jennings, translated by Rodney Livingstone and others. Cambridge, MA, and London: The Belknap Press of Harvard University Press, 2005.
Berleant, Arnold. *The Aesthetics of Environment*. Philadelphia: Temple University Press, 1992.
Berleant, Arnold. *Living in the Landscape: Toward the Aesthetics of Environment*. Lawrence: University Press of Kansas, 1997.
Berleant, Arnold, and Allen Carlson, eds. *The Aesthetics of Natural Environments*. Peterborough, Ont.: Broadview Press, 2004.
Berridge, David. 'Materials of Pastoral'. A Review of Thomas A. Clark's *A Place Apart*. *Ecopoetics* 4/5 (2004–5): 84–90.
'Bindweed'. *Royal Horticultural Society*. https://www.rhs.org.uk/advice/profile?pid=241. Accessed 21 Aug. 2021.
Bishop, Claire. *Installation Art: A Critical History*. London and New York: Routledge, 2005.
Bloomfield, Mandy. 'Landscaping the Page: British Open-field Poetics and Environmental Aesthetics'. *Green Letters: Studies in Ecocriticism* 17, no. 2 (2013): 121–36. http://dx.doi.org/10.1080/14688417.2013.800338.

Board of Regents of the University of Oklahoma. The 1980 Jurors and Their Candidates for the Neustadt International Prize for Literature. *World Literature Today* 53, no. 4 (Autumn 1979): 627–41.

Bold, Alan. *Modern Scottish Literature*. London: Longman, 1983.

Borthwick, David, Pippa Marland and Anna Stenning, eds. *Walking, Landscape and Environment*. London and New York: Routledge, 2020.

Bowring, Jacky. *Melancholy and the Landscape: Locating Sadness, Memory and Reflection in the Landscape*. London and New York: Routledge, 2016.

Brady, Emily. *Aesthetics of the Natural Environment*. Edinburgh: Edinburgh University Press, 2003.

Buell, Lawrence. *Writing for an Endangered World: Literature, Culture and Environment in the U.S. and Beyond*. Cambridge, MA: Harvard University Press, 2001.

Campsie, Alison. 'Scotland's most remote pub to close for good'. *The Scotsman*, 16 Aug. 2019. https://www.scotsman.com/heritage and retro/heritage/scotlands-most remote-pub-close-good-1410420. Accessed 29 Jan. 2021.

Carmichael, Alexander. *Carmina gadelica: Hymns and Incantations*. Edinburgh: T. and A. Constable, 1900.

Casey, Edward S. *The Fate of Place: A Philosophical Inquiry*. Berkeley: University of California Press, 1997.

Casey, Edward S. *Getting Back into Place: Toward a Renewed Understanding of the Place World*. Bloomington: Indiana University Press, 1993.

Casey, Edward S. *Representing Place: Landscape Painting and Maps*. Minneapolis: University of Minnesota Press, 2002.

Clare, John. *Poems Selected by Paul Farley*. London: Faber & Faber, 2007.

Clark, Thomas A. *Adjectives for Grasses*. Pittenweem: Moschatel Press, 1980.

Clark, Thomas A. *Admit one*. Pittenweem: Moschatel Press, 2017d.

Clark, Thomas A. *allt garbh beag/rough little stream*. Pittenweem: Moschatel Press, 2019.

Clark, Thomas A. *An Cidhe Beag*. Pittenweem: Moschatel Press, 2002.

Clark, Thomas A. *and then an island floated past us like a promise of happiness and we rocked in its wake*. Pittenweem: Moschatel Press, 2016.

Clark, Thomas A. *An Lochan Uaine*. Pittenweem: Moschatel Press, 1993a.

Clark, Thomas A. *An Lochan Uaine*. San Francisco: Hawkhaven Press, 2008.

Clark, Thomas A. 'art in the landscape'. 2014a. http://thomasaclarkblog.blogspot.co.uk/2014/12/art-in-landscape.html. Accessed 6 Dec. 2021.

Clark, Thomas A. *before the traffic, the corncrake*. Pittenweem: Moschatel Press, 2021a.

Clark, Thomas A. *Bindweed Stitchwort Knotgrass*. Edinburgh: Essence Press, 2017b.

Clark, Thomas A. *blue remembered hills*. Pittenweem: Moschatel Press, n.d.

Clark, Thomas A. *Bookmarks*. Edinburgh: Morning Star Publications, 2001.
Clark, Thomas A. *By Kilbrannan Sound*. Pittenweem: Moschatel Press, 2012.
Clark, Thomas A. 'Thainig na naoi Sonais, / Le na naoi marannan'. In *Carmichael's Book: A Homage to Alexander Carmichael's* Carmina Gadelica, edited by Alec Finlay. Inverness: Artbook, and Edinburgh: Morning Star Publications, 1997.
Clark, Thomas A. 'CLPW Rights'. 2021e. thomasaclarkblog.blogspot.com/2021/08/. Accessed 3 Nov. 2021.
Clark, Thomas A. *Coire Fhionn Lochan*. Pittenweem: Moschatel Press, 2007a.
Clark, Thomas A. 'A Corncrake in Charlotte Square'. 2014b. http://thomasaclarkblog.blogspot.com/2014/08/a-corncrake-in-charlotte square.html. Accessed 26 Oct. 2021.
Clark, Thomas A. *Curlew Lapwing Plover Whimbrel*. Pittenweem: Moschatel Press, 2021c.
Clark, Thomas A. *A delphinium border*. Nailsworth: Moschatel Press, 1981.
Clark, Thomas A. *Distance & Proximity*. Edinburgh: Pocketbooks, 2000a.
Clark, Thomas A. *Doire Fhearna*. Empty Hands Broadside Series #8. Gardenville, NV: Country Valley Press, 2007b.
Clark, Thomas A. *dun na mairbhe / the fort of stillness*. Pittenweem: Moschatel Press, 2017c.
Clark, Thomas A. *The Earthly Paradise*. Pittenweem: Moschatel Press, 2013.
Clark, Thomas A. *Farm by the Shore*. Manchester: Carcanet, 2017a.
Clark, Thomas A. *a fold*. Pittenweem: Moschatel Press, 2010.
Clark, Thomas A. *folded*. Pittenweem: Moschatel Press, 2010.
Clark, Thomas A. *Folding the Last Sheep*. Pittenweem: Moschatel, 2016.
Clark, Thomas A. *a forest grove*. Pittenweem: Moschatel Press, 2001.
Clark, Thomas A. *The fourfold*. Pittenweem: Moschatel Press, 2017.
Clark, Thomas A. *glade*. Nailsworth: Moschatel Press, c. 1980.
Clark, Thomas A. *glade*. Pittenweem: Moschatel Press, 2017.
Clark, Thomas A. *Glade*. Collection of Greville Worthington, Wall Drawing, 1994.
Clark, Thomas A. *A Grove of Larch*. 2009. http://www.reiachandhall.co.uk/Images/Publication/spacetoheal_sample.pdf
Clark, Thomas A. *The Grove of Delight*. Pittenweem: Moschatel Press, 2014d.
Clark, Thomas A. *The Hundred Thousand Places*. Manchester: Carcanet, 2009.
Clark, Thomas A. *In a fold of hills*. Pittenweem: Moschatel Press, 1999.
Clark, Thomas A. *In Praise of Walking*. Nailsworth: Cairn Gallery, 1988.
Clark, Thomas A. *In Praise of Walking & On Looking at the Sea*. Kirkaldy: Fife Council Central Area Libraries, 2007.
Clark, Thomas A. *In Praise of Walking & Looking at the Sea*. Moschatel Press, 2007.
Clark, Thomas A. 'In Praise of Walking'. In *Distance & Proximity*, 13–22. Edinburgh: Pocketbooks, 2000.

Clark, Thomas A. Interviewed by Glyn Pursglove. *Poetry Information* 18 (Winter-Spring 1977–8): 12–20.
Clark, Thomas A. 'Making Spaces'. Interview with David Herd. *Oxford Poetry* 3, vol. 7 (1993b): 97–102.
Clark, Thomas A. *I say island*. Pittenweem: Moschatel Press, 2003.
Clark, Thomas A. 'In, Among, With and From'. Conversation with Alice Tarbuck. *PN Review* 229, vol. 42, no. 5 (May–June 2016): 36–41.
Clark, Thomas A. *island*. Edinburgh: Essence Press, 2005.
Clark, Thomas A. *Lochan a Bearta*. Pittenweem: Moschatel Press, 2000c.
Clark, Thomas A. *The Lord of the Isles*. Pittenweem: Moschatel Press, 2018.
Clark, Thomas A. 'Meet the Author: Thomas A Clark Discusses *The Threadbare Coat*'. 2020a. https://www.youtube.com/watch?v=KvQNr67u2M4.
Clark, Thomas A. *Names*. Pittenweem: Moschatel Press, 2006.
Clark, Thomas A. *Of Woods & Water. Forty Eight Delays*. Pittenweem: Moschatel Press, 2008.
Clark, Thomas A. *On a Grey Day*. Pittenweem: Moschatel Press, 1999.
Clark, Thomas A. *One Hundred Scottish Places*. 2nd ed. Eindhoven: Peter Foolen Editions, 2021b.
Clark, Thomas A. *One Moment Walk*. Pittenweem: Moschatel Press, 2007.
Clark, Thomas A. 'Pastoral'. *BO HEEM E UM 5* (Dec. 1968): n.p.
Clark, Thomas A. *pli selon pli*. Pittenweem: Moschatel Press, 2013.
Clark, Thomas A. *The Pocket Glade Dictionary*. Toronto: Underwhich Editions, 1980.
Clark, Thomas A. *a recumbent fold*. Pittenweem: Moschatel Press, 2011.
Clark, Thomas A. *A Ruskin's Sketchbook*. London: Coracle Press, 1979.
Clark, Thomas A. *sea hand land foot*. South Street Publications, n.d.
Clark, Thomas A. *a shore is lonely*. Pittenweem: Moschatel Press, 2020b.
Clark, Thomas A. *to redress the loss of the seagrass meadows*. Edinburgh: Essence Press, 2021d.
Clark, Thomas A. *To Scalasaig*. Pittenweem: Moschatel Press, 2000b.
Clark, Thomas A. 'The Standing Poem'. 13 Dec. 2011. http://thomasaclarkblog.blogspot.co.uk/2011/12/standing-poem.html. Accessed 7 Nov. 2021.
Clark, Thomas A. *The teachings of Huang Po*. Pittenweem: Moschatel Press, 1991.
Clark, Thomas A. *The thought of a glade*. Pittenweem: Moschatel Press, 2019.
Clark, Thomas A. *The Threadbare Coat: New and Selected Poems*. Manchester: Carcanet, 2020c.
Clark, Thomas A. *Tormentil & Bleached Bones*. Edinburgh: Polygon, 1993.
Clark, Thomas A. *Tràigh Bhalla*. Pittenweem: Moschatel Press, 2007.
Clark, Thomas A. *Twelve Proverbs*. Pittenweem: Moschatel Press, 2001.
Clark, Thomas A. *unfolding brightness*. Pittenweem: Moschatel Press, 2011.
Clark, Thomas A. *water fold fall*. Pittenweem: Moschatel Press, 2012.
Clark, Thomas A. *wing of the ptarmigan: forty eight delays*. Pittenweem: Moschatel Press, 2018.
Clark, Thomas A. *Wintergreen*. Charleston: tel-let, 2004.

Clark, Thomas A. *The World Brought Near*. Eindhoven: Peninsula, 1998.
Clark, Thomas A. *yarrow & marram grass*. Pittenweem: Moschatel Press, 2021.
Clark, Thomas A. *Yellow & Blue*. Manchester: Carcanet, 2014c.
Clark, Thomas A, and Laurie Clark. *About Nothing in Particular*. A Morning Star Folio, first series, vol. 3. Edinburgh: Morning Star, 1990.
Clark, Thomas A, and Laurie Clark. *An Affinity of Eye and Petal*. Pittenweem: Moschatel Press, n.d.
Clark, Thomas A, and Laurie Clark. 'A Box of Landscapes'. *Tenderbooks*. Accessed 25 Aug. 2021. https://tenderbooks.co.uk/products/a-box-of landscapes thomas-a-clarklaurie-clark?_pos=1&_sid=0da62e9fc&_ss=r.
Clark, Thomas A, and Laurie Clark. *A Bright Glade*. Edinburgh: Scottish Poetry Library, 2006.
Clark, Thomas A, and Laurie Clark. *The Bright Glade*. Pittenweem: Moschatel Press, n.d.
Clark, Thomas A., and Laurie Clark. *The Dappled Glade*. Nailsworth: Moschatel Press, 1979.
Clark, Thomas A, and Laurie Clark. *every time you find*. Pittenweem: Moschatel Press, 2019.
Clark, Thomas A, and Laurie Clark. *from* The teachings of Huang Po. Pittenweem: Moschatel Press, 2014.
Clark, Thomas A, and Laurie Clark. *Garvellachs*. Pittenweem: Moschatel Press, 2021b.
Clark, Thomas A, and Laurie Clark. *A gift of wild flowers*. Pittenweem: Moschatel Press, 2011.
Clark, Thomas A, and Laurie Clark. *go to a clearing, come to a glade*. Pittenweem: Moschatel Press, 2011.
Clark, Thomas A, and Laurie Clark. *Hart's Tongue*. Pittenweem: Moschatel Press, n.d.
Clark, Thomas A, and Laurie Clark. *In Praise of Walking*. Pittenweem: Moschatel Press, 2004.
Clark, Thomas A, and Laurie Clark. *In small things, delight is intense*. Pittenweem: Moschatel Press, 2010.
Clark, Thomas A, and Laurie Clark. *Lullaby*. Pittenweem: Moschatel Press, 2018.
Clark, Thomas A, and Laurie Clark. *a promise of happiness*. Pittenweem: Moschatel Press, 2021a.
Clark, Thomas A, and Laurie Clark. *Proverbs of the Meadow and the Mountain*. Milwaukee: Membrane Press, 1986.
Clark, Thomas A, and Laurie Clark. *A Quiet Island*. Pittenweem: Moschatel Press, 2015.
Clark, Thomas A, and Laurie Clark. *Rothiemurchus*. Pittenweem: Moschatel Press, 2021.
Clark, Thomas A, and Laurie Clark. *Ruin Wood*. Nailsworth: Moschatel Press, 1981.

Clark, Thomas A, and Laurie Clark. *A Short Tour of the Highlands*. Pittenweem: Moschatel Press, 1979.

Clark, Thomas A, and Laurie Clark. *The thought of a glade*. Pittenweem: Moschatel, 2019.

Clark, Thomas A, and Laurie Clark. *Two Evergreen Horizons*. Pittenweem: Moschatel Press, n.d.

Clark, Thomas A, and Laurie Clark. *Untitled*. Pittenweem: Moschatel Press, 2016.

Clark, Timothy. '"Renga": Multi-Lingual Poetry and Questions of Place'. *SubStance* 21, no. 2, issue 68 (1992): 32–45. DOI 10.2307/3684900

Cockburn, Henry. *Memorials of His Time*. New York: D. Appleton and Company, 1856. https://quod.lib.umich.edu/cgi/t/text/textidx?c=moa&cc=moa&sid=95e3f6e828e116b80d4cccd93c806bc1&view=tex&rgn main&idno=ABA0859.0001.001. Accessed 26 Oct. 2021.

Cole, Barry. 'Exciting Patterns'. *Ambit* 60 (1974): 21–4. https://www.jstor.org/stable/44331206

Collins, Lucy. '"Only the Dead Can Be Forgiven": Contemporary Women Poets and Environmental Melancholia'. *C21 Literature: Journal of 21st-century Writings* 5, no. 3 (2017): 1–21. doi.org/10.16995/c21.12.

'Colonsay, Riasg Buidhe'. *Canmore. National Record of the Historic Environment*. https://canmore.org.uk/site/38212/colonsay-riasg buidhe. Accessed 31 Oct. 2021.

'Common knotgrass'. *The Wildlife Trusts*. www.wildlifetrusts.org/wildlife explorer/wildflowers/common-knotgrass. Accessed 31 Aug. 2021.

Cook, Richard. 'The Home-Ly Kailyard Nation: Nineteenth-Century Narratives of the Highland and the Myth of Merrie Auld Scotland'. *ELH* 66, no. 4, The Nineteenth Century (Winter 1999): 1053–73.

Cooper, David E. 'Aestheticism and Environmentalism'. In *Spirit of the Environment: Religion, Value, and Environmental Concern*, edited by David E. Cooper and Joy A. Palmer. London and New York: Routledge, 1998.

Cosgrove, Denis. 'Prospect, Perspective and the Evolution of the Landscape Idea'. *Transactions of the Institute of British Geographers* 10, no. 1 (1985): 45–62.

Crichton Smith, Iain. 'A Lust for the Particular: Norman MacCaig's Poetry'. *Chapman* 45 (Summer 1986): 22.

Culler, Jonathan. 'The Call of the Phoneme'. In *On Puns: The Foundation of Letters*, edited by Culler, 1–17. London: Basil Blackwell, 1988.

Curry, Neil. 'Old Maps and New Selected Poems Review'. *Ambit* 76 (1978): 63. http://www.jstor.org/stable/44336891.

Davie, Donald. *Under Briggflatts: A History of Poetry in Great Britain, 1945–1988*. Manchester: Carcanet, 1989.

Deleuze, Gilles. *The Fold: Leibnitz and the Baroque*, translated by Tom Conley. London: The Athlone Press, 1993.

Dent, Peter, ed. *Candid Fields: Essays and Reflections on the Work of Thomas A Clark*. Budleigh Salterton: Interim Press, 1987.

Derrida, Jacques. *The Animal That Therefore I Am*, translated by David Wills. New York: Fordham University Press, 2008.
Derrida, Jacques. *Dissemination*, translated by Barbara Johnson. University of Chicago Press, 1983.
Derrida, Jacques. *On the Name*. Stanford: Stanford University Press, 1995.
Derrida, Jacques. 'Passages – From Traumatism to Promise'. In *Points . . . Interviews, 1974–1994*, edited by Elisabeth Weber, translated by Peggy Kamuf. Stanford: Stanford University Press, 1995.
Derrida, Jacques. *Singéponge/Signsponge*, translated by Richard Rand. New York: Columbia University Press, 1984.
Derrida, Jacques. *Speech and Phenomena: And Other Essays on Husserl's Theory of Signs*, translated by David B. Allison. Evanston: Northwestern University Press, 1973.
Dufrenne, Mikel. *The Phenomenology of Aesthetic Experience*, translated by Edward S. Casey. Evanston: Northwestern University Press, 1973.
Duncan, Andrew. 'Styles of British Poetry 1945–2000'. *Chicago Review* 53, no. 1, British Poetry Issue (Spring 2007). https://www.jstor.org/stable/40784169
Dunn, Douglas. 'As a Man Sees' – On Norman MacCaig's Poetry'. *Verse* 7, no. 2 (Summer 1990): 67.
Dutoit, Thomas. 'Translating the Name?' In Jacques Derrida, *On the Name*, i–xvi. Stanford: Stanford University Press, 1995.
Farrell Krell, David. *Derrida and Our Animal Others: Derrida's Final Seminar, 'The Beast and the Sovereign'*. Indianapolis: Indiana University Press, 2013.
Fazzini, Marco. 'At the back of my ear': A Note on Seamus Heaney and Scottish Poetry'. *Journal of European Studies* 46, no. 1 (Mar. 2016): 51–9. https://doi.org/10.1177/0047244115617710
Fazzini, Marco. *Crossings: Essays on Contemporary Scottish Poetry and Hybridity*. Venice: Supernova, 2000.
Fink, Eugen. *Sixth Cartesian Meditation: The Idea of a Transcendental Theory of Method*, translated by Ronald Bruzina. Bloomington and Indianapolis: Indiana University Press, 1995.
Finlay, Alec. *Avant-Garde English Landscape. Some Versions of Landscape*, edited by Alec Finlay and Alex Hodby. Wakefield: Yorkshire Sculpture Park, 2005c.
Finlay, Alec, ed. *Carmichael's Book: A Homage to Alexander Carmichael's Carmina Gadelica*. Inverness: Artbook, and Edinburgh: Morning Star Publications, 1997.
Finlay, Alec. *A Company of Mountains. 14 Views on the Isle of Skye*. Portree: Atlas Art, 2013.
Finlay, Alec. 'Gathering'. 2018b. http://gathering-alecfinlay.blogspot.com/2018/10/aplace aware walk.html.
Finlay, Alec. 'Down to Earth But Close to Heaven'. Introduction to In *Atoms of Delight. An Anthology of Scottish Haiku and Short Poems*, 17–26. Edinburgh: Pocketbooks, 2000.

Finlay, Alec. *A Far-off Land*. Edinburgh: Morning Star, 2017.
Finlay, Alec. 'From *A Place-Aware Dictionary*'. In *Antlers of Water: Writing on the Nature and Environment of Scotland*, edited by Kathleen Jamie, 245–60. Edinburgh: Canongate, 2020.
Finlay, Alec. *Gathering*. Zürich: Hauser & Wirth Publishers, 2018a.
Finlay, Alec. Interview with Lilias Fraser. *Scottish Studies Review* (Mar. 2001): 100–9.
Finlay, Alec. Interview on *Navigations*. London: Animate Projects, 2014b. http://www.animateprojects.org/.
Finlay, Alec. *Living Things*. https://www.alecfinlay.com/livingthings?pgid=jozxtal2-613cd0a9-0403-42a8-96fc-7a381a3bdc18. Accessed 22 Oct. 2022.
Finlay, Alec. 'Poet Alec Finlay on His Battle with Coronavirus and Finding Solace in Art'. Interview with Alan Riach. *The National*, 13 Aug. 2020. https://www.thenational.scot/news/18650172.poet-alec-finlay-battlecoronavirus-finding-solace-art/
Finlay, Alec. *Studio Alec Finlay*. 2018c. https://mailchi.mp/alecfinlay/youre-invitedto-alec finlays-book-launch?e=[UNIQID.
Finlay, Alec. *Shared Writing: Renga Days*. Edinburgh: Platform Projects, 2005b.
Finlay, Alec. *Some Colour Trends*. Huntly: Deveron Arts, 2014.
Finlay, Alec. *Three Rivers Crosswords: A Cryptic Word-Map of the North-East*. Edinburgh: Morning Star, 2005a.
Finlay, Alec. *Two Fields of Wheat Seeded with a Poppy Poem*. Milton Keynes: Milton Keynes Gallery, 2006.
Finlay, Alec. *Wild City / Fiadh-Bhaile / Orasul Salbatic*. Edinburgh: Morning Star, 2018.
Finlay, Alec, and Ken Cockburn. *The Road North*. Bristol: Shearsman Books, 2014.
Finlay, Alec, and Ken Cockburn. 2010–11. *The Road North*. http://www.theroadnorth.co.uk.
Finlay, Alec, with Gill Russell. *th' fleety wud*. Edinburgh: Morning Star, 2017.
Finlay, Alec, Hanna Tuulikki and Lucy Duncombe. *Minnmouth*. Newhaven: North Light and Dunbar: Morning Star, 2016.
Finlay, Alec, with Linda France. *Mesostic Remedy*, illustrated by Laurie Clark. Jupiter Artland/Morning Star/Ingleby Gallery, 2008.
Freeman, John. 'Paradise & the Real: The Poetry of Thomas A Clark'. In *Candid Fields: Essays and Reflections on the Work of Thomas A Clark*, edited by Peter Dent, 5–18. Budleigh Salterton: Interim Press, 1987.
Frykman, Erik. '"Unemphatic Marvels": A Study of Norman MacCaig's Poetry'. *Gothenburg Studies in English* 35. Gothenburg: Acta Universitatis Gothoburgensis, 1977.
Fulton, Robin. *Collected Poems* Review. *World Literature Today* 60, no. 3 (1986): 507. doi:10.2307/40142392.
Fulton, Robin. *The Equal Skies* Review. *World Literature Today* 54, no. 4 (1980): 684. doi:10.2307/40135557.

Fulton, Robin. '"Unemphatic Marvels": A Study of Norman MacCaig's Poetry by Erik Frykman'. *World Literature Today* 51, no. 3 (Summer 1977): 486.
Gairn, Louisa. 'Clearing Space: Kathleen Jamie and Ecology'. In *Contemporary Scottish Literature*, edited by Berthold Schoene, 236–44. Edinburgh: Edinburgh University Press, 2007.
Gairn, Louisa. *Ecology and Modern Scottish Literature*. Edinburgh: Edinburgh University Press, 2008.
Gan, Elaine, Nils Bubandt, Anna Lowenhaupt Tsing and Heather Anne Swanson. Introduction to *Arts of Living on a Damaged Planet: Ghosts and Monsters of the Anthropocene*, edited by Elaine Gan, Nils Bubandt, Anna Lowenhaupt Tsing and Heather Anne Swanson, 1–14. Minneapolis: Minnesota University Press, 2017.
Gibson, James J. *The Ecological Approach to Vision Perception*. Boston, MA: Houghton Mifflin Company, 1979.
Gibson, James J. *The Ecological Approach to Visual Perception*. Classic Edition. New York and London: Routledge, 2015.
Gilman, Rachel. 'Reading the Word: Spirit Materiality in the Mountain Landscapes of Nan Shepherd'. *Dialogue: A Journal of Mormon Thought* 52, no. 4 (Winter 2019): 29–38.
Goodwin, Gavin. 'Beyond the Page: The Formal Possibilities of Thomas A. Clark'. *Writing in Practice* 5 (March 2019). https://www.nawe.co.uk/DB/wip editions/articles/beyond-the page-the formal possibilities-of-thomas-a.clark.html. Accessed 10 Sept. 2019.
'Greater Stitchwort'. *The Wildlife Trusts*. www.wildlifetrusts org/wildlife explorer/wildflowers/greater-stitchwort. Accessed 31 Aug. 2021.
Green, Ian, 'Subtle Motions'. In *Candid Fields: Essays and Reflections on the Work of Thomas A Clark*, edited by Peter Dent, 19–23. Budleigh Salterton: Interim Press, 1987.
Greig, Andrew. *At the Loch of the Green Corrie*. London: Quercus, 2010.
Hair, Ross. *Avant-Folk: Small Press Poetry Networks from 1950 to the Present*. Oxford University Press, 2017.
Hair, Ross. 'Opening the Folds: Thomas A Clark, Ian Hamilton Finlay, and Pastoral'. *Journal of British and Irish Innovative Poetry* 5, no. 2 (2013): 13–14.
Hart, George. 'Postmodernist Nature/Poetry: The Example of Larry Eigner'. In *Reading Under the Sign of Nature: New Essays in Ecocriticism*, edited by John Tallmadge and Henry Harrington, 315–32. Salt Lake City: The University of Utah Press, 2000.
'Hart's tongue fern'. *The Woodland Trust*. www.woodlandtrust.org.uk/trees-woods-and-wildlife/plants/ferns/harts tongue-fern/. Accessed 18 Oct. 2021.
Heine, Steven, and Dale S. Wright. *The Koan: Texts and Contexts in Zen Buddhism*. Oxford University Press, 2000.
Heise, Ursula K. *Imagining Extinction: The Cultural Meanings of Endangered Species*. Chicago and London: The University of Chicago Press, 2016.

Hendry, Joy. 'The Metaphysical and Classical Humours of Norman MacCaig'. In *Norman MacCaig. Critical Essays*, edited by Joy Hendry and Raymond Ross. Edinburgh: Edinburgh University Press, 1990.
Hepburn, Ronald. *Wonder and Other Essays: Eight Studies in Aesthetics and Neighbouring Fields*. Edinburgh: Edinburgh University Press, 1984.
Higgins, Dick. *Pattern Poetry: Guide to an Unknown Literature*. State University of New York Press, 1987.
Hodby, Alex. Introduction to *Avant-Garde English Landscape. Some Versions of Landscape*, edited by Alec Finlay and Alex Hodby. Wakefield: Yorkshire Sculpture Park, 2005.
Horozco, Sebastián de. *Teatro universal de proverbios*, edited by José Louis Alonso Hernández. Salamanca: Ediciones Universidad de Salamanca, 2005.
Howard, Peter, Ian Thompson, Emma Waterton and Mick Atha, eds. *The Routledge Companion to Landscape Studies*. 2nd ed. London and New York: Routledge, 2019.
Ingold, Tim. 'Earth, Sky, Wind, and Weather'. *The Journal of the Royal Anthropological Institute. Wind, Life, Health: Anthropological and Historical Perspectives* 13, no.1 (2007): 19–38. https://doi.org/10.1111/j.14679655.2007.00401.x.
Ingold, Tim. 'Footprints through the Weather-World'. *Journal of the Royal Anthropological Institute* 16 (2010): 121–39. https://doi.org/10.1111/j.14679655.2010.01613.x
Ingold, Tim. *The Perception of Environment*. London and New York: Routledge, 2000.
Ingold, Tim. 'The Temporality of the Landscape'. *World Archaeology* 25, no. 2 (1993): 152–74. http://www.jstor.org/stable/124811.
Ingold, Tim, and Jo Lee Vergunst, eds. *Ways of Walking: Ethnography and Practice on Foot*. London and New York: Routledge, 2008.
Irigaray, Luce. *Between East and West*. New Delhi: New Age Books, 2002.
Irigaray, Luce. *The Forgetting of Air in Martin Heidegger*, translated by Mary Beth Mader. Austin: University of Texas Press, 1999.
Jamie, Kathleen. *Among Muslims: Meetings at the Frontiers of Pakistan*. London: Sort of Books, 2002.
Jamie, Kathleen. *The Bonniest Companie*. London: Picador, 2015.
Jamie, Kathleen. *Findings*. London: Sort of Books, 2005.
Jamie, Kathleen. Introduction to *Antlers of Water: An Anthology of Scottish Writing on Nature*, edited by Kathleen Jamie, xi–xvii. Edinburgh: Canongate, 2020.
Jamie, Kathleen. *The Overhaul*. London: Picador, 2012.
Jamie, Kathleen. *Sightlines*. London: Sort of Books, 2012.
Jamie, Kathleen. *Surfacing*. London: Sort of Books, 2019.
Jamie, Kathleen. *The Tree House*. London: Picador, 2004.
Johnson, B. S. 'Measure, Chaos and Indifference'. *Ambit* 24 (1965): 45–6.
Kant, Immanuel. *The Critique of Judgement*, translated by Werner S. Pluhar. London: Hackett, 1987.

Kapalo, James, Éva Pócs and William Francis Ryan, eds. *The Power of Words: Studies on Charms and Charming in Europe*. Budapest: Central European University Press, 2013.

Keats, John. *Letters*. 'To John Hamilton Reynolds'. 9 Apr. 1818, I, 268. https://www.gutenberg.org/files/35698/35698-h/35698-h.htm.

Kell, Richard. 'Collections of British Poetry 1962'. *Critical Survey* 1, no. 2 (Spring 1963): 73–5.

Kelsey, Robin. 'Landscape as Not Belonging'. *Landscape Theory*, edited by James Elkins and Rachael Delue. London and New York: Routledge, 2007.

Kindrick, Robert L. '*Selected Poems* by Norman MacCaig and Douglas Dunn'. *World Literature Today* 72, no. 4, Focus on Nuruddin Farah: The 1998 Neustadt Prize (Autumn 1998): 834–5.

Kleinberg, Ethan. Prologue to *Presence: Philosophy, History, and Cultural Theory for the Twenty-first Century*, edited by Ranjan Ghosh and Ethan Kleinberg, 1–7. Ithaca and London: Cornell University Press, 2013.

Kotva, Simone. 'Attention: Thomas A. Clark and Simone Weil'. *Journal of British and Irish Innovative Poetry* 11, no. 1 (2019). https://doi.org/10.16995/bip.732

Kotva, Simone. *Effort and Grace: On the Spiritual Exercise of Philosophy*. London and New York: Bloomsbury Academic, 2020.

Kripke, Saul A. *Naming and Necessity*. Cambridge, MA: Harvard University Press, 1972.

Kristeva, Julia. *Revolution in Poetic Language*, translated by Margaret Waller. New York: Columbia University Press, 1984.

Lakoff, George, and Mark Johnson. *Philosophy in the Flesh: The Embodied Mind and Its Challenge to Western Thought*. New York: Perseus, 1999.

Lawlor, Leonard. 'Jacques Derrida'. *The Stanford Encyclopedia of Philosophy*, edited by Edward N. Zalta. 2019. https://plato.stanford.edu/entries/derrida/

Leask, Nigel. *Stepping Westward: Writing the Highland Tour, c. 1720–1830*. Oxford: Oxford University Press, 2020.

'Lesser Stitchwort'. *The Wildlife Trusts*. https://www.wildlifetrusts.org/wildlife explorer/wildflowers/lesser-stitchwort. Accessed 31 Aug. 2021.

Lilley, Deborah. 'Kathleen Jamie: Rethinking the Externality and Idealisation of Mature'. *Green Letters: Studies in Ecocriticism* 17, no. 1 (2013): 16–26. doi.org/10.1080/14688417.2012.750841

Lippit, Akira Mizuta. *Electric Animal: Toward a Rhetoric of Wildlife*. Minneapolis: University of Minnesota Press, 2000.

Lyon, John. 'Helluva Hard Tay Read'. Review of *outside the narrative: Poems 1965–2009* by Tom Leonard. *PN Review* 192, vol. 36, no. 4 (2010): 54–5.

Mabey, Richard. *Weeds: The Story of Outlaw Plants*. London: Profile Books, 2010.

Macauley, David. *Elemental Philosophy: Earth, Air, Fire and Water as Environmental Ideas*. New York: SUNY Press, 2009.

MacCaig, Ewen. Editorial Note to *The Poems of Norman MacCaig*, edited by Ewen McCaig, xix–xxv. Edinburgh: Polygon, 2005.
MacCaig, Norman. 'My Way of It'. In *As I Remember: Ten Scottish Authors Recall How Writing Began for Them*, edited by Maurice Lindsay, 79–88. London: Robert Hale, 1979.
MacCaig, Norman. *The Poems of Norman MacCaig*, edited by Ewen McCaig. Edinburgh: Polygon, 2005.
MacDiarmid, Hugh. 'The Norman Conquest'. *The Voice of Scotland* 6, no 2 (July 1955): 20.
Macfarlane, Robert. Introduction to *The Living Mountain* by Nan Shepherd, ix–xxxvii. Edinburgh: Canongate, 2011.
MacIntyre, Duncan Ban. *Praise of Ben Dorain*, translated by Alan Riach. Newtyle: Kettilonia, 2012.
MacKenzie, Garry. 'Lines, Walks and Getting Lost: Contemporary Poetry and Walking'. In *Walking, Landscape and Environment*, edited by David Borthwick, Pippa Marland and Anna Stenning, 15–27. London and New York: Routledge, 2020.
MacLaren, Ian. Review of *The Imprint of the Picturesque on Nineteenth-Century British Fiction* by Alexander M. Ross. *English Studies in Canada* 14, no. 1 (Mar. 1988): 108–12.
Macrae, Alasdair. *Norman MacCaig*. Tavistock: Northcote House Publishers, 2010.
Mallarmé, Stéphane. *Divagations*, translated by Barbara Johnson. Cambridge, MA, and London: The Belknap Press of Harvard University Press, 2007.
Malpas, Jeff. *Heidegger and the Thinking of Place: Explorations in the Topology of Being*. Cambridge, MA: MIT Press, 2012.
Malpas, Jeff. *Place and Experience: A Philosophical Topography*. Cambridge: Cambridge University Press, 1999.
Malpas, Jeff, ed. *The Place of Landscape: Concepts, Contexts, Studies*. Cambridge, MA: The MIT Press, 2011.
Manfredi, Camille. *Nature and Space in Contemporary Scottish Writing and Art*. New York: Palgrave Macmillan, 2019.
Manfredi, Camille. 'Scottish Petroliterature 1993–2013: Poetics of an Oil Spill'. *Environmental and Ecological Readings: Nature, Human and Posthuman Dimensions in Scottish Literature and Arts (XVIII–XXI c.)*, edited by Philippe Laplace, 249–61. Besançon: Presses universitaires de Franche-Comté, 2015.
Marland, Pippa. 'The Gannet's Skull versus the Plastic Doll's Head: Material "Value" in Kathleen Jamie's "Findings"'. *Green Letters: Studies in Ecocriticism* 19, no. 2 (2015): 121–31.
Marland, Pippa. 'Deep Time Visible'. *Cambridge Companion to Literature and the Anthropocene*, edited by John Parham, 289–303. Cambridge: Cambridge University Press, 2021.
Massey, Doreen. *For Space*. Thousand Oaks: SAGE Publications, 2005.

Massey, Doreen. 'Landscape as Provocation: Reflections on Moving Mountains'. *Journal of Material Culture* 11, issue 1–2 (1 July 2006): 33–48.
Matless, David. *The Regional Book*. Axminster: Uniformbooks, 2015.
McEwen, Christian. Review of Thomas A. Clark *In Praise of Walking*. *The Dark Horse* 23 (Summer 2009): 42–7.
McGrath, Sean J. *Thinking Nature*. Edinburgh: Edinburgh University Press, 2019.
McGuire, Matt. 'Kathleen Jamie'. In *The Edinburgh Companion to Contemporary Scottish Poetry*, edited by Matt McGuire and Colin Nicholson, 141–53. Edinburgh: Edinburgh University Press, 2009.
McGuire, Matt, and Colin Nicholson, eds. Introduction to *The Edinburgh Companion to Contemporary Scottish Poetry*. Edinburgh: Edinburgh University Press, 2009.
McNeill, Marjory. *Norman MacCaig: A Study of His Life and Work*. Edinburgh: Mercat Press, 1996.
Mels, Tom, ed. *Reanimating Places: A Geography of Rhythms*. London and New York: Routledge, 2004.
Merleau-Ponty, Maurice. 'Eye and Mind'. In *The Primacy of Perception and Other Essays on Phenomenological Psychology, the Philosophy of Art, History and Politics*, edited by James M. Edie, translated by Carleton Dallery, 159–90. Evanston: Northwestern University Press, 1964.
Merleau-Ponty, Maurice. *Nature Course: Notes from the College de France*, translated by Robert Vallier. Evanston: Northwestern University Press, 2003.
Merleau-Ponty, Maurice. *Phenomenology of Perception*, translated by Colin Smith. London and New York: Routledge, 2002.
Merleau-Ponty, Maurice. *Sense and Nonsense*, translated by Hubert L. Dreyfus and Patricia Allen Dreyfus. Evanston: Northern University Press, 1991.
Merleau-Ponty, Maurice. *The Visible and the Invisible*, edited by Claude Lefort, translated by Alphonso Lingis. Evanston: Northwestern University Press, 1968.
Merleau-Ponty, Maurice. *The World of Perception*, translated by Oliver Davis. London and New York: Routledge, 2004.
Middleton, Peter. 'The British Niedecker'. In *Radical Vernacular: Lorine Niedecker and the Poetics of Place*, edited by Elizabeth Wills. Iowa City: University of Iowa Press, 2008.
Mitchell, W. J. T., ed. *Landscape and Power* [1994]. Chicago and London: The Chicago University Press, 2002.
Mœglin-Delcroix, Anne. *Ambulo ergo sum: Nature as Experience in Artists' Books / L'Expérience de la nature dans le livre d'artiste*. Cologne: Verlag der Buchhandlung, 2015.
Mœglin-Delcroix, Anne. 'Little Books & Other Little Publications'. *Little Critic* 15. Tipperary: Coracle, 2001.

Monaghan, Jim. 'Alec Finlay – Manifesto for Urban Crofts'. *Bella Caledonia*, 14 Oct. 2021. https://bellacaledonia.org.uk/2021/10/14/alec-finlay-manifesto-for-urbancrofts/. Accessed 22 Oct. 2021.
Morgan, Edwin. *Crossing the Border: Essays on Scottish Literature*. Manchester: Carcanet, 1990.
Morrison, Gavin. '14 Views of the Isle of Skye'. 2013. http://www.company-of-mountains.com/p/essay.html.
Morse, Samuel French. 'Veterans and Recruits'. *Poetry* 102, no. 5 (Aug. 1963): 330–4.
Murray, Isobel, and Bob Tait. 'A Metaphorical Way of Seeing Things: Norman MacCaig'. In *Scottish Writers Talking*. East Linton: Tuckwell Press, 1996.
Nagel, Thomas. 'What Is It Like to be a Bat?' *The Philosophical Review* 83, no. 4 (1974): 435–50.
Nancy, Jean-Luc. *After Fukushima: The Equivalence of Catastrophes*, translated by Charlotte Mandell. New York: Fordham University Press, 2015.
Nicholson, Colin. 'Modern Scottish Poetry'. *Scottish Literary Review* 1, no. 2 (Autumn/Winter 2009): 104–6.
Nicholson, Colin. *Poem, Purpose and Place: Shaping Identity in Contemporary Scottish Verse*. Edinburgh: Polygon, 1992.
'North Uist, Dun Na Mairbhe'. *Canmore. National Record of the Historic Environment*. https://canmore.org.uk/site/10342/north-uist-dun-na-mairbhe. Accessed 1 Nov. 2021.
Nowell, April. 'Upper Paleolithic Soundscapes and the Emotional Resonance of Nighttime'. In *Archaeology of the Night: Life after Dark in the Ancient World*, edited by Nancy Gonlin and April Nowell, 27–44. Boulder: University Press of Colorado, 2018.
O'Gorman, Ned. 'Three Poets'. *Poetry* 91, no. 4 (Jan. 1958): 268–73. 'OS1/2/70/41'. *ScotlandsPlaces*. https://scotlandsplaces.gov.uk/digital volumes/ordnance survey name books/argyll os-name-books-1868 1878/argyll-volume-70/42. Accessed 7 Nov. 2021.
Parham, John, ed. *Cambridge Companion to Literature and the Anthropocene*. Cambridge: Cambridge University Press, 2021.
Peacock, Charlotte. *Into the Mountain: A Life of Nan Shepherd*. Cambridge: Galileo Publishers, 2017.
Peacock, Charlotte. 'Quiet Pioneer: The Novels of Nan Shepherd'. *The Bottle Imp* 27 (2020). https://www.thebottleimp.org.uk/2020/12/quiet-pioneer-the-novels-of-nan shepherd 1893-1981/. Accessed 31 Oct. 2022.
'Placenames'. *Comunn Eachdraidh Shlèite/Sleat Local History Society*. 2021. http://www.sleatlocalhistorysociety.org.uk/index.php/placename/50. Accessed 28 Oct.
Pow, Tom, and Joy Hendry, eds. *Norman MacCaig. A Celebration: Tributes from Writers in Honour of Norman MacCaig's 85th birthday*. Edinburgh: Chapman Publishing, 1995.

Pratt, Vernon, Jane Howarth and Emily Brady. *Environment and Philosophy*. London and New York: Routledge, 2000.
Pryor, Sean. *W. B. Yeats, Ezra Pound and the Poetry of Paradise*. Farnham: Ashgate, 2011.
'Ptarmigan'. *Game and Wildlife Conservation Trust*. Accessed 4 Feb. 2022. https://www.gwct.org.uk/game/research/species/ptarmigan/.
Quigley, Peter, and Scott Slovic. *Ecocritical Aesthetics: Language, Beauty, and the Environment*. Indianapolis: Indiana University Press, 2018.
Riach, Alan. 'Affinity and Beyond: Alan Riach on Robert Garioch and Norman MacCaig'. *The National*. 27 Aug. 2018. https://www.thenational.scot/culture/16600389.affinity-and-beyond-alan-riach-on robert-garioch-and-norman-maccaig/
Riach, Alan. 'In Conversation with Norman MacCaig'. *PN Review* 120 (24), no. 4 (Mar.–Apr. 1998). https://www.pnreview.co.uk/cgibin/scribe?item_id=164.
Riach, Alan. 'The Poetics of Devolution'. *The Edinburgh Companion to Contemporary Scottish Poetry*, edited by Matt McGuire and Colin Nicholson, 8–20. Edinburgh: Edinburgh University Press, 2009.
Riley, Peter. 'Quick—Slow'. Review of *The Hundred Thousand Places*. *PN Review* 192 (36), no. 4 (2010): 55–6.
Rillie, Jack. 'Net of Kins, Web of Ilks: MacCaig Phantasmagoria'. *Chapman* 66 (Autumn 1991): 51.
Roberts, Andrew Michael. 'Time, Attention and the Gift in the Work of Thomas A. Clark'. *Journal of British and Irish Innovative Poetry* 11, no. 1 (2019). doi: https://doi.org/10.16995/bip.766.
Rohl, Darrell J. 'The Chorographic Tradition and Seventeenth and Eighteenth-Century Scottish Antiquaries'. *Journal of Art Historiography* 5 (2011): 1–18.
'Round-leaved Sundews'. *The Wildlife Trusts*. https://www.wildlifetrusts.org/wildlife explorer/wildflowers/round-leaved sundew. Accessed 21 Oct. 2021.
Roy, G. Ross. *The Equal Skies* Review. *World Literature Today* 54, no. 3 (1980): 474. doi:10.2307/40135250.
Ryden, Kent C. *Mapping the Invisible Landscape: Folklore, Writing, and the Sense of Place*. Iowa City: Iowa University Press, 1993.
Sallis, John. *Force of Imagination: The Expanse of the Elemental*. Bloomington and Indianapolis: Indiana University Press, 2012.
Scott, Mary Jane W. 'Neoclassical MacCaig'. *Studies in Scottish Literature* 10 (1973): 137–44.
Shepherd, Nan. *In the Cairngorms*. Cambridge: Galileo Publishers, 2014.
Shepherd, Nan. *The Living Mountain*. [1977]. Edinburgh: Canongate, 2011.
Shepherd, Nan. *The Quarry Wood*. [1928]. Edinburgh: Canongate, 2018.
Shepherd, Nan. *The Weatherhouse*. [1930]. Edinburgh: Canongate, 2017.
Shepherd, Nan. *Wild Geese: A Collection of Nan Shepherd's Writing*. Cambridge: Galileo Publishers, 2018.

Shklovsky, Victor. 'Art as Device (1917/1919)'. In *Victor Shklovsky: A Reader*, edited and translated by Alexandra Berlina, 73–96. New York and London: Bloomsbury, 2017.

Sloterdijk, Peter. 'The Anthropocene: A Process-State at the Edge of Geohistory?' In *Art in the Anthropocene. Encounters among Aesthetics, Politics, Environments and Epistemologies*, edited by Heather Davis and Etienne Turpin, 327–40. London: Open Humanities Press, 2015.

Slovic, Scott, Swarnalatha Rangarajan and Vidya Sarveswaran. *The Bloomsbury Handbook to the Medical-Environmental Humanities*. London: Bloomsbury Academic, 2022.

Smith, Stewart. 'Basho Borne on the Carrying Stream: The Word-Mapping of Scotland and the Ecopoetics of Wind Power in Alec Finlay's *The Road North* and *Skying*'. https://books.openedition.org/pufc/9183. Accessed 31 Aug. 2022.

Sneddon, Andrew. *Guest: Alec Finlay; Host: Andrew Sneddon*. Transmission: Host. London: Artwords Press, 2008.

Solt, Mary Ellen. *Concrete Poetry: A World View*. Bloomington: Indiana University Press, 1968.

Spence, Alan. *Edinburgh Come All' Ye*. Edinburgh: Scotland Street Press, 2022.

Stacey, Robert. 1987. '"Into the Order of Things": The Relations of Painting to the Poetry of Thomas A Clark'. In *Candid Fields: Essays and Reflections on the Work of Thomas A Clark*, edited by Peter Dent, 24–36. Budleigh Salterton: Interim Press.

Stephen, Ian. *Waypoints: Seascapes and Stories of Scotland's West Coast*. London: Adlard Coles, 2017.

'Sundews'. *The National Wildlife Federation*. https://www.nwf.org/Educational Resources/Wildlife-Guide/Plants-and-Fungi/Sundews. Accessed 21 Oct. 2021.

Tarbuck, Alice. '"A Stone Within": Visual Poetry & Wellbeing in the work of Alec Finlay and Thomas A. Clark'. *Journal of British and Irish Innovative Poetry* 9 (1), no. 3 (2017). https://doi.org/10.16995/biip.11.

Tarbuck A. 'a place apart: Papers from the Edinburgh Symposium on the Poetry and Practice of Thomas A. Clark'. *Journal of British and Irish Innovative Poetry* 11, no. 1 (2019).

Tarbuck, Alice, and Simone Kotva. 'The Non-Secular Pilgrimage: Walking and Looking in Ken Cockburn and Alec Finlay's *The Road North*'. *Critical Survey* 29, no. 1 (2017): 33–52.

Tarlo, Harriet, ed. *The Ground Aslant: An Anthology of Radical Landscape Poetry*. Exeter: Shearsman Books, 2011.

Tarlo, Harriet. 'Open Field: Reading Field as Place and Poetics'. *Spatial Practices* 15 (1 Jan. 2013).

Taylor, Alan. 'Norman MacCaig: An Introduction'. In *The Poems of Norman MacCaig*, edited by Ewan MacCaig, xxvii–xxxix. Edinburgh: Polygon, 2005.

Thornton, R. D., Roderick Watson, J. MacInnes and M. Byrne. 'Scotland, Poetry of'. In *The Princeton Encyclopedia of Poetry and Poetics*, edited by Roland Green, Stephen Cushman and Clare Cavanagh. 4th ed. Princeton: Princeton University Press, 2012. https://nls.idm.oclc.org/login?url=https://search.credoreference.com/content/ntry/proetry/scotland_poetry_of/0?institutionId=238
Thrift, Nigel. *Non-Representational Theory: Space, Politics, Affect*. London and New York: Routledge, 2007.
Tilley, Christopher. *A Phenomenology of Landscape: Places, Paths and Monuments*. Oxford and Providence: Berg, 1994.
Toadvine, Ted. 'The Elemental Past'. *Research in Phenomenology* 44 (2014): 262–79. 10.1163/15691640-12341288.
Toadvine, Ted. 'Our Monstrous Futures: Global Sustainability and Eco-Eschatology'. *Symposium* 21, no. 1 (2017): 219–230, https://doi.org/10.5840/symposium201721113.
Tucker, Alan. Preface to *Moschatel Press. Exhibition Catalogue. December 1st 1979 – January 5th 1980*. London: Coracle Press, 1979.
Verbeek, Peter-Paul. *What Things Do: Philosophical Reflections on Technology, Agency and Design*. University Park: The Pennsylvania State University Press, 2005.
Wakeman, John. Board of Regents of the University of Oklahoma. 'The 1980 Jurors and Their Candidates for the Neustadt International Prize for Literature'. *World Literature Today* 53, no. 4 (Autumn 1979): 627–41.
Walker, Marshall. 'Interview with Norman MacCaig'. In *Seven Poets: Hugh MacDiarmid, Norman MacCaig, Iain Crichton Smith, George Mackay Brown, Robert Garioch, Sorley MacLean, Edwin Morgan*, edited by Christopher Carrell, 33–8. Glasgow: Third Eye Centre, 1981.
Walpert, Bryan. *Poetry and Mindfulness: Interruption to a Journey*. London: Palgrave, 2017.
Walton, Samantha. *The Living World: Nan Shepherd and Environmental Thought*. London: Bloomsbury Academic, 2020.
Ward, Geoffrey. Review of *Twenty Poems* by Thomas A Clark. *PN Review* 37 (1984): 57–8.
Watson, W. J. *Place-Names of Ross and Cromarty*. Inverness: The Northern Counties Printing and Publishing Company, 1904. https://her.highland.gov.uk/Monument/MHG7769. Accessed 8 Nov. 2021.
Weil, Simone. *Gravity and Grace*, translated by Emma Crawford and Mario von der Ruhr. London: Routledge, 2002.
Welton, Matthew. 'Some Thoughts on Form'. In Thomas A. Clark, *The Threadbare Coat: Selected Poems*, ix–xv. Manchester: Carcanet, 2020.
Westling, Louise. *The Logos of the Living World: Merleau-Ponty, Animals, and Language*. New York: Fordham, 2014.
Westling. Louise. 'Merleau-Ponty's Ecophenomenology'. In *Ecocritical Theory: New European Approaches*, edited by Axel Goodbody and Kate Rigby, 126–38. Charlottesville: University of Virginia Press, 2011.

Weston, Daniel. *Contemporary Literary Landscape and the Poetics of Experience:* London and New York: Routledge, 2016.
Whiston Spirn, Anne. *The Language of Landscape.* New Haven and London: Yale University Press, 1998.
Williams, Raymond. *The Country and the City.* London: Chatto & Windus, 1973.
Williams, Tony. 'Blog Review 15: Tony Williams Reviews Alec Finlay's *Be My Reader*'. *Magma* 72 (2012). https://magmapoetry.com/blog-review 15-tony williams reviews-alecfinlays-be-my-reader/. Accessed 19 Jan. 2019.
Willis, Elizabeth, ed. *Radical Vernacular: Lorine Niedecker and the Poetics of Place.* Iowa City: University of Iowa Press, 2008.
Wolfreys, Julian, ed. *The Derrida Reader*: *Writing Performances.* Lincoln: University of Nebraska Press, 1998.
Wylie, John. 'An Essay on Ascending Glastonbury Tor'. *Geoforum* 33 (2002): 441–54.
Wylie, John. 'The Distant: Thinking toward Renewed Senses of Landscape and Distance'. *Environment, Space, Place* 9, no. 1 (Spring 2017): 1–20. Minneapolis: University of Minnesota Press. https://www.jstor.org/stable/10.5749/envispacplac.9.1.0001
Yeung, Heather. *Spatial Engagements of Poetry.* New York: Palgrave, 2015.
Zukofsky, Louis. 'Program: Objectivists and Sincerity and Objectification: With Special Reference to the Work of Charles Reznikoff'. *Poetry* (Feb. 1931): 268–84. https://www.poetryfoundation.org/poetrymagazine/browse?volume=37&iss=5&page=38.

Index

The index contains proper names of authors and critics, titles of work directly referred to, place-names of significance, and the principal concepts that recur throughout the book. Where certain words are consonant with the main entry (e.g. being, identity, subject, self), these are gathered together under the principal heading, to indicate if not an interchangeability, then a relation, perhaps analogy (i.e., the relation between non-relation), in order to preserve the singularity of each term without presuming to separate and atomise the terminology, as if each were utterly separable from the others.

Adorno, Theodor, 93
Agamben, Giorgio, 52, 111
    anthropological machine, 111
    Homo Sacer, 52
Alaimo, Stacey, 52
Albrecht, Glenn, 151
    'Solastalgia and the New Mourning', 151
aletheia/unconcealedness, 141, 142, 175–82
analogical apperception, 158
Andrews, Kerri, 19
    Wanderers: A History of Women Walking, 19
animism, 64, 96
Anthropocene, 21, 101
anthropogenesis, 7, 13, 61, 67, 101, 119, 120, 154, 166
anthropomorphism, 20, 44, 46, 56, 76, 83, 104, 112, 181
Ascherson, Neil, 86, 87, 97, 98
Assynt, 8, 14, 63, 64, 65, 67, 68, 74, 80, 81, 87, 90, 99, 170
Auchterarder, 192
Auden, W. H., 129
    'Musée des Beaux Arts', 129
Aviemore, 169

Bach, Edward, 207
Bain, Jean, 204
Barbaras, Renaud, 31
Bashō, Matsuo 15, 187, 195

Oku no Hosomichi (Narrow Road to the Deep North), 15, 188
Bateman, Meg, and John Purser, 15, 66, 96, 195
    Windows to the West: Culture and Environment in the Scottish Gàidhealtachd, 15
Beat Movement, 142
Beaton, John, 174
beauty, 5, 28, 37, 40, 64, 66, 72, 73, 74, 80, 96, 132, 134, 143, 145, 149, 154, 157, 160, 182
becoming, 6, 8, 28, 30, 31, 33, 38, 42, 44, 46, 50, 51, 58, 59, 78, 86, 87, 92, 96, 100, 104, 118, 128, 130, 137
being/being-in-the-world/identity/subject/self, 1, 2, 3, 4, 5, 6, 9, 10, 11, 12, 13, 14, 15, 17, 18, 20, 21, 22, 23, 24, 25, 26, 27, 28, 29, 31, 30, 31, 32, 34, 35, 36, 37, 38, 41, 42, 43, 45, 46, 47, 48, 49, 52, 53, 54, 56, 57, 58, 59, 60, 63, 64, 65, 67, 68, 70, 72, 73, 74, 75, 76, 77, 78, 79, 81, 82, 84, 85, 86, 87, 88, 89, 90, 91, 92 93, 94, 95, 96, 97, 98, 101, 102, 103, 104, 108, 111, 112, 113, 114, 115, 116, 117, 118, 120, 122, 123, 124, 125, 126, 127, 128, 130, 133, 134, 135, 136, 138, 147, 158, 164, 165, 166, 177, 180, 181, 187, 190, 191 192, 194, 201, 211; *see also* identity

Bender, Barbara, 1, 2, 100
Benjamin, Walter, 141, 203
  'dialectics of happiness', 141
  'In the Sun', 203
Bennett, Jane, 29
Berleant, Arnold, 5, 98
biodiversity, 7, 8, 9, 101, 113, 188
Black Mountain Poets, 191
Blake, William, 156
  Jerusalem, 185 n.26
Blau DuPlessis, Rachel, 144
Bloomfield, Mandy, 191–2
Bluecoat, Liverpool, 192
body/embodiment, 4, 5, 9, 15, 20, 23, 24, 25, 28, 30, 31, 32, 33, 34, 35, 41, 42, 46, 47, 49, 50, 52, 53, 54, 57, 63, 64, 65, 67, 73, 74, 75, 86, 87, 88, 89, 96, 99, 103, 105, 110, 113, 114, 129, 130, 131, 135, 140, 146, 147, 148, 149, 154, 158, 160, 175, 178, 188, 189, 190, 191, 193
Book of Kells, 95
Boulez, Pierre, 176
  pli selon pli: Portrait de Mallarmé, 176
Bowring, Jacky, 9
Bragar, 118
Brainard, Joe, 208
Brogdale, Kent, 210
Brough of Birsay, 118, 130
Brown, George Mackay, 121
Bruegel, Pieter, 129
  Landscape with the Fall of Icarus, 129
Burns, Robert, 97 n.7

Cairn Gallery, 144, 184
Cairngorms, 11, 16, 19, 20, 24, 65, 135, 166, 169, 202, 203, 204, 206
Caithness, 116
Carmichael, Alexander, 174, 175
  Carmina Gadelica, 174
Casey, Edward S., 6
Charlotte Square (Edinburgh), 16, 151, 152
chiasm, 6, 25, 89
chorography/chora, 189, 196–9, 203, 204, 211
Clare, John, 152
Clark, Laurie, 18, 139
Clark, Thomas A, 8, 14, 15, 16, 17, 18, 128, 135, 139–87
  A Box of Landscapes, 148, 175
  A Bright Glade, 179
  A Corncrake in Charlotte Square, 151, 152
  A delphinium border, 161

a forest grove, 177
a gift of wild flowers / is the gift of a gift, 160
a promise of happiness, 162
A Ruskin Sketchbook, 143
A Short Tour of the Highlands, 170
adjectives for Grasses, 162
'Admit one', 167
After Marvell, 160
After Andrew Marvell, 160
Allt Garbh Beag, 166, 170
An Affinity of Eye and Petal, 158
An Cidhe Beag, 167
An Lochan Uaine, 139, 146, 169
and then an island floated past us like a promise of happiness and we rocked in its wake, 171
At Loch Grinneabhat, 165
Bindweed Stitchwort Knotgrass, 162
BO HEEM E UM, 150
Bookmarks, 177
By Kilbrannan Sound, 146, 165, 170
Coire Fhionn Lochan, 165, 169
'Creag Liath', 165, 166
Curlew Lapwing Plover Whimbrel, 153–4
'Do You know the Land', 154
Doire Shòlais, 166
Dun na mairbhe, 166, 170
every time you find, 164
Farm by the Shore, 155
Folding the Last Sheep, 151, 188
Garvellachs, 173
Glade, 178
glade, 180
Hart's Tongue, 159
I say island, 171
In a fold of hills, 176
'In Praise of Walking', 148, 184
In small things / delight is intense, 160
'Lochan a Bearta', 169
Lullaby, 156
Names, 163
'Nine paces', 156
Of Woods & Water: Forty Eight Delays, 182
On a Grey Day, 177
One Hundred Scottish Places, 148, 152, 155, 179
One Hundred Thousand Places, 179
pli selon pli, 176
Proverbs of the Meadow and the Mountain, 159
'Riasg Buid', 167, 170, 174
Rothiemurchus, 182

Clark, Thomas A (*cont.*)
 Sea hand land foot, 149
 Selected Poems, 182
 Some Particulars, 157
 Suspicion of beauty / is the new Puritanism, 160
 'Thainig Na Naoi Sonais', 174
 The Bright Glade, 181
 The Dappled Glade, 178
 The Grove of Delight, 166, 170
 The Earthly Paradise, 172
 'The High Path', 179
 The Hundred Thousand Places, 155
 The Lord of the Isles, 172
 The Pocket Glade Dictionary, 178
 The teachings of Huang Po, 185 n.22
 The thought of a glade 178
 The Threadbare Coat: New and Selected Poems, 155, 172
 The World Brought Near, 181
 to redress the loss of the seagrass meadows, 154
 'To Scalasaig', 168
 'Tobar Na Cailleach', 167
 Tormentil & Bleached Bones, 167
 Tràigh Bhalla, 166, 170
 Twelve Proverbs, 159
 Twenty Poems, 150
 Two Evergreen Horizons, 155
 wing of the ptarmigan: forty eight delays, 152, 186
 Wintergreen, 144
 Wood Notes Wild: Essays on the Poetry of Ian Hamilton Finlay, 151
 yarrow & marram grass, 161
 Yellow & Blue, 155
Coire an Lochain, 38, 41
Colonsay, 167, 168
Cockburn, Henry, 151–2
 Memorials of His Time, 151–2
Cockburn, Ken, 14, 188, 195, 210
Cole, Barry, 66, 97
Coleridge, Samuel Taylor, 117
consciousness, 8, 11, 24, 25, 26, 27, 29, 30, 31, 33, 34, 36, 45, 48, 50, 54, 58, 59, 63, 71, 74, 75, 78, 86, 88, 89, 91, 101, 112, 133, 143, 158, 169, 175, 176, 190, 191, 192, 193
Cooper, David E., 134
corporeality, 4, 20, 66, 75, 84, 91, 106, 127, 141, 147, 188, 189, 190, 191, 194
Cosgrove, Denis, 2
Covid Memorial, Pollock Country Park, Glasgow, 16, 208

Creeley, Robert, 142, 211
Crieff, 122
Critchley, Simon, 157
Cruikshank, Helen, 202
 'Shy Geordie', 202
 Up the Noran Water, 202
Cùl Beag, 91
Cùl Mòr, 91
Culler, Jonathan, 133
cultural landscape, 106–7, 122
Cunsolo, Ashlee, and Karen Landman, 151
 Mourning Nature: Hope at the Heart of Ecological Loss, 151

Davidson, James Dyas, 204
Davie, Donald, 68, 97, 98
Deeside/River Dee, 49, 52 200, 202, 203, 204
De Horozco of Toledo, Sebastián, 82
Deleuze, Gilles, 175, 188
De Nardi, Sarah, 206
Derrida, Jacques, 124, 152, 197, 201
 On the Name, 212 n.7
 Signéponge / Signsponge, 212 n.7
 'The Battle of the Proper Name', in *Of Grammatology*, 212 n.7
Devereux, Hannah, 204
Dickinson, Emily, 199
Donne, John, 98 n.9
Donside, 200
Dufrenne, Mikel, 74, 75, 94
 The Phenomenology of Aesthetic Experience, 74, 75, 94
Dunn, Douglas, 64
dwelling, 21, 28, 30, 35, , 53, 106, 107, 109, 110, 112, 166, 202, 203, 208

Écart, 85, 89
Edinburgh International Book Festival, 151
Eliot, T. S., 71, 98, 105
 'The Love Song of J. Alfred Prufrock', 105
embodied self, 1, 15, 28, 31, 32, 34, 38, 46, 52, 53, 54, 57, 58, 59, 86
Emerson, Ralph Waldo, 199
Enclosures/Enclosure Acts, 7, 109 152
enmeshing, 24, 27, 149
entanglement, 12, 18, 27, 29, 30, 36, 114, 116, 137
entwining, 11, 25, 45, 58, 61, 63, 65, 85, 155, 189, 207, 211
environmental aesthetics, 5, 192
environmental humanities, 5, 6
European Landscape Convention, 6

Fazzini, Marco, 79, 80, 99
Finlay, Alec, 8, 9, 14, 15, 16, 17, 98, 135, 149, 165, 166, 173, 187–212
  A Far-off Land, 202
  A Variety of Cultures, 210
  'A-GEL03 circlesthroughthepath', 198
  Atoms of Delight, 14, 211
  Avant-Garde English Landscape, 192, 198
  Carmichael's Book, 174
  Còmhlan Bheanntan / A Company of Mountains, 14, 194, 200
  Ebban an'flowan, 187
  'From *A Place-Aware Dictionary*', 188
  Gathering, 165, 187, 190, 202, 203, 204, 205, 206, 207
  I Hear Her Cry: anagrammatic poem-clues for The Oaks, Wellesley, 199
  I Remember: Scotland's Covid Memorial, 203, 208
  'Kinder North', 194
  Manifesto for Urban Crofts, 16, 209
  Mesostic Herbarium, 203
  Mesostic Remedy, 207
  Nether Hive, 210
  Paths for All, 209
  Shared Writing: Renga Days, 190, 200
  Siren, 192
  Some Colour Trends, 190
  Some Versions of Landscape. A survey of artist projects in the landscape (1998–2006), 192, 198, 211
  Specimen Colony, 192
  'SVOL06 Mesostic Herbarium—naMes makE Stems chOsen wordS Their growIng branChes', 198
  Taigh: a wilding garden (Edinburgh Botanic Gardens), 16, 207, 208
  The Bee Libraries, 210
  The Beehives, 210
  The' fleety wud, 187, 189
  The Road North (with Ken Cockburn), 14–15, 188, 195
  Three Rivers Crossword, 200
  White Peak, Dark Peak, 194
  Wild City / Fiadh-Bhaile / Orasul Salbatic, 15, 203, 210
Finlay, Sue, 185
First World War, 61
flesh, 20, 25, 29, 30, 31, 32, 34, 48, 58, 88, 89, 91, 110, 113, 114, 118, 175
France, Linda, 207
Freeman, John, 157, 160
Frege, Gottlob, 201

Frykman, Erik, 96 n.3, 98 n.10
  Norman MacCaig, 96 n.3
fold, the/unfolding, 11, 59, 61, 90, 92, 126, 141, 142, 146, 150, 153, 160, 168, 172 175–82, 183, 186
Fulton, Hamish, 184 n.18
Fulton, Robin, 66, 75, 96, 99

Gaelic, 13–14, 60, 64, 65, 68, 74, 79, 80, 81, 94, 97, 142, 156, 165, 167, 172, 173, 200, 202, 203, 204, 205, 206, 207, 208, 212
Gairn, Louisa, 12, 137
  Ecology and Modern Scottish Literature, 12
Garioch, Robert, 98 n.9
Gaye, Marvin, 154
  'Abraham, Martin and John', 154
gaze/the eye/sight, 1, 3, 3, 9, 20, 24, 28, 30, 31, 32, 33, 34, 35, 36, 38, 40, 41, 43, 44, 46, 48, 50, 51, 53, 56, 57, 61, 73, 81, 82, 83, 84, 85, 90, 91, 92, 93, 96, 101, 108, 112, 130, 132, 134, 158, 160, 164, 176, 177, 179, 181, 188, 194, 195, 197, 202
Geddes, Patrick, 8
Georgic, 151
Gibbon, Lewis Grassic, 20
Gibson, James, 9, 86, 91
Gilman, Rachel, 62 n.6
  'Reading the Word: Spirit Materiality in the Mountain Landscapes of Nan Shepherd', 62 n. 6
Glen Mor, 130
Glenmore, 169
Godfrey, Nanette, 149
Goethe, Johann Wolfgang von, 154, 155
  'Kennst do das land', 154
Goodwin, Gavin, 144, 150, 184, 185
Green, Ian, 160
Green Loch, 169
Greig, Andrew, 184 n.18
Gunn, Neil M., 14, 20
  The Atom of Delight, 14

haecceity, 41
haikai no renga, 195
Hair, Ross, 151, 183
  Folding the Last Sheep, 183 n.1
Hamilton Finlay, Ian, 142, 150, 151, 155, 187, 194, 203, 210
  Eclogue, 151
  Jupiter Artland, 210
  Beehives, 210
  Little Sparta, 210

Hardy, Thomas, 66, 83, 137
  A Pair of Blue Eyes, 137
Harris, 63, 76, 91, 103, 109, 115, 117
Hart, George, 192
Hazlitt, William, 148
Hearn, Lafcadio, 62 n.4
  Gleanings in Buddha Fields, 62, n.4
Heat-Moon, William Least, 197
  PrairyErth: (a Deep Map), 197
Heddon, Dee, 210
Heidegger, Martin, 180, 184, 186, 202
  Lichtung (clearing), 180
  Erschlossenheit, 182
  the fourfold, 186, 202
  Holzwege, 184 n.18
Heise, Ursula K., 138 n.21
  Imagining Extinction: The Cultural Meanings of Endangered Species, 138 n.21
Hepburn, Ronald, 5
  'Contemporary Aesthetics and the Neglect of Natural Beauty', 5
  Wonder and Other Essays, 5
Herbert, George, 98 n.9
Highland Clearances/Clearances, 8, 13, 80, 81, 201, 205
Highlands and Islands, 8, 11, 16, 142, 148
Hoare, Philip, 112
Hodby, Alex, 189, 198
Hokku, 195
Hopkins, Gerard Manley, 36, 67
Hughes, Ted, 66, 97
Husserl, Edmund, 22, 34, 88, 124, 125, 186
  Verweltlichung, 88
  'living-present', 124

identity, 12, 13, 21, 31, 36, 37, 43, 47, 78, 89, 120, 136, 165, 187
imagination, 10, 12, 63, 76, 77, 78, 98, 103, 104, 123, 125, 127, 133, 192
Ingold, Tim, 11, 100, 184
Inner Hebrides, 167, 174
  Islay, 174
International Exhibition of Science, Art and Industry (1886), 116
intertwining, 5, 10, 15, 18, 20, 25, 27, 29, 29, 41, 44, 51, 54, 59, 60, 85, 86, 87, 89, 109, 110, 121, 127, 148, 157, 158, 160, §75, 177, 178, 180, 187, 198, 199, 200
Irigaray, Luce, 53
islands, 104, 105, 115, 118, 135, 142, 148, 171–5

Jamie, Kathleen, 8, 14, 15, 16, 17, 64, 81, 96, 100–38
  'A Tibetan Dog', 138 n.22
  'A Woman in the Field', 100
  'Aurora', 112
  'Cetacean Disco', 112
  'Crex Crex', 152
  'Darkness and Light', 126
  Findings, 82, 101, 123, 132, 136, 137
  Frissure (with Brigid Collins), 135 n.7
  'In Quinhagak', 111, 132, 133
  'Links of Noltland I', 120, 126
  'Migratory III' 137 n.18
  'On Rona', 119, 120
  Sightlines, 100, 101, 121, 123, 130, 135
  'The Snow Petrel', 121
  'The Storm Petrel', 119
  The Tree House, 8–9
  'The Hvalsalen', 112, 119
  'The Wind Horse', 138 n.22
  'Three Ways of Looking at St Kilda', 105, 120
  'Voyager, Chief', 112, 119, 136
Johnson, B. S., 71, 161
  The Unfortunates, 161
Johnson, Mark, 76
Johnstone, Julie, 154, 184
Journal of Scottish Name Studies, 212 n.8

Kant, Immanuel, 4–5, 6, 62, 72, 73
Keats, John, 3
Kelsey, Robin, 4
Kenyon, Simone, 19
  Into the Mountain, 19
Kotva, Simone, 184, 185, 194
  Effort and Grace: On the Spiritual Exercise of Philosophy, 185 n.27
Kleinberg, Ethan, 111
Kripke, Saul, 201
  Naming and Necessity, 201
Kristeva, Julia, 197
  Revolution in Poetic Language, 197
Kunitz, Stanley, 136 n.14
  'Elegy for a Whale', 136 n.14
  The Wellfleet Whale, 136 n.14

Lakoff, George, 76
landscape
  commodification of, 4, 170
  intertwining of self and, 5 18, 25, 27, 29, 31, 51, 54, 86, 99, 110, 121, 148, 158, 160, 175, 177, 178, 187, 196, 199, 200
landscape poetics, 1, 9

Index

representation, 2, 4, 5, 6, 10, 12, 25, 29, 36, 37, 69, 71, 72, 83, 104, 110, 134, 140, 147, 160, 161, 182, 191, 193, 196
Law, Mhairi, 204, 210
Leask, Nigel, 186 n.33
   Stepping Westward: Writing the Highland Tour, c. 1720–1830, 186 n.33
Leibniz, Gottfried Wilhelm, 175
Lewis, 116
light/darkness, 20, 24, 27, 30, 42, 43, 44, 45, 46, 47, 48, 49, 50, 51, 56, 86, 87, 94, 95, 126, 127, 132, 133, 158, 168, 178, 179, 180, 182, 185
Linne na Dunach, 166
Lippit, Akita Mizuta, 111, 114
Lochinver, 65, 74, 75
Loch Sligachan, 166
Long, Richard, 195
   Line Made by Walking, 195
Loose, Gerry, 210
Lorrain, Claude, 3

McAllan, Kate, 210
Macauley, David, 158
McCaig, Norman, 8, 14, 15, 16, 63–99
   'A.K. MacLeod', 73
   'A Man in Assynt', 8, 80, 99
   'A man I agreed with', 94
   'A voice of summer', 94
   'Above Inverkirkaig', 68, 85
   'An Ordinary Day', 65
   'At the foot of Cùl Mòr', 94
   'By the Graveyard, Luskentyre', 93
   'Caterpillar going somewhere', 76, 78
   'Ceann Loch Aeoineart', 14
   'Centre of centres', 88
   'Climbing Suilven', 91
   'Crofter', 81
   'Crossing the border', 81
   'Culag Pier', 66
   'Dying landscape', 93
   'Estuary', 89
   'High mountain loch', 81
   'High up on Suilven', 91
   'Highland funeral', 73
   'Illumination: on the track by Loch Fewin', 95
   'Instrument and agent', 84
   'Inverkirkaig Bay', 85
   'Landscape and I', 89, 95
   'Landscape outside and in', 88, 89, 95
   'Languages', 96
   'Loch of the Wolf's Pass, the Loch of the Green Corrie', 85
   'Loch Scionascaig', 68
   'Looking down on Glen Canisp', 68, 85, 137
   'My Way of It', 68, 70
   'On the north side of Suilven', 88
   'On the pier at Kinlochbervie', 89
   Riding Lights, 84, 97
   'Ringed Plover by a Water's Edge', 92
   'Signs and Signals', 85
   'Small round loch', 73
   'Sound of the sea on a still evening', 85, 95
   'Summer farm', 89
   'Swimming lizard', 78
   'the Cause', 77
   'The Loch of the Peevish Creek', 79
   The Poems of Norman McCaig, 66
   'Treeless landscape', 82, 83
   'Two skulls', 82
   'Walking to Inveruplan', 90
   'Wester Ross, West Sutherland', 81
MacDiarmid, Hugh, 20, 82, 88, 97
Macfarlane, Robert, 19, 20, 22, 25
MacIntyre, Duncan Ban, 18
   Praise of Ben Dorain, 18
MacKenzie, Garry, 184 n.18
   Walking, Landscape and Environmenti, 184 n.18
MacLean, Sorley, 14, 195
   'Ceann Loch Aeoineart', 195
   An Cuillithionn ('The Cuillin'), 195
MacNeice, Louis, 86
Macrae, Alasdair, 96 n.3
Maes Howe, 126–7
Malpas, Jeff, 2, 4, 6, 11, 13, 100
Marland, Pippa, 11, 101, 120
Martin, Martin, 130
McGuire, Matt, 64, 101, 119, 135, 137
McNeill, Marjory, 66, 70, 84, 86, 91, 98, 99
Mabey, Richard, 163
Mallarmé, Stéphàne, 161, 172, 186
   'Un coup de dés jamais n'abolira le hasard', 161
   'L'avant-dire au Traité du verb de René Ghil', 171
   'Variations sur un sujet', 171
   Divagations, 171
   'Crise de vers', 171
Manfredi, Camille, 12, 184, 203
   Nature and Space in Contemporary Scottish Writing and Art, 11

Marr, Andrew, 135 n.5
Massey, Doreen, 6, 11
Matless, David, 84
memory, 4, 13, 187–212
Middleton, Peter, 184 n.11
Mill, John Stuart, 201
　A System of Logic, 201
Miller, J. Hillis, 189
　Topographies, 189
mind, 4, 20, 24, 29, 30, 31, 31, 34, 35, 36, 40, 46, 49, 50, 54, 57, 58, 62, 63, 65, 71, 73, 78, 84, 85, 87, 90, 103, 117, 130, 143, 157, 171, 185
Mingulay, 104
Modern British Nature Writing, 1789–2020, 19
Merleau-Ponty, Maurice, 5–6, 9, 15, 17, 20, 21, 22, 24, 25, 26, 28, 29, 31, 32, 34, 35, 38, 42, 50, 53, 57, 58, 77, 81, 82, 85, 89, 91, 92, 128, 141, 158, 165, 176, 180, 181, 189, 194
　Phenomenology of Perception, 17, 176
Moeglin-Delcroix, Anne, 17, 149
Moreton, Guy, 204
Morgan, Edwin, 69, 70, 73–4, 75, 76, 78, 80, 97
Morrison, Gavin, 200, 201
　'14 Views of the Isle of Skye', 200
Moschatel Press, 139, 155, 169, 183, 184
Muir, Edwin, 20
Muir, Willa, 20
Myers, Misha, 210

Nagel, Thomas, 112, 136
naming/the name/place names /proper names, 14, 24, 36, 37, 60, 74, 79, 80, 81, 88, 89, 104, 106, 136, 139, 142, 152, 156, 159, 161, 162, 163, 164, 165, 167, 168, 170, 171, 172, 176, 178, 183, 186, 187–213, 197, 201, 212
Nancy, Jean-Luc, 2, 108, 126
Napoleonic Wars, 61
National Museum of Scotland, 117, 124
National Trust for Scotland, 106
New Stobhill Hospital (Glasgow), 16, 185 n.19
Nicolaisen, W. E. H., 205
　'Celtic Toponymics in Scotland', 205
Nicholson, Colin, 97 n. 7
Niedecker, Lorine, 143–4, 184, 186
North Berwick, 103, 118
North Mains, 122, 126
North Uist, 166, 174
Northern Lights, 46, 127

Olson, Charles, 142
open-field poetics, 191
openness/radical openness, 10, 14, 20, 29, 31, 45, 58, 85, 91, 141, 157, 161, 182, 199
Orkney, 16, 103, 118, 123, 130, 135
otherness, 63, 76, 95, 102, 114
Oulipo, 161

Pabbay, 104
Palmer, Samuel, 151, 158
parallelism, 32, 52, 73, 74, 85, 89, 90, 92, 98, 100
Parham, John, 138 n.1
particularity, 142, 156, 178
pastoral, 4, 12, 15, 76, 103, 105, 150, 151, 185, 210, 211
Peacock, Charlotte, 19, 62, 63
　Into the Mountain: A Life of Nan Shepherd, 19
Peak District National Park, 194
Pentland Hills, 11, 16
perception, 1, 2, 4, 6, 9, 11, 12, 13, 15, 17, 18, 22, 23, 25, 28, 29, 30, 33, 34, 38, 44, 50, 64, 75, 76, 77, 78, 79, 81, 84, 85, 86, 87, 88, 87, 88, 89, 84, 98, 104, 111, 122, 124, 128, 137, 140, 145, 157, 158, 168, 176, 188, 189, 191, 193, 211
permanence, 79, 86, 101–38
Perthshire, 103, 122, 125
phenomenology/phenomenality, 1–19, 21, 22, 23, 25, 36, 41, 64, 65, 75, 76, 82, 87, 107, 127, 129, 148, 168, 191, 193, 196, 197
picturesque, 3, 9, 10, 13, 15, 56, 134
place, 1–62, 63–76, 80–9, 97–111, 114–39, 142–212
Plath, Sylvia, 199
provisionality, 12, 90, 131, 197, 198, 211
Pryor, Sean, 141
Poetry (journal), 142
Pound, Ezra, 141
Pursglove, Glyn, 139, 140, 141, 145, 146, 156, 158, 160, 163, 175

Queneau, Raymond, 161

Ramsay, Allan, 97 n.7, 185 n.20
　The Gentle Shepherd: A Pastoral Comedy, 185 n.20
Renga, 190, 192, 194, 195, 211
Riach, Alan, 64, 75, 79, 97, 98, 99, 187, 208
Riley, Peter, 147, 150

rock, 23, 25, 28, 40, 44, 52, 68, 87, 90, 95, 102, 128, 129, 131, 135, 159, 166, 167, 207
Rohl, Darrell J. 196, 197, 211
Romanticism/Post-Romanticism, 3, 4, 15, 21, 67, 69, 70, 80, 86, 97, 98, 101, 105, 112, 140, 142, 176
Rona, 16, 101, 103, 104, 109, 119, 120, 121, 129, 139, 136
Rothiemurchus Forest, 60
Roubaud, Jacques, 161
Roy, Ross, 97 n. 6
Royal Botanic Garden, Edinburgh, 208
Rule Water, 189, 212
Ruskin, John, 143
Russell, Bertrand, 201
Russell, Gill, 204, 221

Sallis, John, 133–4
Salter, Jo, 192
 Specimen Colony, 192
Samperi, Frank, 142
Scalasaig, 168, 170
Scalpay, 63
Scarinish, 167
Schelling, F.W.J., 133
Schiehallion, 89
Schuyler, James, 199
 'October', 199
Scott, Mary Jane, 69
Scottish National Gallery of National Art, 179
Scottish Covid Memorial (Pollock Country Park), 16
Second World War, 19, 61, 62, 96
senses/experience/the sensual, 1, 2, 4, 5, 6, 9, 11, 12, 15, 17, 18, 20, 23, 25, 26, 28, 30, 31, 32, 33, 34, 35, 36, 37, 38, 40, 41, 42, 43, 44, 47, 48, 49, 52, 54, 55, 57, 58, 61, 63, 64, 65, 66, 67, 71, 72, 73, 74, 78, 81, 82, 83, 86, 87, 88, 89, 94, 100, 101, 102, 106, 107, 110, 111, 113, 124, 125, 126, 127, 128, 131, 132, 133, 134, 135, 142, 143, 147, 149, 158, 160, 161, 168, 171, 177, 181, 185, 188, 189, 190, 191, 193, 197, 208, 209
Shepherd, Nan, 8, 14, 15, 16, 19–63, 79, 130, 132, 133
 A Pass in the Grampians, 19
 In the Cairngorms, 19, 20
 The Living Mountain, 19–63
 The Quarry Wood, 19, 27, 28, 30, 38, 45, 49, 52, 54, 62

The Weatherhouse, 19, 36, 43, 46, 53, 56, 63, 130
Wild Geese, 20
Shetland, 103, 113, 116, 121
Shiant Isles, 104
Shklovsky, Viktor, 144
 'Art as Device/'Art as Technique', 144
singularity, 18, 21, 40, 41, 61, 62, 63, 64, 72, 83, 90, 92, 94, 128, 157, §64, 166, 178, 179, 202
Skye, 14, 166, 195, 200
Sleat, 166
Sloterdijk, Peter, 101
Smith, Iain Crichton, 96, 195
Solnit, Rebecca, 195, 196
Solt, Mary Ellen, 147
sound, 8, 28, 50, 52, 53, 57, 58, 59, 65, 74, 76, 80, 84, 85, 90, 91, 95, 96, 104, 114, 124, 127, 128, 130, 131, 133, 135, 146, 153, 162, 165, 169, 170, 174, 190, 192, 207
South Hebrides, 173
 Garbh Eileacha, 173
 Eileach an Naoimh, 173
Speyside, 200
Spirn, Anne Whiston, 15–16
St Brendan, 141, 173
 Navigatio Sancti Brendani Abbatis, 173
St Kilda, 13, 16, 103–9, 120, 127, 135
Stac Pollaidh, 65, 91
Stafford, Fiona, 144, 148, 184 n.15
 Local Attachments: The Province of Poetry, 184 n.15
Stacey, Robert, 160
Stein, Gertrude, 148
Stevens, Wallace, 87, 88, 157
Stevenson, Robert Louis, 145, 148, 160
 A Child's Garden of Verses, 145, 160
Stoer Point, 91
Strathallan Estate, 122
Strathbogie, 200
Strath Deveron, 200
Strathearn, 122
Strang, Rose, 19
Stroma, 104, 115
sublime, 3, 15, 27, 48, 62, 73, 101, 105, 117, 122, 123, 124, 125
Suilven, 72, 85, 87, 88, 90, 91
Sulla Sgeir, 104
Sumburgh Head, 116
Sutherland, 64, 72, 80, 81
Szuba, Monika, 10
 Contemporary Scottish Poetry and the Natural World: Burnside, Jamie, Robertson and White, 10

Taigh na Caillich, 208
Tarbuck, Alice, 143, 185, 186, 191, 194
Tanzaku, 187, 188, 191
Tarlo, Harriet, 9, 17, 146, 147, 191
Tay, 103
temporality/time, 2, 4, 6, 10, 11, 12, 13, 15, 18, 19, 21, 22, 23, 25, 26, 30, 31, 32, 33, 34, 36, 38, 41, 44, 45, 47, 48, 51, 54, 55, 56, 57, 59, 61, 65, 72, 73, 74, 75, 78, 79, 82, 83, 87, 92, 96, 100, 101, 102, 123, 127, 196, 207
Thoreau, Henry David, 135, 148, 199
Tilley, Christopher, 5, 100, 192, 193, 196, 203
Tiree, 166, 167
Toadvine, Ted, 82, 100, 128
topography, 122, 165, 189, 193, 207
topophilia, 10
trace, 53, 54, 61, 108, 110, 113, 115, 118, 120, 124, 196, 206
Treaty of Perth (1266), 172
transience, 100–39
transcendence, 25, 31, 74, 87, 157, 177
trompe l'œil, 38

Uist, 82, 166, 174
Umwelt, 33, 77, 85
UN Climate Change Conference (COP26), 9, 154
Uncanny, the, 2, 43, 46, 48, 58, 109, 119
Upper Teviot, 187, 189, 212

Verbeek, Paul, 88
Vico, Giambattista, 123
Virgil, 105
    Georgics, 105
vision, 2, 4, 7, 8, 24, 16, 31, 32, 33, 35, 38, 40, 41, 42, 43, 48, 49, 50, 51, 54, 55, 56, 61, 66, 69, 70, 74, 84, 85, 103 108, 127, 129, 133, 137, 175, 176, 189, 194, 200

walking, 10–11, 15, 19, 26, 27, 28, 32, 33, 34, 47, 49, 57, 85, 90, 103, 147, 148, 149, 161, 176, 177, 184, 190, 193, 194, 195, 201

Walking Library, 210
Walpert, Bryan, 76, 99
Walton, Samantha, 19, 21–3
    The Living World: Nan Shepherd and Environmental Thought, 19, 21
Ward, Geoffrey, 140, 150
Watanabe, Eiji, 169
Watson, Adam, 202, 204
    The Place Names of Upper Deeside (with Elizabeth Allen), 202, 204
Watson, Chris, 135, 192, 210
    Siren, 192
Watson, Roderick, 195
Watson, William, J., 186, 205
    Place-Names of Ross and Cromarty, 186 n.31
    The Celtic Place-Names of Scotland, 205
weather/weather-world, 20, 24, 26, 36, 44, 54, 55, 56, 72, 83, 91, 100, 101, 105, 107, 119, 121, 127, 130, 131, 159, 194
Weil, Simone, 143, 184, 185
    Gravity and Grace, 184 n.8
Welton, Matthew, 142, 156
West Highlands, 63, 65, 79, 87, 89
Westling, Louise, 94
Weston, Daniel, 123
Whitby, 116, 117
White, Gilbert, 102, 135
Wild Being, 141, 180
wilderness, 4, 15, 74, 103
Williams, Raymond, 2
Williams, Tony, 193
witnessing, 9, 13, 15, 16, 94, 96, 101, 107, 109, 113, 118, 160, 206
Wordsworth, William, 3, 98
    The Prelude, 98 n.10
Wylie, John, 2, 5

Young, Andrew, 86, 98

Zen, 14, 16, 40, 62, 64, 140, 142, 159, 203
Zukofsky, Louis, 142, 186
    'Program: "Objectivists"', 142, 188
    'Sincerity and Objectification: With Special Reference to the Work of Charles Reznikoff', 142

EU representative:
Easy Access System Europe
Mustamäe tee 50, 10621 Tallinn, Estonia
Gpsr.requests@easproject.com

www.ingramcontent.com/pod-product-compliance
Lightning Source LLC
Chambersburg PA
CBHW051121160426
43195CB00014B/2284